Routledge Revivals

THE STRUGGLE FOR SOUTH AMERICA

THE STRUGGLE
FOR SOUTH AMERICA
ECONOMY AND IDEOLOGY

by

J. F. NORMANO

WITH AN INTRODUCTION

by

CLARENCE H. HARING
Professor of Latin-Am erican History and Economics,
Harvard University

Routledge
Taylor & Francis Group

First published in 1931 by George Allen & Unwin Ltd.

This edition first published in 2018 by Routledge
2 Park Square, Milton Park, Abingdon, Oxon, OX14 4RN
and by Routledge
711 Third Avenue, New York, NY 10017

Routledge is an imprint of the Taylor & Francis Group, an informa business

A Library of Congress record exists under ISBN: 31028475

ISBN 13: 978-1-138-55142-8 (hbk)
ISBN 13: 978-1-315-12406-3 (ebk)

THE STRUGGLE FOR SOUTH AMERICA

THE STRUGGLE
FOR SOUTH AMERICA

ECONOMY AND IDEOLOGY

by

J. F. NORMANO

WITH AN INTRODUCTION

by

CLARENCE H. HARING
Professor of Latin-American History and Economics,
Harvard University

LONDON
GEORGE ALLEN & UNWIN LTD
MUSEUM STREET

FIRST PUBLISHED IN 1931

PRINTED IN GREAT BRITAIN BY
UNWIN BROTHERS LTD., WOKING

TO

HER

INTRODUCTION

A century ago the South American nations entered upon independent statehood at a period in their social development when they were peculiarly devoid of the requisites for a genuine national life. Methods of industry were antiquated, trade was backward, communications were inadequate or non-existent. The population was sparse, and generally scattered in isolated communities, separated by mountains or by great open spaces, where conditions of life were primitive, education was meagre, and the mental horizon bounded by the Indian or the desert. These peoples had achieved political independence, but economically they remained in the status of a colony.

Accustomed to the military government of a viceroy and to the absolutism of a distant king, they had had no experience whatever in self-government—such as was vouchsafed to the English colonists in America—and no tradition of popular control. Their democratic and republican constitutions were theoretical performances, foreign abstractions, the work of well-meaning doctrinaires, who wanted to create for the new *patria* an ideally perfect government, regardless of any considerations of its adaptability to local needs. Their common characteristic was a naïve faith in the written instrument to work political and social miracles.

As a spirit of public service had never had opportunity to develop, the device of majority rule was not understood, and political and religious intolerance were unchecked. In the new-found equality each leader was as good as his fellow, and convinced of his special capacity to manage the State. Governments in consequence became the prey of ambitious generals and politicians, public finance was erratic, and revolutions were frequent. Constitutions, it is true, were lengthy and numerous, but politics were at best a scramble for personal power.

These countries needed everything: capital, immigrants, example, and advice. And what they received came in those days mostly from Europe, and in the beginning especially from Great Britain. England continued till the close of the nineteenth century to enjoy a commercial and financial preponderance in the markets south of Mexico, and a certain political leadership as well.

Yet to Europeans generally, as to North Americans, the southern continent remained an uncharted area, on the fringe of civilization, a source of the raw materials of industry and a stage for *opéra bouffe* governments. The average man was scarcely aware that these peoples existed, except when he took a "flyer" in South American bonds or mining securities, and lost! He certainly had the vaguest idea of South American political geography.

By the first decade of the present century the scene had wholly changed. Brazil, Chile, and Argentina had attained to a degree of political stability and economic progress that compared favourably with conditions in the Latin nations of Europe. Uruguay followed closely after, and more recently Colombia. Railways and other public utilities had been constructed with foreign aid, at a time when the export of European capital was becoming an increasingly spectacular feature of international relations. Continental nations began to compete actively for the South American markets, and Great Britain saw her pre-eminence seriously challenged by the banks, shipping lines, and export houses of Germany. After the Spanish-American War the United States emerged as a world power, and began to reach out beyond Mexico and the Caribbean for the trade of more distant republics. The circumstances of the World War only hastened its evolution as an exporter of goods and capital, a development which in any case was inevitable. For a time North America possessed a virtual monopoly of South American markets. After the War, as the European belligerents recovered from their extreme prostration, they were bound to come back and seek again the patronage of their former customers. An intense economic rivalry has ensued, a drive on a new "western front" to recover the ground lost to the Yankee. The British Industrial Exposition in Buenos Aires is its most recent and notable manifestation. Latin-American Institutes have been organized in Germany, France, and England, to serve as centres of geographical and historical research, but also to train future salesmen in the language, history, literature, and economy of the South American nations. Spain has conjured up the ideal of Pan-Hispanic cultural union as a cloak for her ambitions to recover economic and even political leadership among her former subject provinces. France and Italy, with analogous aims, play up the broader cultural issue of Pan-Latinism. England sends the heir to the throne as a sort of super-salesman, to recall to Chileans and Argentines the traditional bonds that have allied them with the merchants and bankers of Britain. And in all of these "drives" commercial and intellectual Europe has not been unaware of the advantages derived from he persistence of that spectral "Peligro Yanqui," conjured up in the minds of many Latin Americans by recent interventions in some of the more backward and irresponsible republics about the Caribbean Sea.

Dr. Normano possesses peculiar qualifications for handling the problems involved in this intense international competition for commercial and financial leadership in the South American continent. Born a Brazilian, but trained in the best schools of economic thought abroad, long a resident in Europe and in the United States, he approaches with detachment, and yet with sympathetic understanding, the issues, psychological and economic, involved in the attitude both of the "seducers" and of the "courted." He analyses the relations between the Latin-American trade and investments of the United States and the new economy of mass-production of which the United States is the chief exemplar; he directs our attention to Cuba as a republic in which the impact of diverse cultures and economic forces may ultimately reveal a friendly and satisfactory solution; and he has much of significance to suggest regarding the future. It is a pleasure to contribute these introductory words to his brilliant and stimulating study.

C. H. HARING

HARVARD UNIVERSITY
April 1931

PREFACE

The World War has not only disturbed Europe's position as the centre of humanity, but it has also brought into prominence the question of the downfall of Europe and its culture. Since the War Europe has been politically split up, financially indebted, morally humiliated, and, as Russia no longer belongs to Europe, territorially reduced. That "Continental Europe is now a reproduction of the Balkan peninsula on a large scale," is Francesco Nitti's description.[1] The pessimistic philosophy, with Spengler at its head, natural to modern Europe, finds echoes throughout the world. Ortega y Gasset from the perspective of his peninsula, and Keyserling from his organized "school of wisdom," prophesy the migration of the centre of the world. And now a pessimistic prognosis has also been made concerning Europe's economic future. Sombart, who in Schlegel's sense of the word is certainly to be regarded as a prophet, paints a picture of the exhaustion of modern capitalism, of *late*-capitalism in Europe. Europe is no longer a "going concern."

Where is the new centre of human culture and economy to spring up? In North America? But common opinion emphasizes the solely materialistic aspect of the United States—its striving for gain alone—and one is not inclined to concede the possibility of that country's universal supremacy. In Asia? She has to combat her internal disorganization. Africa is still purely colonial. And Australia, the little continent of the white man, is an appendage of Great Britain.

By eliminating the other continents, the eye turns to South America.

"The present century is the century of South America, as the nineteenth century has seen the tremendous development of the United States," said Theodore Roosevelt; and a South American President registers his agreement by stating: "I consider the future of humanity of the twentieth century to be in Latin America."[2]

It is coming into vogue to preach the theory of the special destination and the Messianic mission of the South American continent. An English writer looks forward to a new economic order and a social solution which it shall be the appointed fate of this continent to fulfil. "Is it inevitable that an intelligent and Europeanized people must pass through the industrial phase before any form of social equilibrium can be secured, or is there any other way?"[3] "What is their special mission then? It might conceivably be in bringing to being a newer type of economic life."[4] One remembers the great social experiments undertaken by the Jesuits in Paraguay and the Incas in Peru. The Churches now are seeking new spheres of influence, especially on this continent. The Catholic Church is attempting to maintain and to strengthen its influence; Protestantism is launching a counter-offensive. The Latin race is hoping that a new, great future may lie here. In this trend of thought the Peruvian Calderon, rich in ideas and words, finds himself on common ground with a calm Englishman who also believes that "The future of the Latin race rests, to a large extent, with Latin America."[5] France and Italy are spreading Latin-Americanism; the former mother countries are endeavouring by means of Hispano-Americanism and Ibero-Americanism to regain their influence. The sober Pan-Americanism of the United States tries to adapt itself to the mentality of South America; and in a manner characteristic of this attitude Waldo Frank, in the style of a Biblical prophet and with the energy and pathos of a New England Puritan, writes of his "brothers" on the other continent.

Such ideas are flooding the South American continent, finding loud echo but little criticism there; at the same time, however, they are tending to counterbalance the deep pessimism which during the last decades has dominated the sociological literature of that continent. Ideas of this sort have their economic basis. The new importance which the continent acquired during and after the War, the hope of sharing in its economic potentialities, of recovering, maintaining, or expanding trade—these are the impelling motives of the different ideologies.

And thus the future of the South American continent involves a great number of important political and economic problems of our time.

But what is South America to-day? The most frequent definitions have been commonplaces—the continent of the future, a continent with a future, El Dorado, a country of lights and shadows, a country in the making, the land of promise, the land flowing with milk and honey, the continent of the One Thousand and One Nights, wealth in poverty, the neglected continent, the unknown continent—the list could be prolonged indefinitely. They are not only the titles of books, but generally, in their lack of clarity and precision, they also symbolize the content of the major part of the literature on South America. It is good form for writers on South America to record the wealth and inexhaustible possibilities of the continent, to wax lyrical about the beauties of Rio de Janeiro, and to point out that there is no need for the Monroe Doctrine.

The continent is constantly represented as an infant prodigy. The child has grown up, however, and is now of marriageable age. And suitors of dubious intentions are wooing the new Helen with phrases and ideas expressed in a style adapted to her South American character. Ideas and sentiments are often used as powerful weapons in the economic struggle for the continent.

This problem—the intentions and plans of the wooer, the position of the wooed, and the economic aspect of their relations—is the subject of the first two chapters of this book. Many burning questions of the hour are raised in the course of these pages. The principal questions, however, are whether the Anglo-Saxon and Iberian peoples can live together in mutual regard on the American continent, and what form relations will eventually assume (Chapters III–V).

The subject is intentionally restricted to South America, so as to exclude Mexico, the Central American and Caribbean countries of Latin America. The exception made of Cuba in Chapter IV is merely an attempt to study and understand how the two societies live together.

There are many descriptions of official Pan-Americanism, a deluge of propagandists of Hispano-Americanism, a number of good performances in the kindred field of international law, in all European languages. There exists to my knowledge only one article in the German language which treats of the economic problem of Pan-Americanism. So far there has been no attempt at a critical comparative study of all these movements.

One more remark. The lyricism which appears to have swayed the most matter-of-fact people in their relations with South America unfortunately prevails also in most investigations of the continent.

Neither in South America itself nor abroad has any attempt so far been made to answer the question which Sarmiento, one of the greatest minds of South America, asked some eighty-five years ago: "What is America? What are we?"[6] Scientifically, perhaps even more than economically, South America is still a desert with oases near the coast. Ultimate rediscovery is to be made, not by means of prophetic pilgrimages, nor the visits of statesmen, nor banquet eloquence, but rather in the study.

And the conscientious investigator will find that, *mutatis mutandis*, this continent also is subject to the universal economic tendencies, and that here, too, in the more progressive countries, one can already find the beginnings of industrialism. The realities of daily life, the economic needs, and the urge for gain are gradually gaining victory over the romanticism of yesterday. The South American "heart" and "soul" are to be relegated to the same historical category as the Russian Slavophils, and as the "spirit of the people," that much-bantered phrase of German jurisprudence at the beginning of the nineteenth century (Puchta and Savigny). And in the same way, Cecil Jane's latest psychological, monistic attempt to prove irrational the social and political organism of South America fails completely.[7] The types of South Americans of the future are not the ruling "generals and doctors," the landlords and the *gaucho*, but the manufacturer from São Paulo, the meat-jerker in Rio Grande do Sul and Uruguay, the wholesale merchant in Buenos Aires and Valparaiso, the *almacén* owner in the interior, the labourer; they are the *porteño* and *paulista*, and not the man from the country. Industrialization is still only beginning, but under the tropical sun everything grows rapidly.

It may be rash to prophesy the imminent downfall of capitalism in Europe; but there is a real basis for the forecast that the new capitalism of South America will clear away the remains of the Middle Ages. The current crisis and illness of the continent are the birth-pangs of the new economic order.

To-day there is still place for a Loti,[8] a Farrère, or a Maurand; but the man who is entranced by the romantic exoticism of the continent in its glory must make haste. It will not remain long.

For all the kind assistance, without which my book might never have reached its present stage, my thanks are sincere and many: to Professor Edwin R. A. Seligman and Professor Harry Elmer Barnes for encouraging my first steps as economist in this country; to Professor Seligman also for his stimulating suggestions on Alexander Hamilton; to Professor Clarence H. Haring for my thought-provoking conversations with him; to my friend Mr. Idelfonso d'Abreu Albano for his inspiring help and important materials; and to Mr. Edgar M. Hoover, Jr., for assistance in collecting material and compiling statistical tables.

My appreciation is especially deep for the work of Mr. Miron Burgin and Mr. Sidney S. Korzenik, whose work on this English text was indispensable.

B

I owe a debt of gratitude to many organizations, too many to recount here; but especially to the Pan-American Union at Washington, and the United States Department of Commerce; to the World Peace Foundation, Boston; the Foreign Policy Association of New York; and to the Widener Memorial Library and the assistants there who have patiently done their utmost to satisfy the wishes of a troublesome reader.

CAMBRIDGE, MASS
September, 1930

CONTENTS

CHAPTER I

THE ECONOMY

(*a*) TRADE[1]

In South America foreign trade is the breath of life. All economic activity—the satisfaction of the needs of the population by imports (for domestic industry is inadequate); currency stability; continuance of interest and amortization payments; peace and order in domestic politics; and even the foreign policy—all is dependent upon commerce with the outside world.

Inability to export is the bugaboo of South American governments. And so this continent pursues deliberately an export policy, often in the style of that formulated by the Russian Finance Minister Wischnegradsky in the 'eighties of the last century: "It is better not to stuff our bellies full, but *export* we must." The same problem was stated by the Brazilian statesman, Cincinato Braga, as "to export, to export, and to export."[2]

This is the formulation of the balance-of-trade policy of capital-importing nations.

This foreign trade with South America has been always the object of strenuous rivalry. Modern industrial countries have sought and still are seeking to attract this market, to cajole it, to conquer and possess it. They foresaw and felt the potential capacity for investment capital on this continent; they followed its development and attempted to profit by it. The South American states owe their independence in part to England's avowed wish to take possession of these markets—an attitude that found an ally in the United States. Canning was reasonably clear and outspoken in his statements, and must be placed on Monroe's side in opposition to the peril of the Holy Alliance.[3]

The import trade from South America also was a bone of contention due to the wealth of products and to the continent's quasi-monopoly in certain commodities.

The nineteenth century exhibits a panorama of movements on the part of all the countries. Each new industrial power turned its eyes to this continent and struggled to win a place in the South American sun. The United States obtained entry at the end of the 'eighties, Germany was striving to come in, in order to divide the market with the old suppliers and the old customers: England and France. But the other nations as well—kindred Spain and Portugal, Italy, those historical colonizers the Dutch, the descendants of the Scandinavian Vikings, and others—all tried as best they might to get a share of the business.

The situation prior to the World War was as follows:

TABLE 1

THE TRADE WITH SOUTH AMERICAN REPUBLICS

(*Unit*: $1,000,000 *U.S.*)

	1910	1911	1912	1913
UNITED KINGDOM—				
Exports to South America ..	244	262	273	286
Imports from South America..	238	237	269	282
UNITED STATES—				
Exports to South America ..	111	130	153	168
Imports from South America..	192	195	243	204
GERMANY—				
Exports to South America ..	142	166	179	189
Imports from South America..	125	139	157	162
FRANCE—				
Exports to South America ..	70	77	84	90
Imports from South America..	93	98	104	105

Source: *Bulletin of the Pan-American Union*, annual trade summaries.

England held traditionally the first place; a moderate quota of the business went to France. The South American trade of the other Latin countries was inconsiderable and fluctuating, though Italy could point to a certain degree of accomplishment. The young industrial powers, the United States and Germany, were struggling to compete with their decadent rivals. The United States, in a relatively unspectacular fashion, on account of possessing an immense domestic market, were not regular exporters, but merely tried to find an outlet for their surplus in times of overproduction. Germany has since developed into a regular exporter and was trying to educate her impetuous young industry. The United States was active and successful in Latin North America and the Antilles.[4]

So the business was gone. South America profited by the competition of purveyors, made friendly connections with several, and built up a clientèle for her own products. She came to enter more and more into the money economy, into international economic relations. Business has added one new territory after another to the zone of modern economic life. The process of, as we used to say before the War, gradual Europeanization of the South American continent was set under way.

The War was an economic earthquake for this continent, which was not in the least prepared for the sudden simultaneous stoppage of maritime traffic, investment, commerce, immigration, and credit advancement.

The routine of life was broken. The providers had disappeared. The agents of the German firms no longer went in quest of orders; the French luxuries so much in demand were no longer to be had; the English houses had no more stocks; South America was thrown over by her old friends. Even trade with the neutral countries was checked. The usual exports ceased. And in South America foreign trade is the breath of life.

At this juncture the United States leapt into the breach. It was a triumphal entry. We saw a tremendous growth get under way in America's merchant shipping, trade, and the credit and investment markets. Pro-Allies and anti-Allies—both sides bought goods from North America—both rejoiced over this "aid."

And the United States made the most of it. With their well-known energy and willingness "to try," the Yankees sought to satisfy every demand. In all parts of the world there was feverish activity; United States goods were distributed to the most remote corners of the planet, with the help of former rivals: for England, France, and Italy, for military reasons, were obliged to facilitate the process in every way they could.

The decade 1914–24 saw an uninterrupted crusade of United States industrialism, which extended itself without let or hindrance, and which—through its profitable business—augmented the domestic market, and so promoted its own extension internally as well as externally. No other period in the world's history has witnessed the capture of foreign markets on such a scale. Never before had a nation had such an opportunity offered it, or utilized it to equal advantage. The whole world was flooded with United States goods.

The exports to Europe reached their highest point in 1919 ($5,187 million as compared with $1,499 million in 1913), and those to the other continents attained their maximum in 1920 (Africa, $165 million as against $28 million in 1913; Oceania, $171 million as against $79 million in 1913; and North America, $1,929 million as against $601 million in 1913).[5]

The growth of the United States trade with South America was in proportion; here, too, 1920 marked the high point (see Table 2).

South America has attempted to adapt herself to the changed circumstances, and has also—following the lead of the United States—sought to turn them to her own advantage, and to build up some industries. In this connection—even when the immediate consequences were not always of importance—this tempestuous period was an instructive one, during which the South American continent was introduced to the spirit

TABLE 2

GROWTH OF UNITED STATES TRADE WITH SOUTH AMERICA
(*Unit:* $1,000)

Year	Exports	Percentage Ratio to 1913	Imports	Percentage Ratio to 1913
1913	146,515	100	198,259	100
1914	91,013	62	229,520	116
1915	144,129	99	322,282	163
1916	220,267	152	427,610	216
1917	311,893	212	598,819	302
1918	302,710	206	610,931	308
1919	441,748	302	687,525	347
1920	623,917	425	760,999	384
1921	273,325	186	295,623	149
1922	226,075	154	358,763	181
1923	269,318	184	467,421	236
1924	314,252	214	466,074	235

Source: *Foreign Commerce and Navigation of the United States*, annual summary tables.

TABLE 3

GROWTH OF THE FOREIGN TRADE OF THE SOUTH AMERICAN REPUBLICS
(*Unit:* $1,000,000 *U.S.*)

Year	Exports	Percentage Ratio to 1913	Imports	Percentage Ratio to 1913
1913	1,160	100·0	1,020	100·0
1914	864	74·5	654	65·0
1915	1,177	101·5	524	51·4
1916	1,265	109·0	639	62·6
1917	1,431	123·5	899	88·1
1918	1,724	148·9	1,080	106·0
1919	2,187	188·9	1,368	134·0
1920	2,086	180·0	1,800	176·5
1921	1,329	114·5	1,365	134·0
1922	1,363	117·6	1,174	115·1
1923	1,665	143·7	1,470	144·1
1924	2,058	177·1	1,562	153·2

Source: *Bulletin of the Pan-American Union*, annual trade summaries. Percentages computed.

of capitalism. South America has indeed entered a new epoch. New opportunities in export and home trade have been discovered; new needs have arisen; and the continent has shared in the ups and downs of the great post-War speculation period.

The increased importance of the United States in the economic existence of the separate countries is shown by the figures in Table 4.

The period of storm and stress has now come to its close. The end of the German inflation, in 1924, must be regarded as marking the turn back to normalcy. Events no longer convulse the world. The heroic epoch of the War, the speculative frenzy that succeeded it, are closed chapters. Now settled normal existence asserts its sway. We try to live once more as before the War, exporting and importing, reappraising our friendships and enmities. There is even a demand for political peace; interests have been turned more to business, to art and culture—a natural reaction.

How is South America's foreign trade made up at the present time? What are the positions of the individual countries and their traders? Has the United States been able to retain the exceptional position she occupied in 1914–24? The answer is to be sought in the statistics for the period 1925–28 relative to 1913, with reference to the changes wrought by the War.

The figures for the total of South American foreign trade are necessarily subject to wide fluctuations. The extent to which this trade is dependent on crop yields and on the price situation, and the influence of the mono-production characteristic of these countries, appears in the figures shown in Table 5.

The export trade, which exceeded $1,000 million for the first time in 1913, underwent violent fluctuations in the 1914–24 period (reaching a high point in 1919); and in the subsequent period has begun to stabilize itself once more. The same holds true for the import trade, and for the balance of

TABLE 4

TRADE OF THE UNITED STATES WITH INDIVIDUAL SOUTH AMERICAN REPUBLICS

(*Unit:* $1,000)

(*Per cent. denotes percentage ratio to* 1913)

	1913	1920	1924
Argentina	79,759	421,502	192,391
Percentage	100	529	241
Bolivia	941	15,068	4,206
Percentage	100	1,600	447
Brazil	162,794	384,328	244,544
Percentage	100	236	150
Chile	43,732	175,791	129,661
Percentage	100	402	296
Colombia	23,378	112,775	85,493
Percentage	100	483	366
Ecuador	5,592	26,724	12,234
Percentage	100	478	219
Paraguay	246	2,994	935
Percentage	100	1,218	380
Peru	17,009	110,715	46,729
Percentage	100	650	274
Uruguay	9,973	67,502	25,292
Percentage	100	676	254
Venezuela	16,589	51,593	34,106
Percentage	100	311	206

1913, fiscal year ending June 30; 1920 and 1924, calendar years.

Source: *Foreign Commerce and Navigation of the United States.* Percentages computed.

TABLE 5

FOREIGN TRADE OF THE SOUTH AMERICAN REPUBLICS

(*Unit:* $1,000 *U.S.*)

Year	Exports	Percentage Ratio to 1913	Imports	Percentage Ratio to 1913
1913	1,166,065	100	1,022,009	100
1925	2,005,079	172	1,804,669	176
1926	1,911,811	164	1,771,552	174
1927	2,135,959	183	1,765,866	173
1928	2,282,113	196	1,915,835	188

Source: *Bulletin of the Pan-American Union,* annual trade summaries. Percentages computed.

TABLE 6

FOREIGN TRADE BALANCE OF THE SOUTH AMERICAN REPUBLICS

(*Unit:* $1,000 *U.S.*)

Year	Exports	Imports	Excess of Exports
1913	1,166,065	1,022,009	144,056
1925	2,005,079	1,804,669	200,410
1926	1,911,811	1,771,552	140,259
1927	2,135,959	1,765,866	370,093
1928	2,282,113	1,915,835	366,278

Source: *Bulletin of the Pan-American Union,* annual trade summaries. Balance computed.

TABLE 7

EXPORTS OF THE SOUTH AMERICAN REPUBLICS

(*Unit:* $1,000 *U.S.*)

	1913	1925	1926	1927	1928
Total	1,166,065	2,005,079	1,911,811	2,135,959	2,282,113
Percentage	100	100	100	100	100
Argentina	468,999	841,892	768,413	979,045	991,351
Percentage	40	42	40	46	43
Bolivia	36,551	46,522	47,846	43,717	42,306
Percentage	3	2	2	2	2
Brazil	315,165	483,758	455,729	430,900	474,743
Percentage	27	24	24	20	21
Chile	144,653	228,582	201,357	205,633	239,052
Percentage	12	11	10	10	10
Colombia	34,316	81,832	108,366	105,729	115,500
Percentage	3	4	6	5	5
Ecuador	13,690*	35,241	12,714	19,206	19,676
Percentage	1	2	1	1	1
Paraguay	5,462	15,196	15,033	13,854	15,410
Percentage	1	1	1	1	1
Peru	44,410	105,708	116,475	151,621	153,181
Percentage	4	5	6	7	7
Uruguay	65,142	102,657	98,564	100,541	105,251
Percentage	6	5	5	5	5
Venezuela	29,484	63,690	76,313	85,714	117,644
Percentage	2	3	4	4	5

* 1912.

Source: *Bulletin of the Pan-American Union*, annual trade summaries. Percentages computed.

TABLE 8

Imports of the South American Republics

(*Unit:* $1,000 *U.S.*)

	1913	1925	1926	1927	1928
Total (100 per cent.)	1,022,009	1,804,669	1,771,552	1,765,866	1,915,835
Argentina	408,712	850,542	797,822	831,100	873,719
Percentage	40·0	47·1	45·0	47·1	45·6
Bolivia	21,358	26,545	27,624	22,740	27,462
Percentage	2·1	1·4	1·6	1·3	1·4
Brazil	326,429	406,162	386,452	387,036	441,826
Percentage	31·9	22·5	21·8	21·9	23·0
Chile	120,274	148,844	157,318	130,583	146,044
Percentage	11·8	8·2	8·9	7·4	7·6
Colombia	28,536	83,255	107,370	121,993	135,500*
Percentage	2·8	4·6	6·1	6·9	7·0
Ecuador	10,355†	26,844	9,415	11,410	15,858
Percentage	1·0	1·5	0·5	0·6	0·8
Paraguay	7,672	17,123	11,839	11,618	13,876
Percentage	0·8	0·9	0·7	0·7	0·7
Peru	29,591	88,807	95,059	94,110	85,665
Percentage	2·9	4·9	5·4	5·3	4·5
Uruguay	50,666	97,937	99,064	85,103	97,479
Percentage	5·0	5·4	5·6	4·8	5·1
Venezuela	18,030	58,609	79,590	70,173	80,406
Percentage	1·8	3·2	4·5	4·0	4·2

* Estimated. † 1912.

Source: *Bulletin of the Pan-American Union*, annual trade summaries.

foreign trade. It is definitely a stabilization period for the whole continent, as well as for the individual countries.

The shares of the various South American republics are shown in Table 7.

In the export trade Argentina's share, which during the War varied between 37 per cent. and 49 per cent., has become stabilized at around 44 per cent. Brazil's share, which varied between 17 per cent. and 38 per cent., has become stabilized at around 24 per cent. to 21 per cent. Chile's proportion, too, has decreased somewhat.

These three countries shipped in 1914 84 per cent. and in 1928 75 per cent. of the total exports of South America.

Conspicuous gains have been made by Peru, Venezuela, and Colombia, which in 1928 accounted respectively for 7, 5, and 5 per cent. of the total South American exports, as compared with 4, 2, and 3 per cent. in 1913.

This consequence of the War—the opening-up of new territories—we shall look into further.

In the import trade Argentina's share, after fluctuating in the former period between 33 per cent. and 57 per cent. of the total, has become stabilized at 45 per cent. to 47 per cent.; Brazil's varied from 16 per cent. to 31 per cent., and now has settled around 22 per cent. to 23 per cent. Chile's declined from 12 per cent. in 1913 to 8 per cent. in 1925 and 7 per cent. in 1927, but increased again slightly in 1928.

The ABC countries together received in 1913 79 per cent. and in 1928 77 per cent. of all the imports of South America. This small loss, as well as loss of other countries, are gained by the countries of the northern coast.

	1913	1928
Colombia	2·8	7·0
Venezuela ..	1·8	4·2

These two countries, with their increased shares of export and import trade, appear to be experiencing also in import trade the benefits of newly opened-up countries.

TABLE 9

FOREIGN TRADE OF SOUTH AMERICAN REPUBLICS

(*Unit:* 1,000 *U.S.*)

	1913	1925	1926	1927	1928
UNITED STATES					
Imports from South America	204,287	522,145	559,676	512,907	571,920
Percentage Ratio to 1913	100	256	274	251	280
Exports to South America	167,523	498,525	543,661	531,807	581,524
Percentage Ratio to 1913	100	298	324	317	347
UNITED KINGDOM					
Imports from South America	281,988	409,361	363,937	470,317	482,866
Percentage Ratio to 1913	100	145	129	167	171
Exports to South America	285,555	381,995	320,864	330,392	364,117
Percentage Ratio to 1913	100	134	112	116	128
FRANCE					
Imports from South America	104,971	155,456	111,032	138,407	148,494
Percentage Ratio to 1913	100	148	106	132	142
Exports to South America	89,520	107,748	113,858	112,795	127,326
Percentage Ratio to 1913	100	120	127	126	142
GERMANY					
Imports from South America	162,026	161,168	154,698	268,775	273,196
Percentage Ratio to 1913	100	100	95	166	169
Exports to South America	188,901	211,887	205,481	198,672	225,008
Percentage Ratio to 1913	100	112	109	105	119
ITALY					
Imports from South America	26,166*	81,585	69,415	—	—
Percentage Ratio to 1913	100	312	266	—	—
Exports to South America	58,908*	113,743	108,497	—	—
Percentage Ratio to 1913	100	193	184	—	—

* Not including trade with Uruguay—no data.

Source: *Pan-American Union*, Foreign Trade Series and bulletins.

TABLE 10

Total Foreign Trade and South American Trade of Leading Countries

(Unit: $1,000,000 U.S.)

	1913			1928		
	Total Foreign Trade	Trade with South America		Total Foreign Trade	Trade with South America	
	(Value)	(Value)	(Percentage of Total)	(Value)	(Value)	(Percentage of Total)
U.S.A.	4,279*	364*	8·5	9,220*	1,050*	11·4
United Kingdom	6,830†	542‡	7·9	9,931†	487§	4·9
France	2,953†	197‡	6·7	4,108†	276§	6·7
Germany	4,970†	336‡	6·8	6,264†	498§	8·0
Italy	1,189†	—	—	1,923†	—	—

Sources: * *Foreign Commerce and Navigation of the United States.*
† *World Almanac*, 1930.
‡ *Bulletin of the Pan-American Union.*
§ *Bulletin of the Pan-American Union*, March, 1930, pp. 256–59.

We come to the crucial question: How have the relative standings of the competitors on the South American market changed?

A comparison of Tables 5 and 9 shows that before the War South America sent about 20 per cent. of her exports to the United States. In the War and post-War years this proportion fluctuated violently, going as high as 42 per cent. before settling down in the 1924–28 period about a new level of 25 per cent.

The movement in the case of the United Kingdom was just the reverse. Her share in South American commerce, which was 25 per cent. in 1913, had fallen to 21 per cent. in 1928. This percentage kept relatively steady even during the War; connections were not interrupted.

France's position is somewhat improved at the return of stability. Germany, despite the annihilation of her trade by the War, has regained her former place.

South America has not kept the United States as a customer on the quantitative level of the War and immediate post-War period. During the War, however, the figures offer a sort of optical illusion, in that the United States was purchasing goods also *for* the other countries.

The chief buyers of South American exports are the same as before the War, with the difference that the United States and the United Kingdom have changed places.

The picture of the imports of South America shows us that the share of the United States therein, after reaching 44 per cent. during the War, has settled down in the 1925–28 period to about 30 per cent. A part of this War-time increase is to be ascribed to the importation of goods from other countries under United States labels. But it remains as a numerical fact that the share of the United States is practically double what it was; it has gained fully 14 per cent.

A part of the increase in imports from the United States is to be ascribed to the opening up of new markets in Venezuela and Colombia.

But it is not sufficiently clear if this 14 per cent. has been gained also at the expense of Europe, in spite of the fact that the United Kingdom's share has shrunk from 28 per cent. to 19 per cent., France's from 9 per cent. to 6 or 7 per cent., and Germany's from 19 per cent. to 12 per cent. (This last figure represents a great accomplishment on the part of Germany, in spite of cessation of business during the War and reduction of territory.)

Let us see what constitutes these imports from the United States. What are the chief classes of goods that the United States has been shipping to South America? What commodities within these classes are mainly responsible for the growth? What sort of import trade in the same commodities was there from other countries prior to the War? Has the importation of these goods from other countries diminished, i.e., have United States goods displaced their foreign competitors? Or is it a question of the satisfying of *new* wants by *new* sorts of commodities?

The chief bulk of the United States' exports is shown in Table 12, page 36.

The Department of Commerce makes the following interpretation:

The development of new export fields, and the increasing distribution of new products which were little known and less widely used before the War, testify to the increasing purchasing power of the Latin-American peoples as well as their intention to avail themselves of all those varied items which have ceased to be regarded as luxuries and are accepted as necessary to a more comfortable everyday existence. With the improvement in Latin-American purchasing power there has been an increased demand for quality merchandise, even in those markets which are regarded as essentially price markets. Moreover, in addition to the extensive advertising and greater coverage of the markets by salesmen, the increasing stream of Latin-American visitors to the United States has carried back the desire to obtain the latest types of merchandise, electrical equipment, office appliances, the newest lacquers, high-grade machinery both agricultural and industrial, fine hardware, and similar articles, in which American mass production makes possible increased quality and lower prices, have enjoyed considerable increases each year.

The continued development of such articles and the more intensive

TABLE 11

UNITED STATES DOMESTIC EXPORTS TO SOUTH AMERICA BY COMMODITY CLASSES

(*Unit:* $1,000,000)

Year	Total	Crude Materials	Crude Foodstuffs	Manu-factured Foodstuffs	Semi-Manu-factures	Finished Manu-factures
1905–09*	74	1	1	9	12	53
1910–14*	121	3	1	12	22	83
1915–19*	248	11	5	21	47	16
1921–25†	294	8	4	22	46	214
1923‡	268	6	3	19	47	192
1924‡	312	9	3	23	53	223
1925‡	400	6	5	33	65	291
1926‡	441	16	12	31	68	314
1927‡	436	6	7	28	77	317
1928‡	478	3	7	30	72	365

* Average of five fiscal years ending June 30th.
† Average of five calendar years.
‡ Calendar years.

Source: *Foreign Commerce and Navigation of the United States.*

TABLE 12

VALUES OF CERTAIN UNITED STATES EXPORTS

(*Unit:* $1,000,000)

	1913	1925	1926	1927	1928
Passenger automobiles	25·3	184·9	176·4	208·0	263·6
Automobile engines	1·6	15·3	12·5	10·9	13·0
Tyres and tubes ..	4·6	27·9	31·6	40·8	36·9
Electrical machinery	27·0	53·3*	84·4	84·8	89·0
Petroleum and products	159·8	473·0	554·5	485·9	525·5

* 1922.

Source: *Commerce Year Book*, 1929, Vol. I, pp. 323, 441, 459, 485.

TABLE 13

VALUES OF CERTAIN UNITED STATES EXPORTS

(*Unit:* $1,000,000)

	Average 1910–14	1913	1922	1925	1926	1927	1928
PASSENGER AUTOMOBILES							
Total exports..	—	25·3	—	184·9	176·4	208·0	263·6
Exports to South America ..	2·9*	—	—	37·7	35·6	38·9	52·9
Percentage of total	—	(11·4)	—	20·4	20·2	18·7	20·1
ELECTRICAL MACHINERY							
Total exports..	—	27·0	53·3	—	84·4	84·8	89·0
Exports to South America ..	—	—	7·5	—	—	17·8	17·8
Percentage of total	—	—	14·0	—	—	21·1	20·0

* Partial figure (seven chief republics only).

Source: *Commerce Year Book*, 1929, Vol. I, pp. 147–54, 461.

study of the market are expected to compensate for any decline that may occur in the value of long-established staples.[6]

(It would be interesting to compare the positions of the United States and the United Kingdom in South American import trade *after deducting automobiles*.)

This 14 per cent. which the United States has gained in the South American trade is partially a result of the development of her natural markets on the north coast of the continent, but is mainly *one of the manifestations of her winning of world markets in individual export commodities which go to fill new and previously non-existent wants*.

Table 14 opposite shows where the gains have been made in the foreign trade of the United States: automobiles, oil, machinery; "King Cotton" has a backward development to show.

It is a known fact that the growth in United States' exports is chiefly in finished manufactures;[7] that all other commodity classes are losing in relative importance; and that about 45 per cent. of total exports is made up of these finished manufactures.

In this category first place is taken by motor vehicles and petroleum, with a few particular mass-production manufactures. It is remarkable that no writer has yet depicted Uncle Sam for us, riding to the world market in his own automobile with a stock of gasolene, tires, and parts, equipped with radio, telephone, and telegraph, with a cash register and a typewriter; nor has he neglected to bring along his safety-razor blades and his motion pictures.[8]

Just as the textile industry was the foundation of British imperialism, and just as the German rise to world economic power was based on chemistry, so the *automobile* brings the United States to her position on world markets.

It is no wonder that this branch of the export trade is growing, when we recall that out of a world production of 5,203,139 cars, 4,358,759 were made in the United States, and that of the remainder a considerable fraction was merely *assembled* abroad.

TABLE 14

PERCENTAGE CHANGE IN LEADING EXPORTS, AND PERCENTAGE WHICH EACH FORMS OF THE TOTAL VALUE OF EXPORTS

	Value, Percentage Change in 1928 from:		Percentage of Total Value of Exports in:		
	1910–14	1921–25	1910–14	1921–25	1928
Petroleum and its products	+311·4	+29·7	6·0	9·4	10·4
Automobile parts and accessories	+1971·8	+182·3	1·1	4·1	9·9
Machinery	+214·2	+54·9	7·4	7·4	9·9
Cotton	+66·7	+14·3	25·9	18·7	18·3

Source: *Commerce Year Book*, 1929, Vol. I, p. 116.

No single branch shows such a growth!

TABLE 15

PERCENTAGES OF TOTAL UNITED STATES EXPORTS, CONSISTING OF AUTOMOBILES AND OF UNMANUFACTURED COTTON

(*Unit:* 1 *per cent. of total exports*)

	Automobiles*	Cotton
1910–14 (average of fiscal years)	1·1	25·9
1921–25 (average of calendar years) ..	4·1	18·7
1928 (calendar year)	9·9	18·3

* Including parts and accessories.

Source: *Commerce Year Book*, 1929, Vol. I, Table 18, p. 116.

"We do not fear competition if the commodity concerned is made by machinery and not by hand," declares the Department of Commerce.[9]

Among the finished manufactures the foreign demand is in general largest for highly elaborated articles produced by mass methods. In the case of many such articles, however, the high standards of living in the United States create a market much greater than that of all the rest of the world combined, although in a few instances exports constitute a large proportion of the output. We export over half of our annual output of motor cycles, over one-third of the typewriters, one-fourth of the sewing-machines, and about one-fifth of the agricultural machinery. In the case of cash registers and automobiles the proportion exported is about one-eighth. There is no conspicuous tendency toward change in these proportions.

Exports constitute a considerable fraction of the output of refined mineral oils; the proportion is largest in the case of kerosene, although foreign markets are taking a smaller part of the output of that commodity in recent years than formerly.[10]

In 1912–13, grains, machinery, cotton cloths, wood products, meats, and leather stood higher than in 1928. In the past year vehicles have gained an even stronger hold upon first place, the increased demand for automobiles and parts having resulted in these products becoming the most important item in the trade to-day. Cotton cloths and grains still remain, and will continue to remain commodities of great importance in the trade; but automobile tires, which were practically nothing in 1913, have increased, until in 1928 they were valued at approximately one-fourth the value of cotton cloths. . . .

Notwithstanding the competition in many staple lines, we have continually forged ahead in creating new markets for the latest products of our industries. Automobile sales, which increased approximately 34 per cent. over those of 1927, indicate the increase in purchasing power which has taken place in Latin America. Sales of such goods, which were formerly regarded as luxury items, but which have become integral parts of everyday life, continue to mount, in spite the fact that many countries have undergone and are now undergoing periods of severe, and in many cases protracted, depression, which has temporarily limited their purchases.[11]

Or else these goods were *relieved of competition*, which idea is definitely corroborated in another place in the same publication:

The remarkable increase in our sales of automotive products, together with the rapid expansion in shipments of many new commodities, indicates that, notwithstanding the keen competition offered by our major European competitors, there is little evidence that our proportion of the trade was reduced in 1928.[12]

. . . Practically every type of automotive product was exported in much larger volume in 1928 than in any earlier year, and export records were also numerous among the office machinery and petroleum products groups.[13]

. . . Argentina ranks second only to Canada among the foreign markets for American automotive products, and automobiles, tractors, and gasolene were the principal commodities which were exported in that country in larger quantities in 1928 than the year before. These same commodities accounted for most of the increase in our exports to Brazil.[14]

It is only to countries within her sphere of influence that the United States sells other products as well in considerable quantities.

The expansion of trade with Colombia, on the other hand, was widely distributed, including such diverse commodities as lard, flour, shoes, rubber tires, cotton textiles, steel rails, and automobiles.[15]

The United States' success is almost entirely a question of non-competitive exports manufactured under United States mass-production methods.

The real difficulty is with the merchandising of competitive commodities. Americans have creditably succeeded in foreign markets in special lines such as typewriters, adding-machines, and cash registers, but success in these lines is no test of what can be done in iron and steel products, lumber, hardware, textiles, automobiles, paper, etc. It is in marketing such competitive articles that the exporter meets with vital competition, and it is in marketing them that a permanent export policy is not only desirable but imperative.[16]

It is not at all a question of the United States eliminating her erstwhile competitors, completely emancipating herself from Europe, and taking over the South American trade. It is simply that where an article is adapted to methods of mass-production under mass-organization, the United States will win out in the export of that article, to South America or to anywhere in the world.[17] The United States has become the world's workshop *for these articles*. But the United

States is the workshop for all the continents except Europe; exports to Europe consist chiefly of crude materials and foodstuffs.

This result conceals the revival of European competition in South America, a particularly keen competition, since European

TABLE 16

SOUTH AMERICA'S CHIEF EXPORTS TO THE UNITED STATES IN 1928

(*Unit:* $1,000,000)

Commodity	Total Value	Value Exported from Principal Sources
Coffee	272·5	Brazil, 189·9; Colombia, 69·6; Venezuela, 12·2
Hides and skins..	55·8	Argentina, 39·3; Brazil, 8·8; Uruguay, 3·7
Crude petroleum	42·8	Venezuela, 21·3; Colombia, 17·2; Peru, 2·7
Sodium nitrate ..	36·3	Chile (all)
Flaxseed	26·1	Argentina, 26·0
Crude copper ..	25·2	Chile, 12·7; Peru, 12·4
Raw wool ..	11·7	Argentina, 7·2; Uruguay, 2·7
Meat	10·4	Argentina, 6·4; Uruguay, 3·2
Rubber	5·7	Brazil, 5·1
Quebracho extract	4·3	Argentina, 4·2

Source: *Foreign Commerce and Navigation of the United States*, 1928, pp. 207, 212, 233, 236, 239, 243, 252, 266, 276, 284.

industry is in need of markets during periods of depression, and the great market at the east of the European continent is at present not in a position to take anything.

It is really worth noting that, amidst the belligerent spirit in which economic factors and the war propaganda of both sides helped the United States while she was yet playing the rôle of *tertius gaudens*, the success of the United States was assured only in and by extreme specialization. We shall later have occasion to come back to this point.

In 1920 it looked as if the United States were monopolizing the trade: 33 per cent. of the export and 42 per cent. of the import business of South America was in her hands. But times have changed. European competition has been staging a successful come-back.

A consideration of the distribution of United States' imports from South America, Table 16, p. 42, shows that the character of South America's specialized lines of production is advantageous for the United States' interests, which are in the market primarily for certain crude staples, and which not infrequently consolidate or organize thereby a control of the international market in these goods.[18]

The tariff policy of the United States has attracted these raw materials. The percentage of goods sent free of duty into the United States in 1928 was 63·9; for imports from South America it rises to 88·6 per cent., and for imports from the North Coast to the impressive figure of 98·5. From the West Coast less of imports—94·8 per cent.—are free, and from the East Coast still less—82·7 per cent. Colombia and Venezuela each send 99·7 per cent. of their exports to the United States without payment of duty; Brazil, Chile, and Bolivia between 95·5 per cent. and 98·5 per cent.; and Ecuador and Peru about 90 per cent. The corresponding percentage for imports from the continent of Europe is only 38·2 per cent.[19]

The United States' particular customers in South America are as shown by the following figures for 1928:

TABLE 17

IMPORTS FROM THE UNITED STATES

(*Unit:* $1,000,000)

Argentina	178·9
Brazil	100·1
Colombia	58·6
Chile	40·4
Venezuela	37·8

The principal commodities imported from the United States are shown in the table which follows:

TABLE 18

SOUTH AMERICA'S CHIEF IMPORTS FROM THE UNITED STATES IN 1928

(*Unit:* \$1,000,000)

Commodity or Class	Total Value	Chief Importing Countries
Automobiles, parts and accessories	93·0	Argentina, 45·3; Brazil, 24·9; Colombia, 5·8; Uruguay, 5·5; Chile, 5·3
Refined oils	48·1	Brazil, 17·2; Argentina, 16·2; Chile, 7·2; Uruguay, 5·5
Industrial machinery ..	37·8	Argentina, 9·5; Venezuela, 7·0; Brazil, 6·2; Colombia, 5·4
Steel-mill products (includes pipe)	25·4	Venezuela, 7·2; Argentina, 5·7; Colombia, 3·7
Agricultural machinery..	23·2	Argentina, 20·8; Uruguay, 1·1; Brazil, 0·8
Cotton manufactures ..	22·9	Colombia, 6·1; Argentina, 5·2; Chile, 3·7
Electrical machinery and apparatus	17·7	Argentina, 6·6; Brazil, 4·8; Chile, 2·0
Iron and steel semi-manufactures	10·3	Argentina, 3·2; Brazil, 2·9; Colombia, 1·4
Wheat flour	9·9	Brazil, 5·2; Venezuela, 1·6; Colombia, 1·1
Oil machinery	6·8	Venezuela, 3·8; Argentina, 1·4

Source: *Foreign Commerce and Navigation of the United States*, 1928, pp. 36, 65, 101, 113, 115, 135, 145, 151, 164, 169.

Therein is the dissimilarity between the import and the export situations. The former suppliers of South America have not been willing to give over the market there to the United States.

South America has kept to her old customers of 1914–24, not having been enterprising enough to extend her old markets and conquer new ones. Then, too, new competition has arisen by reason of the quasi-monopoly (only quasi) position. There has been growth of internal competition as well (coffee!)

The conservatism of this market, which was an aid to Europe in the regaining of her position after the War, has held back the exploration of new markets for the South American export trade.

The situation of Brazil is specially peculiar:

TABLE 19

EXPORTS OF BRAZIL IN 1928 (DOMESTIC)

		Values in $1,000
To:	United States	215,992
	United Kingdom	16,363
	Germany	53,216
	France	43,566
	Italy	23,582
	Argentina	28,211

Source: *Commerce Year Book*, 1929, Vol. II, p. 94.

TABLE 20

IMPORTS OF BRAZIL IN 1928 (GENERAL)

		Values in $1,000
From:	United States	117,511
	Argentina	51,035
	Germany	55,142
	United Kingdom	95,219
	France	28,076
	Italy	16,425

Source: *Commerce Year Book*, 1929, Vol. II, p. 94.

Argentina and Uruguay are in a better position, for they are at least dependent not on a single *product*, but on a single *branch of economic activity*: agriculture. In 1928 this accounted for 56 per cent. of the Argentine and about 62 per cent. of the Uruguayan total exports.

In Brazil, exports of coffee are 75 per cent. of the total; in Chile, nitrate and copper are 78 per cent.; in Bolivia, tin is 92 per cent.; in Ecuador, cacao and coffee are 50 per cent.; in

Peru, petroleum is 35 per cent. (the rest is well distributed among cotton, sugar, and copper); in Venezuela, petroleum is 73 per cent.

As we shall see, although no foreign peril, no danger of commercial monopolization, appears to threaten South America, rather another danger is at hand: the whole continent, and each separate country, are suffering from their mono-production and mono-export.

There is no monopolization of the South American market going on, either on the part of the United States or on that of any other country, either in export or in import trade.

Relations are much the same as before the War so far as the sharing of business by the chief industrial powers is concerned.

There is only one difference: the *new* market in automobiles, tires and accessories, motion pictures, radio and other electrical apparatus, etc., is under the control of the United States (as it is more or less over the rest of the world as well). Even in these products there is no conquest of the continent involved; it is merely one of the manifestations of the world-wide expansion of particular branches of the United States mass-production system.

"After we established freedom of commerce, Great Britain was the great new supplying country; it was only during the Great War of 1914–18 that the United States came into the list of new importers.

"Since the Peace Treaty Great Britain has regained her position, while the United States, which had come to be our principal supplier, maintained its position in 1925, 1926, and 1927. Purchases of automobiles, gasolene, petroleum, and other articles have contributed greatly to this dislocation of trade favouring the United States."[20]

The foregoing is true not alone of Brazil. It is the same story for the whole South American foreign trade.

Of course, the situation is different in the different countries, especially in the north of the continent. The United States trade has found a new centre of gravity. Venezuela and Colombia—the geographical extension of the northern continent—are the new fields of their general activity.

On the Atlantic coast the United States maintains the most extended trade relations with Brazil; but Europe plays the principal part in the business with the Atlantic states.

On the Pacific coast the situation is about the same, despite the growth of commerce with the United States.

. . . . .

What are the results of the struggle for the South American trade for the United States? The monopolization is not accomplished (was not intended, as we shall see further), but the real success lies in the fact that the supply of raw materials for the domestic industries has been assured, and a new market for the newest mass-production industries created and brought into permanent connections. Both of the factors which Charles E. Hughes speaks of in reference to the trade with South America have come to fulfilment.[21]

In comparison with the beginning of the twentieth century, the great progress of the United States is evident. As late as 1911 attention was called in North American literature to the absence in South America of United States' commerce,[22] especially in comparison with the position of Great Britain and Germany's gains.

As an official publication of 1916 declares, "Exporting has meant little more to them than peddling abroad unsold wares."

Such is no longer the case. The United States has come into this market and has won an important part in it. The high record set during the War, however, has not been maintained, which was to some extent foreseen.[23]

(*b*) INVESTMENTS

Accurate statistics on the migrations of capital do not exist. The compilation of such information is made especially difficult by the fact that there are neither political nor customs frontiers for this most duty-free of exports. Yet *mobile* capital is characteristic of modern capitalism, and the first modern European institution of credit was the *Crédit Mobilier*. Capital is easily portable, its wanderings invisible, and its amounts cannot be stated definitely. It is not always possible to compute the volume of moving capital, or to establish its nationality.[1]

Statistical estimates on the movement of capital and investments have often been attempted. But these were only attempts, were summaries of unrelated facts and figures, and more or less round approximations. These studies are still in an embryonic stage.[2]

In the literature of South America one finds very few attempts at ascertaining even these statistics. Only for Argentina do such approximations exist (offered by Alejandro E. Bunge).[3] On the other hand, during the last few years in the United States several efforts were made to ascertain the volume of investments in South America (really in Latin America).

For Mexico, Central America, and the Antilles, data is abundant, and a thorough piece of research could be made on these countries in the near future. For the greater part of South America, however, materials are poor, and the work is still at that early stage where a careful and diligent collection of facts is necessary.

The published investigations by Frederick M. Halsey,[4] Robert W. Dunn,[5] Max Winkler,[6] as well as special research inquiries into particular countries (similar to that of Margaret A. March's work on Bolivia[7]) and several official publications, form the basis of the following observations.

(Among these works, only Halsey gives any virtually new material. Dunn dedicates infinite care to the collection and correlation of existing material, while Winkler offers a popularization of the data. A study of these books shows the necessity of organizing a broad programme for a systematic inquiry for data among American officials in South America, and sponsored perhaps by the Department of Commerce.)

The fact that United States' investments have increased enormously during and since the War is beyond dispute. The aim of this chapter is to analyse on a comparative basis the investments of various nations, the essential features of each, and to point out the specific character of United States' investments. This is not a mere matter of statistics, nor of description, nor of "Idiography," but rather consists of attempting to locate the *typical* in the methodological sense of Max Weber.

South America is homogeneous in its lack of capital. Rich or poor, small or great, on the Atlantic or the Pacific coast, all countries on this continent are indebted to foreign countries, and depend continually on the influx of foreign capital to make their natural resources productive and often to bolster up their state finances.

The national formation of capital is limited, and the organization of their domestic capital market does not exist. Most of the material and social ills of South America are due to insufficiency of capital and especially the transportation problem—*falta caminos* is the cry of every country, community, and village.

The Anglo-Saxon nations dominated in the field of capital exports to South America for over a hundred years. During the nineteenth century England was pre-eminent and without a comparable second. In the 'eighties French capital began to strike out paths toward South America. At the close of the century Germany followed. One after another the political rivals made their entrance on the continent—the French nation of "rentiers," and the German industrial state. But there was room enough for the smaller countries too—Belgium, Holland, Spain, and Italy. In the War they all must give place to the new financial power—the United States.

Financial relations between *England* and South America had their origin in the support given to the colonial revolts against the peninsula. In the quest for markets, the former workshop of the world had a special interest in winning and educating South America as a customer. In this manner England became the first market for South American governmental credit. The states-in-the-making went to England *à la Polonaise* to exchange their indebtedness for London gold. (In 1822 came Peru, 1824 Brazil and Argentina, and so forth.)

Often England had to share the griefs and worries of the borrowers. The still unwritten history of these relations is in part a story of difficulties and agreements over new and more lenient terms and forms of payments. For generations it was a prolonged affair between an old astute and experienced money-lender and a youth with a golden future, and it reached a dramatic climax in the Baring Crisis of the 'nineties.

England had invested altogether £3,800,000 up to 1913. This was estimated in 1929 to be £4,500,000. In Argentina the English ranked first, as they did before. Bunge gives the estimates for 1927 in Argentina as follows:

English	4,700,000 pesos m/n
United States	1,150,000 ,,
Others	1,175,000 ,,

In Brazil in 1928 English capital was estimated to be £282,000,000.[8]

French relations with South America do not date back as far as the English. French investments are estimated by Dunn to be $425,000,000 in Argentina and smaller amounts in other countries. France was not a regular professional financier for Argentina and Brazil in spite of her continued relations with these countries. She participated only in occasional transactions. The primary interest of the French political policy lay in east Europe, where French savings were being directed. England often invited France to join in the larger financial operations, and these were frequently accepted with alacrity, as they were entirely consistent with the French principle of inactive participation. French capital is more often bondholder than stockholder, preferring to sleep well rather than eat well.[9]

German capital exports were proportionally small, younger in origin, but spasmodically heavy. Germany sought to win an historical handicap over her rivals in this field. A debtor in Europe, the German Empire tried to enter upon the American scene as a creditor. Germany, being usually a borrower of short-term loans, became a lender in the long-term foreign markets. The amounts she offered were still small, but her competition was keen. In many countries she succeeded in gaining a foothold. The strong bank organization prepared and managed these investments. Dunn estimates the German investments in Argentina to have been about $375,000,000; more or less exact figures for Brazil do not exist; in Bolivia $20–25,000,000; in Peru $22,000,000.

Prior to the War *Italy*, as well as the other Latin countries, *Spain* and *Portugal*, was insignificant as a capital-exporting nation, in spite of several investments in South America, which were effected through private family relations and friendships, and which cannot be estimated. Dunn's figures for Spain's capital in Argentina is $60,000,000. Besides the usual money transfers from and to immigrants, the great social intercourse of these three Latin countries with South America stimulated surely in several instances the beginnings of continued financial relations.

Dunn's appraisal of Italian investments in Argentina at $25,000,000 appears to be an underestimation, especially in comparison with Italy's estimated $40,000,000 in Peru.

Larger but not of great importance were the investments of *Belgium* and *Holland.* According to Dunn, these amounted in Argentina to $135,000,000 and $150,000,000 respectively.

The *United States* appeared on the scene in an important rôle only in the twentieth century, in spite of occasional transactions prior to this time. Only in the Latin countries of North America were there substantial investments by the United States.

John Hay, Secretary of State, interpreted in 1902 the state of mind prevailing in business circles when in a moment of enthusiasm he exclaimed: "The debtor nation has become the chief creditor nation. The financial centre of the world, which required thousands of years to journey from the Euphrates to the Thames and the Seine, seems passing to the Hudson between daybreak and dark."[10]

This prophecy was fulfilled only in the World War. In Hay's time the United States was not ripe for this evolution. In 1913 Enock emphasized German competition, but observed that "North American interests have been practically unpresented, but there are indications that American groups are to enter the field."[11] The United States heeded the wartime exhortation by F. A. Vanderlip: "The United States should cease to be a financially provincial people."[12]

The United States' investments in South America were estimated in 1913 to be $173,000,000, against $2,294,000,000 in 1929. Great Britain's rose from $3,800,000,000 to $4,500,000,000. During this period Great Britain could only foster and furnish with capital the already existing relations. France did not invest any amounts of importance. German investments were wiped out, and the country became the greatest debtor in world history. The extension of the success of the United States and its accelerated tempo are singular in world economy.

The War and the period following led other capital exporters to South America. Italy in connection with the active policy of its young industrialism and its new imperialism, Spain invigorated by gains of the War and stimulated by political aims, promoted their influence and importance. Undoubtedly the investments of Holland and Sweden will reach higher amounts than before the War. Belgium, however, did not return.

The increase of the United States' investments is without parallel. The United States has not only sent her own new capital to South America, but has also taken over English, French, and German interests. The United States did not eject Europe from South America but leaped into her position.[13]

It is with increasing interest that one reads the papers of the first financial Inter-American Conference. The question of a United Bank organization throughout all Latin America through the twelve Federal Reserve Banks was in the fore.[14] Buying up Latin-American debts and securities which had been placed in Europe was a subject of serious discussion.[15]

The United States was a saviour in time of distress.

All the countries of Latin America had to pass in review before the conference and display their strength—their financial balances. The representatives of the United States at the conference understood well enough the purpose of their mission. Disregarding the official declarations of brotherhood and their customary enthusiasm, the committee proceeded to award ratings to the credit-seekers according to their financial strength. The aim of the conference was selfish, and no efforts were made to conceal it. In the words of a member of the conference:

"What is the principal object of this conference? The commercial expansion of the United States in Latin America, taking advantage of the situation created by the European War. All the rest is subsidiary.

"From the standpoint of the Latin countries the corollary of that premise should be: Given the situation created by the European War and the mutual necessity of extending American commerce in the Latin Republics of the continent, to request of American finance the necessary elements for the development of our natural resources and of our national commerce."[16]

The general picture changes in different countries. Judging geographically, European capital still ranks first on the Atlantic seaboard. On the Pacific coast the rivals enjoy about equal standing. The United States is predominant on the northern coast, in Colombia, and in Venezuela. The last two can in this respect also be considered as an economic extension of Central America and the Antilles. One can find here many oft-recurring names in the story of expansion in Central America and the Antilles, such as the United Fruit Company, Atlantic Fruit, Caribbean Oil Syndicate, Caribbean Coal Company, and others, including, of course, the Standard Oil Company.

On the entire continent, however, the European rivals are no longer able to expand with the same rapidity as the United States after 1913.

The following tabulation furnishes a comparison between the United States and Great Britain, one of the few countries for which anything like accurate figures exist, thanks to the brilliant statistical investigation of foreign investments by Sir George Paish.[17]

TABLE 21

INVESTMENTS IN SOUTH AMERICA

In Millions of Dollars

	United States		Great Britain	
	1913	1929	1913	1929
ATLANTIC COAST				
Argentina	40	611	1,860	2,140
Brazil	50	476	1,161	1,413
Uruguay	5	64	239	217
PACIFIC COAST				
Chile	15	395	331	389
Equador	10	25	14	22
Peru	35	150	133	140
NORTHERN COAST				
Colombia	2	260	34	37
Venezuela	3	161	41	92
INTERIOR				
Bolivia	10	133	2	12
Paraguay	3	15	15	18
Total	173	2,294	3,834	4,485

A study of the nature of these investments leads to a division into two categories. The first class consists of

Government, municipal, and industrial bonds and stocks, which found their way to the stock exchanges of the capital-exporting countries and are listed there. A great many South American securities are listed and traded in London; many can be found in Paris; and recently several in New York.

Thus on the list of the London Stock Exchange one can find South American Government and municipal, railroad and public utility stocks and bonds, and similar issues. The money for these securities was recruited from savings throughout the country. The old wealth of England would dispatch its yearly income to South America, as well as to other continents, and set it to work there. The English merchant banker, the foreign banker, who understood his market and had studied its conditions for generations past, organized this flow of investments and often participated in it himself. The joint-stock company and its shares of small value were coming to play an important part in capital exports. Investments abroad are the consequences of the operations of merchant bankers who, following the famous English principle of division of banking activity, specialized each in his own particular field.

The list of Paris quotations includes, besides Government bonds, railroads and banks, especially mortgage banks which French capital always favoured. The French *banques d'affaires* organized these investments and offered them for public purchase. They used the *guichets* of the depositing banks. They were seldom interested in any economic side-purposes or auxiliary possibilities of gain.[18]

New York quotations similarly list South American Government and municipal bonds, and occasionally railroad issues. These are likewise investments of the general public. The main objective in the purchase of these securities was their yield. They constitute the loans underwritten by the great houses of issue in the United States, and distributed through dealers and sold by their salesmen to the general public, except for large lots purchased directly from the issue houses by various investment trusts. In the last case one finds an important difference between the European and the United States system. In the former the owner of South American securities remains in direct relation to the debtor. In the system prevailing in the United States this relation is completely impersonal, for investment trusts and holding companies keep the securities in their portfolios and sell to the public their own certificates of issue. This form of investing has in the United States become an organized mechanized system of distribution connected with the yearly reappearance of capital-seeking investment. The dealer, the salesman—these figures are typical of the market organization in this country, but are entirely unknown in Europe.

One can, however, rarely find the United States' industrial investments in South America listed on the stock exchange. They are invisible investments, and therein lies the difference between the system of capital exportation from the United States and that from Europe. Dunn, Winkler, and others tell of millions of United States' investments in South American industry. But whence this money? What are these industries? And who owns them?

These stocks are not listed on the stock exchange; no prospectus exists for them; the general investor has nothing to do with them.

If we travel through the different countries and undertake a review of foreign investments in South America, one can see that each borrower developed certain specific fields for his investments. The French had a predilection for mortgage banks (typically "rentier" and true not only for South America but for the entire world) and railroads. They play mostly the passive rôle of the lender and not of the entrepreneur.[19] These enterprises originate through the capital support of France, and pay tribute to the stockholders, although remaining South American companies.

England made South America fertile with railroads. "The

most active nation in the commercial conquest of Latin America so far has been Great Britain. The development of the principal Latin-American Republics was begun with British gold. It built the railways, opened the mines, and financed the plantations and the banks to an extent greater than that of all other investing nations combined."[20] In South America there are no subsidiaries of the English railroads. Similarly public utility companies are national enterprises founded with the help of the English capital market. The difference in character between the English and French investments is that the English tendency is to retain management. "Scores of offices and boards of directors in London attest the part played by the British merchant and shareholder in those regions."[21] The Englishman is fond of his own activities. "It is his railroads that tie this country together. It is his enterprises that have opened thousands of its square miles; and although the folly of his ancestors a century ago caused him to lose the political control of this 'purple land,' the energy of his more recent forbears has given him a splendid heritage. Not only has he been able to pay large dividends to the British stockholders who have such great faith in the future of Argentina, but he has made many native Argentinos wealthy beyond the dreams of avarice."[22]

An inspection of the industrial enterprises of the United States in South America reveals that they are mostly affiliates and subsidiaries of corporations in the United States. It is not the man in the street who has placed his capital in South American industrial securities, but it is the great United States' concerns which have organized these enterprises with their own funds, neither offering the stocks for sale to the general public, nor issuing certificates representing their holdings in these companies. Instead they keep for themselves this continual participation, and if they need more funds, they procure them through their own issues.

To-day the investors of the United States in South American industry are the world's greatest industrial giants.[23]

A bird's-eye view of the allocations of capital on the continent reveals European investments to be geographically extensive and industrially diversified, railroads being the foundation of these investments; on the other hand, the investments of the United States appear to be concentrated heavily in a few industries. The European investments may be likened to spacious buildings which extend over a great acreage, but are only a few stories high. The investment structures of the United States, however, cover little ground, but are skyscrapers. European investments are more diversified, for the principle of the savings is: "Don't put all the eggs in one basket." In the case of the direct investments of the United States, the intention is to concentrate on one basket. Immediate yield from industrial investments is of no consideration to the United States investor, but it is indispensable to the European.

Everywhere on the continent people drive General Motors' automobiles and Ford cars. They depend on the Standard Oil Company for gasolene and oil. They telephone and telegraph by means of the International Telephone and Telegraph Company and the Radio Corporation of America. They ride the tramways of the American Foreign Light and Power Corporation and the Electric Bond and Share Corporation and use light and power supplied by these companies. In the field of construction the American International Corporation and Ulen and Company are well entrenched. Cement of the International Cement Corporation is used. The United States Steel Corporation, of course, is well represented. In mining, Anaconda Copper and Guggenheim Brothers dominate together with several others. Meat-packing is controlled by Swift and Company, Armour and Company, Wilson and Company and Morris and Company.[24] And banana plantations are cultivated in South America with the same efficiency as in Central America and the Antilles by the United Fruit Company and the Atlantic Fruit Company. There is no exportation of capital from the United States to the industry of South America, which is not an extension of the domestic business of industrial concerns in the United States.[25]

In noting that in her credit organization the United States is represented in South America by branches of her world-wide banking institutions (and no single branch of a purely European bank exists there), one cannot help feeling himself to be in the familiar environment of the giant organizations native to the United States. And in the United States, contrary to the European system, large industry dominates often over banks.

It is always the same concerns which are represented in the various countries. Industrial investments are not interested in the *country*, but in its *own branch of specialization*. Just as before the War Belgium built tramways all over the globe, and after the War Kreuger and Toll conquered the match industry of the entire world,[26] so the largest concerns of the United States are seeking to extend their field of work to cover the earth, and in prospecting about the world they do not neglect South America. Theirs are not investments of savings, and their primary interest does not lie in yield, but in the extension of their domestic business. They are not mainly interested in this continent, nor in any particular country thereof. The Standard Oil Company operates throughout the entire world wherever there is a trace of oil. Swift and Company owns subsidiary companies not only in Argentina, Brazil, Uruguay, Paraguay, but also in Canada, Great Britain, Cuba, Australia, and other countries; Armour and Company in Argentina, Brazil, Uruguay, Australia, Canada, Great Britain, Germany, France, Italy, Denmark, Cuba; Morris and Company in Uruguay, France, Holland, Norway, Germany, Belgium, Great Britain; Wilson and Company in Brazil, Great Britain, and other countries. One can find the General Motors Corporation in the farthest corner of the world.[27]

Except for the case of Ford, who recently placed in Europe a part of the issues of his subsidiaries and who is not typically

American in his financial methods—where are the stocks of the subsidiaries of those concerns issued or traded? Nowhere. Because the aim of those investments is not financial but industrial; banks and stock exchanges have nothing to do with them.

Brazilian Traction is one of the best-known and greatest public utilities operating in South America. The famous Belgian banker, Alfred Loewenstein, aided in the founding of this company. It is a Canadian Corporation whose stocks are listed in London, Paris, Brussels, Montreal, and New York. This company was a typically European investment organized with the help of the public market.

The Electric Bond and Share Corporation bought a controlling block of stock in it. With what aim? For the extension, the rounding-out, and the completion of its field of work. Newspaper accounts of this purchase of control were subsequently denied, but the objective was nevertheless achieved. "American and Foreign Power and Brazilian Traction make two connections, rival companies operating also in São Paulo."[28] European investments abroad are the results of the operations of private wealth, of "rentiers" (not business enterprises), undertaken through intermediary merchant bankers or *banques d'affaires*. A new type of person is pushing himself into the fore and grasps at the straw of British economy. Instead of the entrepreneur, who is rooted at home and bowed down with the weight of buildings and machines, there appears the financier who produces values in order to dispose of them as soon as possible.[29]

The industrial investments of the United States, however, are direct, and originate in the quest of ultra-modern mass-production for new worlds to conquer. Here, on the other hand, it is not the financier, but the industrial corporation which organizes and leads these developments. So in this sense we cannot speak of a pure financial capitalism in the United States.

There are altogether, perhaps, thirty great—nay, greatest—corporations of the world officially domiciled in the United

States, which direct the industrial investments of the United States in South America. The capital market has, as a rule, no connection with these investments.

If we investigate the activity of these enterprises, we are forced to conclude that they are in the main mere outposts of the United States. Their capital is the property of the parent organization. Raw materials are merely supplied by them. Credit is obtained from home banks, while the distribution of the products and the management of the company both reside in the United States. Supervision, methods, practices are all directed in the United States. It is characteristic of such South American enterprises that they do not produce for the national market of the country in which they operate. What, then, is South America's contribution to this business? The land, natural resources, and often the labour, but not always. The South American Company is really in this case a local extension of the parent corporation, and constitutes a point of expansion of industrial United States. It is a material branch of the main office, a piece of the United States abroad. Such world expansion is typical of the modern stage of capitalism, for national boundaries are too narrow for world enterprises.

The machine cannot stop; there is continual pressure to expand the natural boundaries of the domestic market. In order not to be limited by the raw material supply of one country, in order to be freed from its cyclical fluctuations, in order to be insured against the uncertainties of local natural phenomena—the giants of industry seek each in his own specialty to obtain world domination and to secure thereby a rationalization of their activity. For these reasons the Standard Oil is fighting for monopoly; the International Telephone and Telegraph for cable lines and centres of communications; General Motors for distributing facilities and outlets for their products. For these reasons Ford is securing rubber for the future through concessions in Brazil, and Firestone is entering Liberia. For the same reasons capital from the United States is invading Bolivia, after the exportation of tin ore to the United States from the Federated Malay States was prohibited by a heavy tax.[30]

Of course, exceptions can be found. Parallel with this extensive and highly specialized development of the world's industrial giants, one can find examples of a vast extensive development. W. R. Grace and Company exemplifies expansion in commerce, industry, shipping, agriculture, finance, and other fields, and leads one to recall the British type of colonial factory or the similar diversified activities in the style of Cecil Rhodes.[31] In the operations of the founder of this company (who was of Irish origin) in Peru one can discover certain political elements, which permit even a closer comparison with Cecil Rhodes.

However, this case, wherein the personality of the founder was of weighty importance, is not typical of the modern development. The modest beginnings of W. R. Grace, and the startling success of the following generation, the diversified and unspecialized growth, the broad universality of his business interests—all are relics of the past, of the epic days of United States business, of the time when individual personalities created and clashed. The general and unspecialized character of Grace's enterprise was an exception even in his time. For even then there "were principalities of iron, of copper, of oil, of gold and silver, of timber, of meat; and soon a great prince arose in each one of these zones of exploitation."[32]

Where it formerly required Rockefeller's genius for organization, the Standard Oil now has more systematic, precise, and scientific methods, gained through its amassed power, technique, and experience. The difference is that Rockefeller organized national production and conquered the domestic market, while the Standard Oil is concerned with the world production for the world market. A list of all its subsidiaries throughout the world would occupy pages and pages.

Those heroic personalities of former days now belong to history. The names Gould, Rockefeller, Astor, Carnegie are familiar to the entire world. But who, except the specialist, knows the names of the executive chiefs of the great corporations to-day? Leadership became impersonal. The capitalistic spirit has been replaced by the internal necessity for the corporation toward expansion and domination of the market. Methods have become mechanized. While previously the outcome of the struggle for markets was not always certain, it is now merely a question of time and patience. This rivalry in the case of the Standard Oil Company is not at an end because an extraordinarily strong personality leads the competition. Without Sir Henri Deterding the contest would have been decided long ago.[33]

Grace's plans to establish himself industrially in foreign countries might have been the result of an accident, a sudden idea, or inspiration. In the case of the huge corporations of to-day these developments follow from a carefully planned programme. Large staffs of statisticians and business scientists collaborate on these projects. It is no longer the spirit of Kipling's *Seven Seas*, nor of Shakespeare's royal merchant Antonio, which motivates these concerns abroad, as it did those pioneers of the United States in South America, such as Wheelwright and Meiggs. Foreign enterprise is no longer the result of a random idea or chance opportunity, nor personal energy and initiative; but is the automatic consequence of the press and stress of expanding mass-production. It is calculated, established, and directed by business administration. And so it is that the fate of a mining enterprise in distant Bolivia may depend on the investigation carried on by a statistical department on the fifty-second floor of a skyscraper in New York.[34]

. . . . .

The future of the exportation of capital from the United States is still uncertain. One cannot be sure that the United

States will continue its wartime and post-War rate of expansion in the field of passive investments where primary interest lies in yield. Most likely such exports will become more moderate in the near future, for the United States does not possess a great army of "rentiers" like France and Great Britain.[35] And only the "rentier" state has the passive investment as its "rentier" ideal. France with her zeal for thrift seems to be making the greatest exertion to regain her old status among capital-exporting countries. In this field the United States will participate on a larger scale only occasionally and not regularly, like France and Great Britain. Investigation of the distribution of income clearly demonstrates that the United States is not yet a nation of "rentiers." The United States is still not mature enough in this respect.[36] Although she has not yet settled into the position of a "rentier" state, the *direct* active investments of industry seem to give promise of further growth. For, applying an expression of Cecil Rhodes, to the present monsters of industry "extension is everything."

(*c*) FOREIGN TRADE AND INVESTMENTS OF THE UNITED STATES AS AN APPENDAGE OF MASS-PRODUCTION[1]

Let us compare the structures of foreign trade and of investments in South America. The *exports* from the United States in the main include a few articles of modern mass-production. Motor-cars, radios, phonographs, machines are a few products of newly organized large-scale industries, manufactured mainly for the satisfaction of new wants and symbolizing the technological culture of our times. Who produces these articles? Mainly the same "Big Thirty" with which we became acquainted in the foregoing expositions.

The *imports* of the United States from South America are mainly vegetable, mining, raw materials, such as petrol, tin, coffee. Who produces them in South America? Mainly the affiliated organizations of the same "Big Thirty" of the United States. Their investments virtually lie in factories which engage in an export business. Much of the foreign trade of the United States with South America is dominated by the same firms which are regular investors in the local South American industries. These mammoth concerns seem to be foremost not only in investments but also in foreign trade.

The following table presents a typical picture of these relations in Chile. If we compare 1910–14 with 1928, we must conclude that the only increase in exports from the

TABLE 22

PRINCIPAL UNITED STATES EXPORTS TO CHILE

(Unit: $1,000 U.S.)

	1910–14* (Average)	1926†	1928†
Cotton cloth	731	2,996	2,479
Boards	777	587	271
Gas and fuel oil	924	4,289	5,226
Lubricating oil	392	745	860
Paraffin wax	36	453	814
Iron and steel and manufactures of	3,780	7,818‡	5,422
Electrical machinery	371	5,066‡	1,964
Mining machinery	182	2,734‡	757
Construction and conveying machinery	2	1,967‡	672
Other industrial machinery	977	3,323‡	1,744
Motor trucks and buses	11	919	1,386
Automobiles, passenger	710	1,096	3,083
Automobile parts	6	891	780
Railway-cars and parts	263	1,171	208

* Fiscal year ending June 30th.
† Calendar year.
‡ Result of Investments.

Source: *United States Department of Commerce Year Book*, 1929, Vol. I, Table 42, p. 153.

United States to Chile was in the field of mass-production and that all other exports declined. The gross machine exports in 1926 depended on the investments of the manufacturing concerns. Statistics of exports from Chile to the United States show an increase in nitrates and copper, two products developed by United States investments. The entire relationship is circular in structure and movement, and capital investments hold the centre of the circle.

The entire economic intercourse with South America seems to be mainly a result of an incessant expansion of the industrial giants. "Trade follows the Flag"—the policy of conquest—has been replaced by the new formula, "Trade follows Capital"—the policy of economic penetration. The slogan which came into fashion is: "Foreign loans promote business at home." In our case, however, this formula is erroneous. For the moving force in capital exports is large-scale industry,[1] mass-production at its height, the "Big Thirty" concerns which operate throughout the world, but have their official domiciles in the United States. It is they who manage investments, and through these investments direct the export of materials of production such as machines and installations of various kinds. It is they who supervise production itself, and through it the distribution of the manufactured articles. They rarely work abroad for the local market. They operate for the market of the world. "It is no longer demand which regulates the rhythm of production, it is the equipment; it is the furnace which must not be allowed to cool; it is the wheel which must continue to turn; it is the dynamo which does not cease to transform into electrical-motive force—the energy furnished by oil or by streams of water."[2]

Foreign trade and investments are a supplement, an appendage of industry. In our case (and only in our case?) the leaders of industrial expansion of the United States are not in the realm of finance capital, but of big industrial business. The chief figure here is not the New York financier, but the worldwide corporation whose main office is in the United States.[3]

(*d*) COMPETITION

Is South America virtually conquered by the United States? The answer will vary according to the perspective. Taking a close and intimate view, one can understand the psychology of this opinion. A bird's-eye view, however, presents us with a panorama of a land on which there stand numerous economic structures, many already several floors high; and leaping up among them are isolated United States skyscrapers. The growth of these skyscrapers has been vertical in height, but not horizontal in its base. The concerns of the United States, which invest intensively, do not colonize the continent, but cultivate only their own special fields. Their relationship to their new land of operation is slight. They remain isolated from the country and from the people. Their relations are abstract, impersonal. In content their business is purely internal, merely a transaction between the United States and the United States. In form, it is foreign trade and foreign investments. These companies remain alien to their newly adopted field of operations. They do not attempt to familiarize themselves with it, but hold themselves aloof. Having transplanted their customary home atmosphere, they are merely continuing their domestic business abroad. Machines, practices, stationery —all are transferred from the United States. Mass-production is planted in new fields, which are all islands of the United States, but only economically specialized islands, mechanized affiliates of the great concerns. There are neither colonizers nor political aspirants. They take as much pride in selling cheap articles used in every home as the European merchant does in being furnisher to the court. The technological revolution of the twentieth century was the foundation of modern mass-production and extended markets to world-wide proportions. In their triumphal march around the world the "Big Thirty" came, of course, to South America.

Their entrance on this continent was advanced, accelerated,

and even to a certain extent suggested by the World War. The United States was really officially invited and urged at the first financial conference in Washington to invade the continent. Now, twelve years after the signing of peace, we may already state that the United States took advantage of this invitation, but was forced in the post-War development to retreat into fields of specialized activity (except on the northern coast, which should be considered as a prolongation of the natural sphere of influence of United States economy).[1] This retirement has been like the recession of a swollen river after spring floods, which leave only a few deep pools on the banks. Europe began the post-War struggle very energetically, but Europe cannot compete at present in motor-cars, radios, razor-blades, and similar articles of the United States; just as the United States cannot compete in Pforzheim articles, French luxuries, and English cloths.[2]

In practice a division of specialties resulted. This variety of specialties is accompanied by a diversity of methods of the different countries. The Britisher is proud of the far-famed quality of his merchandise, and fills the orders of clients who must adjust themselves to and accept English methods and customs. The German displays samples of his products, and must adapt them to the demands of the market; he must be able to compete by special accommodations through special facilities of credit, and similar means. The Frenchman dictates the laws and fashion and has an undisputed monopoly in the realm of his specialty. Industrial United States produces the articles of common use found in every home, and articles for which a need is only beginning to be felt by the world.

Correspondingly, France trades through local representatives in South America, England through a few large specialized English exporters, and the United States through the affiliates of its industrial concerns. The German organization of foreign trade is widespread, split up, personal (with the exception of the great German concerns, as in the electrical industry, which are in most cases connected with companies in the United

States), and essentially German. The directory of German exporters contains many thousands of names. On the other hand, only three hundred names were contained in a list of firms interested in foreign trade with Latin America published by the National City Bank.[3]

Not considering the huge concerns in the United States, it must be conceded that in the regular type of foreign trade the United States is unable to compete abroad. Reports of the Department of Commerce and other literature make complaint about the fact that the organization for selling is inferior to that for manufacturing.[4] In the United States foreign trade success is to be credited not to the selling organization, but rather to mass-production.[5]

The passing sympathy which South America manifested toward the United States several times during the War is extinguished. Sentiments of favour have migrated to the other side, and are not to be underestimated. In the United States the true character of European competition in South America is beginning to be realized. "The United States faces a formidable array of hostile or competing European interests in South America."[6] "Our manufacturers have to meet in Argentina not merely the competition, i.e. the competition coming from the co-operation of commercial and financial interest of each nation against all others. If American interests are to succeed, they must develop a like solidarity against rival nations."[7]

"Competition in Latin America is not individual but national. The Germans, the English, and the French, each presents a united front of commercial co-operation. Each country, as it were, pools its financial and commercial forces, and with the support of its Government moves into foreign markets united. The individual manufacturer becomes of secondary importance, and the aim of the German steel industry, for example, is success over the English steel industry. All is made to contribute toward this end. The German Government encourages export combinations, the financial and banking interests favour their nations, and strong commercial houses are established which engage in a variety of activities—importing, exporting, steamship and insurance business, local industries, etc."[8]

The advantage of the European position is recognized.

"At the outset it must be recognized that the financial and commercial interests of Europe have many advantages in Latin-American countries. The outlook of these countries is European. They have not only inherited many of their traditions and customs from the Portuguese and Spanish colonial systems, but they still maintain close intercourse, social as well as otherwise, with the Latin countries of Europe. The commercial interests of France, Italy, Spain, and Portugal, therefore, find them a natural field for development into which they go with the advantage of language and an appreciation of the Latin point of view. As for the Germans and the English, they have been in these countries so long that they have had time to learn and adapt themselves to their ways, which, it must be always recognized, are distinctly different from those of Anglo-Saxon countries.

"Suspicion still lingers in the minds of many Latin Americans on account of a misunderstanding of the Munroe Doctrine, and this suspicion is at times aroused to active hostility by European interests, who are jealous of the growth of American trade and who desire to create a prejudice against American merchandise. As common interests draw the Republics of the Americas closer together it becomes less and less possible to arouse this suspicion. The delicacy of this situation, however, should be kept in mind by those seeking markets in Latin America.

"Unfair competition not infrequently takes the form of calumny. Europeans with their long-established trade and personal connections are loth to yield anything to American interests, and they do not hesitate to spread stories similar to the false interpretation of the Monroe Doctrine in the press and elsewhere derogatory to Americans and their goods. Since the beginning of the European War the impression has grown among Latin Americans that the business community of the United States is taking advantage of the present situation which gives it a more or less monopolistic control of merchandising in their markets. Europeans are doing all that they can to encourage this view, hoping that with the coming of peace they will get back the trade which they have lost."[9]

It is also understood that "the advantage which European exporters have over American exporters is more than a matter of tradition and sentiment."[10]

The present situation, however, is relatively peaceful. The sharpness of the competitive struggle has subsided within the past few years. The post-War war has become quiescent. Figures show the relative stability of these relations.

From time to time there are conflicts which are partly local manifestations of world struggles in certain industries (Standard Oil Company and Royal Dutch Shell; Kreuger and Toll, and the Diamond Match Company; the concentration of forces in the meat-packing industry,[11] and other cases). The repeated skirmishes of the past are now infrequent and all is quiet. But how long?

When, however, one thinks in continents, one cannot dispel the notion that if the Pan-European Union becomes a reality (which is prerequisite for Americanized mass-production in Europe), then all the encounters engaged in by the rivals up to now were only preliminary. The new tendency of world-tariff policies shows quite clearly the new whetting of world competition.

. . . . .

Thus flow the streams of merchandise and capital from one continent to another, and thus do they meet and contribute to the new foundation of South American economy. Their courses are not always tranquil, but are often turbulent, like the careers and activities of the contestants. The rivals are struggling over positions, prices, power. They are seeking to extend their influence, and to push out others. They are trying to obtain monopolies and enter favourable alliances. Streams of merchandise from all over the world present a variegated panorama when they meet in the South American market. And he who creates, transports, and organizes the merchandise for sale in the foreign market often tries to press into the service of commerce spiritual arms—the power of ideas. Each contestant is seeking to arm himself and his products with ideas, ideals, which he hopes will find an echo and a harmony on South American soil. Each rival is trying to spread his cultural influence, to place his political power also in the scales, to operate with sentiments, with kinships of race, religion, history, geography, and other such ties. Thus originate interesting intellectual movements, to the study of which we dedicate the next chapter.

CHAPTER II

THE IDEOLOGY

(*a*) THE SEDUCERS

1. The Non-American

In the struggle for the market, the raw materials, and the potentialities of the South American continent, competing parties seek to employ intellectual as well as other weapons. It is supposed that in order to do business with the "backward" peoples of Latin America, one must appeal to feeling and temperament. "Soul" and "heart" always play an important rôle with "these" peoples.

And so the suitors attempt to bring the force of ideas into the field of their rivalry. Figuratively, they adorn themselves with coloured feathers, as in the courtship of the animal world; they seek points of familiarity and relationships. They bring to bear common memories and imagine a common future; they construct their own realm of ideas and combat strangers; they proclaim identity of blood, brotherhood, language, religion, and other grounds. Ideology as a tool in the economic struggle is in and of itself nothing new in history. The practical politician has never underestimated the power of great ideas; and even the practice of materialistically minded socialism has, as we know, been obliged unconsciously to employ this power. The history of modern times has also seen successful and unsuccessful "idea campaigns" of this kind: the founding of the German Empire and the propaganda for Pan-Germanism, Italian unity, the abortive attempts of Pan-Slavism, Pan-Islamism, the present Pan-Europeanism, as well as many other such propagandist movements.

The striving of the great national communities to expand their influence into a Great Germany or a Greater Britain lies in the nature of things. Great nations with great individual cultures and the impulse toward economic expansion endeavour to play the rôle of magnet to the others, and, under certain conditions, often exercise an irresistible drawing power over the smaller, weaker, or younger ones. The little satellites willingly assemble about the great planets, while the latter pursue a conscious policy of concentration and alliance, and attempt to assume the paternal attitude of protector.

These movements combine a number of political, economic, and cultural elements, which change with the course of history. The offensive Pan-Germanism of pre-War days has been obliged to fall back into another position since the War. The earlier, impetuous Pan-Germanism now has an avowedly defensive character. Similarly, Pan-Slavism has lost the axis about which it turned, and is seeking orientation. Each of these movements originates in romanticism, takes nourishment from many roots, and seeks to touch the most emotional chords of the human soul. The contents of these movements are characteristically turbid and unstable.[1] But their lack of clarity and instability is particularly pronounced in the case of the propagandist movements for union concerning the South American continent. A calm and rational analysis asks: Where is the much-touted "Great Fatherland" to be found on the map? Who shall go with whom, and which nations shall be joined in order to build the Great Fatherland? Is it a political ideal, or a purely cultural one? Is an attempt being made to bring about an economic union?

We find no clear, exhaustive answer in the mass of brilliant words and thoughts. Every rival seeks an independent solution and attempts to set up his own ideal; each one intends to win the continent for himself.

The peculiarity of the South American situation lies in the variety of the alleged bases of union and in the very widely differing sources of the ideas, propositions, and proposals submitted to the fair lady by her wooers.

The proud Spaniard, the gallant Frenchman, the passionate Italian vie in declarations of love for their beloved. Sometimes they appeal to her as "daughter" or "sister." The Teuton planned to abduct her by force. The awkward lover from the United States alternates declarations of love with a big-stick policy. Even the Japanese deigns to make sheep's eyes at her. Each one is actuated by different feelings, but all harbour the same secret desire.

These ideas come from Europe, North America, and Asia; they are adapted to the occasion, are more or less sincere and well-founded, and are presented by the wooers each in his own way. The history of these ideas is a story of actions and reactions.

. . . . .

Latin America! Belonging to the line of the old Romans, to the ancient culture of mankind, to the artistic places of Italy, and to France, which is the second home of every educated man! The thought is alluring,and gives pride to every South American, even those dwelling in the far interior of the continent. However, the Iberian peninsula is in this case intentionally excluded from membership in the noble Latin family which traces its genealogy back thousands of years. The racial principle is taken as the basis of this distinction. The mixed population of the South American continent is declared full-bloodedly Latin. The negro in Bahia, and the Indian in the Bolivian Chaco or in Paraguay, the Araucanians in Chile, and the countless half-breeds who populate the continent, are silently tolerated or ignored. This is not the place to discuss the racial question or to examine its justice or injustice. The fact is that the attackers and defenders of family relationships use the same weapons and put forth the same arguments, each in his own favour.

Religious unity is sometimes brought into play, even by "godless" France. Cultural unity is stressed.

Calderon presents Latin-Americanism as follows: "From a racial point of view, it is true, one cannot call the South American republics Latin nations. They are rather Indo-African or Africo-Iberian. Latin culture—the ideas and the art of France, the laws and the Catholicism of Rome—have created in South America a mental attitude analogous to that of the great Mediterranean peoples, which is hostile or alien to the civilization of the Germanic or Anglo-Saxon peoples."[2] He unmistakably emphasizes the modern warlike character of the movement.

It is thus that Latin-Americanism originated. The movement has two sources—Italy and France. The *Italian* source is poorer in the attractiveness of her power of the past, and is nourished mainly by migration to and from the continent. Mussolini's "Roman Concept" does not extend toward South America. This movement is not political, for Italy hardly thinks of political expansion in South America. Culturally it is of importance, because the new Italy, through the millions of her sons in South America, her goal-conscious and constantly growing policy, and the glamour of her new rank as a world power, is in a position to disseminate her ideas, her ancient culture, and her modern achievements. But her aim is purely economic. The newly discovered Italian Latin-Americanism arises out of young Italian capitalism's will to expand, the demand of her industries for new outlets, and the desire to use to the utmost all opportunities to develop the full power of the new Italian imperialism. This movement is still young —younger, naturally, than new-born Italian imperialism.

Heavy Italian immigration may become its support. The Italian is a poor subject for the melting-pot; he is difficult to assimilate, and long continues to feel his attachment for his native country. The presence of segregated Italian colonies, especially in Argentina, where one-fourth of the population is Italian (Buenos Aires is, after Rome, the largest Italian city), in certain parts of Brazil (São Paulo is one-third Italian), and Uruguay, may prepare a field for the extension of Italian influence.[3]

This movement was perhaps romantic in its origin, but its methods are businesslike in their nature, modern, and practical; they are aimed not at political Utopias, but at business success, even though political and cultural results are left out of account.

The usual methods involve: organizing and strengthening of the Italian element overseas, Italian local credit unions, propaganda, institutes, visits of statesmen (Orlando), etc. The vigour of this new movement lies in its freshness, the consciousness of its aim, its energy, and the success of Italians in South America. A Matarazzo in Brazil is of more value to this Italian policy than a thousand holiday speeches. Romantic pathos has as its effect practical activity, not mere lyricism.

This policy possesses tact, and takes into account the temperament of the continent. A typical example is afforded by the foundation, in 1924, of a division of the *Instituto Superiore di Scienze economiche e commerciale* in Genoa for the study of Latin America. According to the Royal decree, the reason for the foundation was "the necessity of rendering more active and intense the commercial relations of Italy with the countries of Latin America." Its goal was given as the "commercial expansion of Italy in Latin America." In 1929 this forthright wording was modified to "the development of the commercial and cultural relations between Italy and Latin America." In the old formula, South America was given as a field for expansion; in the new, it is pictured as a partner.

The literary ideology of Italianism in South America is of the slightest effect. Francesco Nitti once casually said that the future of this continent belongs to Italy. It was not seriously intended. "Italian ambitions are both economic and cultural,"[4] but not political, even though "a new Italy" is talked about now and then.

The importance of this movement for Italy is understood in South America. "Of Italy it suffices to say that she has known how to convert her robust emigratory state into an organism so useful to her national economy that her colony of emigrants in America is the one from which she derives the greatest benefit of all her colonies, with the advantage that it does not cause her the anxieties attached to dominion of a territory."[5]

French policy is different. If Italy bases hers on the exportation of men and dependence on Italian colonies, France uses the exportation of ideas and takes advantage of the French culture of South America. In no other place in the world has everything French such drawing power as in South America, even though France is everywhere considered pre-eminent in ideas, culture, taste, and goods of the finest quality. The French influence is of long standing, and is more deeply rooted than the Italian. Glorification of the French Revolution, already half-forgotten in Europe, figures here on official occasions, and has not lost its tone. Auguste Comte conquered South America. French literature and French taste are the standards: "This crops out in a thousand ways. French is spoken by all educated Latin Americans; French textbooks are used in all the higher schools; French art and literature have served as the standards which Latin-American artists and writers have consciously or unconsciously followed. When Latin Americans go abroad, Paris is their Mecca; France their second patria."[6] As Benjamin Franklin said: every man has two countries, his own and France besides.

In the case of the French suitor, there is no passionate love, no wildly devoted liaison; it is a constant cousinly flirtation, an enduring courtship—regarded as such by the South American side also—which the fair European republic gladly animates and cultivates as a matter of course. It is a French fascination. These relationships are best expressed by Rubén Dario:

> Abuelo, preciso es decíroslo: mi esposa
> es de mi tierra: mi querida de Paris.

The Latin brother in America admires France, and allows himself to be introduced to the world of culture and taste. France does this with especial charm, and at the same time seeks to combine business with it.[7]

France has always acted cleverly in this connection. Here, too, propaganda follows its usual course: banquet speeches, associations, institutes, visits of statesmen, etc.[8] But the personal factor in the dissemination of slogans has always been the reason for France's success. Hanoteau, Caillaux, Viviani, Clemenceau, Anatole France, Jaurès, have laid their personal charm in the balance, and have not only strengthened the cultural influence of their homeland, but have also been of help to French economy and opened up interesting opportunities of investment for the formerly very active French capital market. No other country has understood so well as France how to arouse the sentiments of the South Americans and how to touch at the right moment upon the ties of kinship and cultural unity. France's great asset is her excellent understanding of South American psychology and her facility for entering into it.

In return, South America's affection and admiration are so great that even Louis Napoleon's attempt to establish in Mexico a European monarchy under French patronage left no bad taste; and this attempt "was the most serious menace that republican institutions in the new world have had to face since the schemes of the Holy Alliance were checked by Monroe and Canning."[9]

Paris, however, is and always has been not only a shrine to which pilgrimage is made, but also the meeting-place of South Americans. For South America, where natural barriers separated the peoples—mountains, deserts, forests—where people knew little of each other, *Paris, not Madrid*, was the gathering and meeting-place. In France Miranda made his first efforts for the freedom of South America. His name appears in the Arc de Triomphe in Paris in the list of heroes of the French Revolution. In Paris Francisco Bilbao gathered together South Americans of various countries and laid before them his project of a union. France was among the instigators of the countless associations and unions of a Saint-Simonist cast, which served South America in the first half of the nineteenth century as the focal-point of her intellectual movement. France has always been the refuge of the banished and fleeing revolutionaries and members of the opposition, as well as the traditional playground of the ex-presidents. French romanticism's will to freedom, which Victor Hugo defined as the liberalism of literature, reached the South American coast. The legal systems of various South American states are based on the Code Napoleon. But while France herself welcomed foreign ideas and tendencies, she was always their interpreter to South America. Thus English thoughts have often arrived overseas in French dress and French translation; the strange and foreign first had to get a French stamp.

The French influence has the peculiarities of French economy, and its main power is not directed toward the masses. French economy, art, literature, language, fashions, and even her former political ideals, were all for the educated and cultured classes, the intellectuals, those who were already urbanized, and not for the inferior. It is, in fact, universal in Ibero America, and is perhaps most pronounced in Brazil. But the people, the great masses, do not know or use French products, and are unaccustomed to the finesse of French culture.[10]

This movement has no roots in the native masses of people, nor is it greatly advanced by the few and thinly populated French colonies; it finds no French oases on the South American continent. It is and remains a pronounced cultural tendency of educated society.[11]

But France is modest in her desires; France has forgotten that she "formerly possessed in North America a vast empire which extended from Labrador to Florida and from the shores of the Atlantic to the farthest lakes of upper Canada"—the melancholy and grandiose sentence with which Chateaubriand begins *l'Atala*. The highest of her unexpressed wishes is a "colony without a flag." She really intends to undertake no great political tasks in South America, she does not follow a power-seeking policy, has no economic plans for a union, and seeks no hegemony, but "the social alliance, the intimate mingling of two streams of the Latin family which attract each other as much by the necessity of satisfying reciprocal needs as by an exchange of sympathy."[12] Gabriel Hanoteau only on one occasion said, "une plus grande France."[13] It is error to try to read an opposite meaning into a recent utterance by Poincaré, who said: "Intellectually and morally I feel myself much farther from certain European countries than I do from certain of the great Latin nations of South America. If we are going to attempt to form countries into groups, I do not see why we should group together all the countries of the old world and eliminate all those of the new."[14] This is clearly a remark on Briand's policy and plans, and obviously relates to internal and not to foreign policy.

Spain is opposed to Latin-Americanism. The name is rejected, as a matter of principle. "Spaniards even accuse France of inventing the term 'Latin America' in order to confirm the rupture between the former Spanish colonies and the mother country and substitute herself as an affectionate step-mother."[15]

"One day the term Latin American leaped beyond the Pyrenees, in order to christen Latin (French and Italian) relations with a new name."[16]

"No one has pointed out with such persistence as the French the substantial differences between the Spaniards and the South Americans. Rightly or wrongly, even within the circle of the closest friendship with us, the French regard us as on a plane of intellectual inferiority, because they consider us haughty, fanatical, violent, as representative of our African origin . . . and farewell Latinism."[17]

At the Congreso de Historia y Geografia Hispano Americano in Seville (April 1914) a memorandum was presented "upon the denomination 'Latin' applied to Spanish America." The writer asked: "Who is the author of these new expressions which have been unfairly circulated? From what country have they come to invade us? Who has taken the efforts to spread them? It is not our intention to examine this. But we will call attention to the fact that the French adopt them with rare unanimity and fervour.[18] And he replied to his own question, saying: "The French will claim Latinism in order to win American friendship away from us, to obstruct the advance of our language, and to continue functioning as a shining light; the Italians will favour their own immigration beneath a cloak of Latinism."[19] And seven years later, at the second Congress in Seville (1921), the same informant asserts that: (1) " 'Latin America' is improperly applied to the American nations of Spanish origin; (2) the denomination 'Ibero American' is unnecessary; (3) proposes the name Spanish be given to what belongs exclusively to Spain, and the name Hispanic for everything common to Spain, Portugal, and all of America which originates from both."[20]

The Spaniards show a sharp reaction against Latin-Americanism, and consider the Italian movement an especial danger to themselves. "The Italian colonies, Italian emigration, Italian literature and policy are our greatest enemies in America," says Garcia Caminero.[21] He speaks of "a methodical struggle, conscious and perfectly organized" (p. 96). "The Italian and the Spaniard there are like odd and even, inside and outside, movement and repose, yes and no. Our mission is at least to polarize Italianism, since it is useless to deny its strength" (p. 87).

But Italianism does not worry Constantino Suarez, who says: "The injection of Italianism by Italian emigration is so weak that the sons of Italians are as much Hispano-Americans as are the descendants of Spaniards."[22] But France . . . and this author in his anger tries to show that European influence upon South America actually is exercised more by England and Germany.

Spain is irritated by Latin-Americanism, that "article of luxury made in Paris" according to Camillo Barcia's definition.

Spain's situation is both more and less difficult than that of the other Latin countries. More difficult because there was never any hate against Italy or France, but there was hate for the land of the mother country, for the ruler, the oppressor; because it is not a new approach but an approach following a complete separation; these are attempts to win back a part of the lost riches and somehow to entrench themselves anew on the lost continent. The boldest Utopias of the other nations —political, cultural, and economic—were for the former world power, Spain, for the former mother country an actuality, and not only a dream. Spain's situation is further rendered difficult since she cannot boast of the culture of France, the new energy of Italy, the glamour of victory attending both, the capital power of the Anglo-Saxons, or the industry of the Germans. One is himself in the making; one is not politically stable. Spain's task is made easier by language, customs, religion, the support of the Churches, and by the settlement of Spaniards overseas. And, a fact which should not be underestimated, the task is made easier by the past, by sentiment.

If the fresh Italian Latin-Americanism colours its period of storm and stress with a romantic character, if seductive France is flirting with South America for a second century, there is nevertheless in Hispano-Americanism a peculiar mixture of tragedy and sentimentality.

Is it not tragic: in that when Spain founded universities in America, and possessed the monopoly of ideas on the continent; and now the doctrines of the French Encyclopedists are influencing and preparing the revolt of the colonies and are bringing about the transfer to France of absolute spiritual mastery? "Since then—that is, during the whole of the nineteenth century—the mother country has been losing the greater portion of her ancient intellectual privileges. Political and literary ideas, romanticism and liberalism, faith in reason and poetic enthusiasm, all these have been imported from France."[23]

Is it not tragic for proud Spain, the former ruler of the greater part of the American continent, to be obliged to try to win back by means of sentiment the heart of the former colonies? Is it not tragic for a monument to Simon Bolivar, the liberator *from* Spain, to be erected *in* Spain in the interest of Hispano-Americanism?

This is the spiritual aspect of Hispano-Americanism. It is called Hispano-Americanism for export only; it is the other side of the new Pan-Hispanism, the result of Spanish regeneration of the twentieth century.

The close of the nineteenth century saw the end of the final act of the drama. The last vestiges of the world power and the colonial kingdom of Spain in America were destroyed. The Spanish standard no longer waved over American soil. Spain had to shrink into her European and African boundaries. The historical work of centuries was overthrown, and the proud nation lived through bitter hours. At this time the hour of the new Pan-Hispanism struck, as if history, in its perversity, had waited until the last Spanish colony in America was lost in order to begin the work of regeneration. The War's defeat was a turning-point for the future of Spain.

This period of Spanish history is reminiscent of Germany after Jena; and it is not by chance that Fichte's *Speeches to the German Nation*, translated into Spanish, exercised their magic effect on this people. It was the time when Joaquín Costa summoned the nation to become Europeanized, when a new interest in economics, art, and science arose, and when occurred a renaissance of Spanish economic science.[24]

A new lustre was added to the Spanish coat of arms by Ortega y Gasset in the field of philosophy, by Blasco Ibañez and Pio Baroja in literature,[25] by Zuloaga in painting, and by the Encyclopedist Unamuno in the field of science, to mention only a few names.

The Catholic Church is not to be undervalued as an ally of Spain—her faithful child—in South America. It is not on the side of France and Italy, whom it reproaches for their anti-clerical and anti-Vatican policies respectively; and it is naturally opposed to the Protestantism of the United States.[26] At the same time the economic basis of Spain is being built up. The World War accelerated the economic tempo.[27] Wartime brought unexpected and great possibilities to Spain, programmes similar to those after the loss of her colonies.[28] It was a period of growing economic nationalism,[29] when Spain began occasionally even to enter the field of international financial transactions.

Spain is no longer the traditionally romantic land of warriors, poets, and painters. The romantic mantle is being laid aside, and exchanged for the street dress of the new economic man. The history of Spain "became a long and laborious process of adaptation to a rationalistic and business age."[30] Don Juan is no longer a *grand seigneur*: Figaro is perhaps the head of a dancing school; and if Carmen is still to be found in the same tobacco factory, she is sitting at the cigarette machine. The capitalistic spirit and the entrepreneur impulse are modern phenomena in the new Spain. And—who knows?—perhaps Spain's unconquerable will to develop her national power will in time enable her to overtake the starting lead of the other countries.

The initiative in proclaiming and launching Pan-Hispanism was taken by the University of Oviedo. It is interesting to read Posada's recollections of the rôle played by the University and of the Hispano-American campaign earlier proclaimed by Labra, which it undertook together with Aramburu and Altamira.

"I do not forget—how could I forget?—that Hispano-American Congress of 1900. Aramburu, Altamira, and I represented our dear University of Oviedo, which had initiated a few months before a campaign of literary and intellectual relations with the other Hispano-American professors. The occasion was propitious for the accentuation of the desire shown by Oviedo; and I had to take advantage of it. Furthermore, how could the representatives of Asturias remain mute and indifferent at a Hispano-American Congress?"[31]

A definition of the movement was given at this Congress, which, we learn from Posada, Altamira—the driving force and most active collaborator—drew up.

"Pan-Hispanism . . . means the union of all the countries of Cervantine speech, not solely to attain intimate interpenetration, but also to obtain a strong economic alliance, a kind of

'Zollverein,' with all the political transcendence which that state of things would produce for the united countries, and especially for Spain, who would thus realize her tutelary mission over the American peoples born of her." "Those whom God hath joined together, let no man put asunder," is indeed the byword of this movement.

The official manner of expression is, of course, not so strong. "A great part of the social and economic future of our nation lies in the necessity of cultivating those racial sympathies which Spain possesses in America," proclaims the Ministerio de Estado, April 16, 1900, in its "Exposición" on the Congress.

And so the campaign is begun. In countless meetings, speeches, pamphlets, companies, institutes, voyages, and lectures, in the press and in scientific publications, in Spain and in Spanish America, by pen and orally, reconciliation, understanding, union, were talked about, written about, preached, at time argued, occasionally endangered by common enemies, but all with lyricism and feeling. A way not to reason but to the heart was sought. The new spirit of Spain has permanently abandoned the propagandists. The old practice of flowery phrases is in vogue again.

Whether we read Labra, Altamira, Rueda, Rahola, it is always the same thing: the past is given first place—relationship, brotherliness, language, religion, history. It produced no realistic politicians, no leader, no Bismarck, no Cavour. In practice, the movement has remained a literary game, an essay by professors and poets. It has never yet formulated a concrete programme; there have been only slogans, catchwords, congresses, festivities, declamations, rhetoric. Economics has not taken any part; people were busy at home, and could not afford the luxury of a foreign voyage even to visit relatives.

With the passing of time, this movement has lost its first tragic quality, and it remains merely sentimental and lyrical. There is something of Don Quixote in Hispano-Americanism.

At the same time, it is the only Latin movement which had

some chance of success. Hispano-Americanism, it is true, does not possess the universality of French influence, since it does not extend to Brazil. On the other hand, it is not an object of luxury; it can and does meet with the sympathy of the masses and the immigrants who usually form closed groups and constantly bring new Spanish blood to America. These people are living and active bearers of Hispano-Americanism, unconscious representatives and missionaries of this thought, and not the intellectuals, lawyers, parliamentarians, and writers who have formed the backbone of the movement until now. The mass, however, has not allowed itself to be moved either in the Peninsula or overseas; and the economic impetus of Spain was not sufficient to give these ideas any material foundation.[32]

There has really been no lack of understanding of this fact. The necessity of mobilizing Spanish capital in order to win over South America has been emphasized by several writers.[33] But people have overlooked the main thing: Spain is not a capital-exporting, but still a capital-importing country; and it does not lie within her power to compensate the lack of capital by means of organization as Germany does.

Pan-Hispanism or Hispano-Americanism is best compared with Pan-Germanism of Imperial Germany; but it is a passive, theoretical "ism." It is richer in ideology and poorer in economic strength. It lacks the glamour and the economic growth of German imperialism. The official Hispano-Americanism of Primo de Rivera (1926) was a miscarriage.[34]

In the Hispano-Americanism of Spain we find all possible nuances: the storm and stress of the journalists, the academic imperialism like that of Altamira, the pessimism of Araquistain, which condemns the rhetoric,[35] and the more practical temperament of Posada, whose positive construction no one contradicts, but who confines himself to spiritual interpenetration.[36]

Strengthening of the "cultural interpenetration" is the permanent result of the first period of Hispano-Americanism in the twentieth century. Lyrism thus brought people nearer together, even though only in the cultural sphere. The success of Spanish art and science, their new renaissance, are real and powerful instruments for Spanish cultural expansion. The constantly maintained community of culture is in flow, its energy is renewed.

Politically, the ideal of union was so far from possibility of realization, so Utopian, that not even the most rabid Pan-Hispanists have brought it up for consideration. The dream of a "Great Spain in America" was a dream even to its partisans, in spite of the continual attempts of Spain to seize and conduct an actual campaign.[37]

Economically, the movement broke down at its inception; it was wrecked on material community with South America: lack of capital and insufficient industrialization were the causes.

But if political peace reigns in Spain, if Spain's economy remains aloof from the European decadence and takes a position in the world market, neither France with all her great influence, nor Italy with all her recent success, will have Spain's chance of assuming the leadership in South America.

Spain has, over all the other wooers, the advantages of language, customs, and history. In the Latin family only Spain can declare the mother's right to South America. The real success of Hispano-Americanism was the sealing of spiritual reconciliation. Inasmuch as the motherland no longer seeks to recover her lost political rule, the former colonies have renewed the broken connections.[38]

Pan-Hispanism, in its theoretical impulse to expand "La Patria Grande," attempts to extend its system to the Lusitanians, to include in it Portugal on the European peninsula and Brazil in South America. Unity suffers thereby, it is true; but importance may thus be increased. The leaders are forthcoming in that they rechristen the movement *Ibero-Americanism*. There is less uneasiness than in the case of Latin-Americanism.

This idea is of Spanish origin. The spiritual leader is Camillo Barcia.[39]

The most definite and pragmatic proclamation of Ibero-Americanism is the manifesto to the nation published in 1914 by Juan del Nido y Segalerva, which served also as his political testament.[40] He advocates the formation of "a single nation, from Barcelona to Lisbon" (p. 3); he agitates and argues historical and sociological parallels in the unions of Italy and Germany, seeks an Iberian Cavour, and uses as his strongest argument: "Either Portugal and Spain unite, or Portugal and Spain will be *divided among their protectors*. The Portuguese do not rule in Portugal and the Spaniards do not rule in Spain. Foreigners dominate" (p. 4). He wishes "the Peninsula for the Peninsular dwellers." He even promises the Portuguese allies "the transformation of the present Spanish state into a state which would permit Portugal to live within it and maintain its personality like the other regions" (p. 8).

Other authors also seek to strengthen Ibero-Americanism. Thus Emilio Zurano Muñoz, typical dilettante product of a Latin-American and representative of the intellectual "*almacén* type," says of the historical ties: "Spain and Portugal there find their life transplanted, with no difference other than that of place and name";[41] he emphasizes "the geographical position of the Iberian Peninsula as the base of the future universal market";[42] and seeks to assure Spanish hegemony in the Ibero-American federation: "Spain should be the Rome of the Spanish and Portuguese peoples"; [43] he calls for the establishment of "unions and centres of correspondence with them, and the formation of economic organizations which shall effect the transfusion of moral and economic values" and bring about "Conferencia Internacional de los pueblos Ibero-Americanos."[44]

This course is aided from the Argentine side. Colmo says that Portugal "was a simple sociological remnant of Spain."[45]

Neither in Portugal nor in Brazil does this movement have land and partisans, with a few exceptions.

On the other hand, the theories of A. Herculano and Oliveira Martins, who wished to deny Portugal's right to independent existence, are being strongly opposed. Portuguese common opinion takes the stand that "The eternal divorce between Iberians and Lusitanians is continued by economics."[46]

When during the War Juan del Nido y Segalerva published *La Union Iberia*, there appeared a compendium entitled *A questão Iberica*[47] as an answer to his "romantic policy" and the strongest refutation of the possibility of a union or federation. In the conclusion ("A Licão dos factos") of the latter work, written by Luis de Almeida Braga, the following sentence appears: "Spain is not a sister nation, she is a rival nation."[48] This may perhaps be a writer's exaggeration; but another author preaches Portuguese imperialism, and demands, under the influence of German ideas, "Great Portugal" (p. 281), and an "armed nation." They fear "Iberianism," which they understand to include "absorption" of Portugal, either by force or peaceably; and they all speak of the "historically imperialistic Castilian spirit" (p. 182), say that "Portugal has as much individuality as Castile," decline economic union, because of the resulting "inconvenience to Portugal of an Iberian union, even a customs union, from the agricultural point of view" (p. 171).

Furthermore, the obstacle was not merely economic. They further attempt to show that Portugal differs from Spain in every way—territorially, racially, in language, music, art, economy, law, and has no thought of submission to Spanish imperialism. They see, too, that there would be danger to Spain in union, since "the inclusion of Portugal in the Castilian system would represent an accretion of heterogeneity, of separatism, rather than a strengthening of her precarious unity" (p. 159).

The characteristic of the Iberian movement is the following: "For Spain an independent Portugal is too heterogeneous, particularist, regionalist, Spain the living negation of Peninsula unity" (p. 158). Thus Portugal withdraws from partnership in Ibero-Americanism.[49]

Nido de Segalerva seems to be right when he says himself of

the Iberian union that "Most people think it Utopian. Others consider it a fair illusion. Almost all speak of secular obstacles" (p. 15). *Portugal*, in her anxiety over the new Spanish imperialism, and out of humour because of historical reminiscences, does not think of sharing with Spain her existing friendship with Brazil. The relationship between the Portuguese colonies and their mother country has always been more amicable than that between Spain and hers. Certainly the Brazilian market is potentially the largest on the continent; and Portugal does not wish to place it at the disposal of the "Union." On the other hand, many in the country dream of a "Great Portugal," of union with Brazil, etc.[50]

But this course has almost all the weaknesses of Hispano-Americanism without its great advantages. It seeks economic factors as its basis. This Luso-Brazilian campaign initiated by Paolo Barreto in Brazil and by Pedroso in Portugal had not success in Brazil.[51]

"Economic *rapprochement* of Portugal and Brazil is demanded in the name of the interests of both countries; and the fact that the products of our colonies are similar to those of some regions of Brazil, instead of being an obstacle to this closer contact, is on the contrary a condition of success, since it is undeniably more advantageous for us to co-operate in the competitive struggle in the great world market than to exhaust ourselves through inability to come to a commercial agreement based on the greatest possible economic equality, and to find the formula for mutual understanding and valorization of the natural resources of the two sister republics, seeking the most efficient way to place the products of the two countries in the different world markets."[52]

"Having sought the principal factors which sufficiently demonstrate the impracticability of a Portuguese-Brazilian commercial accord or treaty of a permanent character, which factors have brought to nothing all the steps so far taken in that direction, it remains for us to enunciate those which determine the *latent necessity and viability of an economic pact*, which will result in the establishment of a Portuguese-Brazilian federation for the greater community of political interests. These principal factors are the following: for both countries, the possibility of mutual *conquest and maintenance of the international markets for the union of identical products of Brazil and the Portuguese colonies*; and, principally for Brazil, the *utilization of the excellent commercial and military bases which the geographical situation of the Portuguese colonies affords them for their greater economic expansion*."[53] Thus there is painted an attractive picture of a new colonial empire brought about by full utilization of the Portuguese colonies.[54]

The cultural unity between Brazil and Portugal is somewhat looser than that of Spanish America with its mother country. The greater influence of the University of Coimbra on the history of Brazil is no longer present to the former extent.

This, however, is owing in part to the receptive character of Portuguese culture. The adult nation has begun to draw upon the original source—as a result of the extension and strengthening of French influence—and is also proud of the beginnings of a culture of its own, which, unlike that of Spanish America, is closely related to the original population of the country.

Hispano-Americanism, Latin-Americanism, Ibero-Americanism, Lusitanianism—such are the Latin tendencies influential in South America. They affect one another, combat one another; and there is, on the other hand, no lack of effort to unite, to co-ordinate their strength: "The Franco-American Committee had decided to associate itself with the Ibero-American Union of Madrid and with other institutions having kindred objects in Latin America, in order to unite the forces organized in favour of the interests of the Latin race, of civilization and justice, and of the well-being of humanity."[55] This thought is a partial appearance of the ideal Latin Union. Using as a basis Poincaré's remarks, which we have already mentioned, Louis Guilaine in the *Temps* endeavours to develop this idea. He uses historical reminiscences as a basis. France, Spain, and

Italy were practically united in the eighteenth century through the Bourbon dynasty; Napoleon also attempted to bring about a union, and wished to draw into it the Latin Americans by way of "counter-balancing the Anglo-American hegemony."

He believes that "Great Britain feels less close to Europe than to the great republic of the United States of America, its former colony. . . . With the Dominion of Canada as liaison agent, the formidable grouping together of the two Anglo-Saxon worlds proceeds apace in this grouping, backed up by the Pan-American Union, which the United States established forty years ago over the twenty republics of Latin America, is going to dominate the entire New World more than ever before." Thus it is possible that "through Hispano-Portuguese-America the European Union would be allied to the Pan-American Union."[56] This, however, is all a lovely dream from closet politics. A Latin Union would be a great power; but first the friction among the Latin nations in Europe would have to be eliminated and the question of hegemony settled. And, furthermore, who is to assume the leadership?[57]

South America's non-Latin wooers are not in a position to turn their feelings to account for business ends, although *Japan* is attempting to find certain points of contact. "On the West Coast the Japanese Government seems to be making especial efforts to cultivate the friendship of the Latin nations, particularly Chile, Peru, and Mexico."[58] The point of departure for Japan, however, is not economics but politics: the Pacific.

The Japanese steamship on the Atlantic can hardly have any political importance, and they are welcome in Brazil because they bring neutral labour. Great expansion cannot take place, since Japan is not yet able to export capital and dissipate her resources. The Japanese are welcome also as a means of differentiation of immigration.

Matters are different on the Pacific; the Japanese are already represented in a business way (by fisheries, coaling-stations, etc.) on the Pacific coast of Mexico. The nitrate export from Chile, which is increasing steadily, and the rapid colonization in Peru are only economic facts; but we can imagine far-seeing plans in South America—the wish, in any case, to prepare allies for themselves, or at least benevolent neutrals, and to mobilize opinion in advance. The continent is already prepared: the Yankee peril.

The two great European non-Latin economic competitors in South America are *England* and *Germany*, the only two who must proceed purely and solely in a business way, but who proceed each in her own way: Germany, by adapting herself to the needs of the market and its wishes; England, by means of the fact that the market is accustomed to and educated in the English tradition. The Englishman can hardly imagine a life different from that at home, with other customs and other ideals; and he strives to extend English conservatism. The German delights in novelties, is elastic. It is easier for the German, because in many parts of South America he finds numerous German colonies[59] which afford him a means of personal contact with the population. The Englishman does not seek these contacts, does not look for an outlet; those interested must come to him. He can do this on the basis of his business lead, his moral position, and the quality of his goods. The German has to show his samples; the English goods are known.

Enock characterizes very clearly the peculiarities of the English position. "The educated Englishman who arrives in Latin America must generally assume the prestige as well as the burden of his empire, for he is among a race of idealists. 'La Gran Bretaña' and 'Inglaterra' are names of lasting power. That a man is an 'Ingles' is to stamp him a being worthy of distinction and favour. The British word has always been the British bond in Latin America: the 'palabra de Ingles' has passed into a byword. The Frenchman may command the deserved admiration for art and culture which his country has earned; the German may be the recipient of attention from his faculty of entering into local social life and for his pushing commercial qualities; the American from the United States may begin to reflect some prestige from the power and wealth of his great country; but it is for the Englishman that peculiar regard is entertained: the history of his country and the character of this nation which has pervaded the world. The Englishman in Latin America is still to a certain extent a 'milord.' He comes for great enterprises; his pockets are always overflowing with silver, which he is supposed to dispense liberally. The traits of impartiality and general commercial rectitude of Great Britain have been the cause. Furthermore, Englishmen who travel or reside in Latin-American countries are generally men not falling below a certain standard of education, and if not always of independent means, they have come as representatives of wealthy firms, companies, or syndicates. They are managers of branch houses, engineers, travellers, sportsmen, financiers. The lower-class Briton is rarely encountered, as is the case with immigrants from other European and North American countries. There has been no influx of poor-class immigrants from Great Britain. England is the country which in great part has financed railways, and railways in the Latin-American countries are things which come far closer to the heart of the dweller than is conceivable in England, France, or Germany. An individual who builds a railway in South America is regarded as a benefactor. No honour is too great for him. His praises are sung in the Press, he is toasted at public banquets, he is a Napoleon, a world conqueror. He has 'united our beloved patria with those bands of steel which carry civilization in their path,' as the sentiment is generally expressed. The German and the Frenchman, on the other hand, are generally engaged in much smaller enterprises, and display a less liberal method of conducting business, and, with the Italians, they make money out of the country rather than bring it in. German hardware stores and other shops, and French haberdashers and tailors, are freely encountered in the towns of Mexico and South America, along with Spanish and Italian grocers, restaurant keepers, hotel proprietors—all valuable agents in the growing communities, but of less standing than those foreigners who conduct banks, great wholesale establishments, build railways, open mines, and plant great sugar, cattle, and cotton estates."[60] England does not need to exert herself; tradition, time, and her good name work for her.

But "the imperial idea of Greater Britain" does not apply to South America. Not even in the case of the most realistic and always hungry exponent of this policy—Beaconsfield—do we find any suggestion of this tendency; although "The world of Latin America has always possessed attraction for the man of British race."[61]

At the same time, England's position rests also upon cultural influence. Not so dominating as France, not so popular as Spain, English views have nevertheless prevailed with certain of the intellectual classes of South America. Thus Bello in Venezuela-Chile, Alberdi in Argentina, represent English penetration.[62] But the bulk of English cultural influence is more in Central America, as on the Southern continent; the influence of Bentham in the first is not to be underestimated.

Like the others, England tries through visits of her statesmen to invigorate the relations: missions like those of Sir Ernest Shackleton, Sir Maurice de Bunsen, Lord D'Abernon were of great importance.

German culture is no propagandist of German goods in South America. It is almost unknown. It was not and is not in a position to force Spanish culture out of favour with the masses; and it has acquired no position with the cultured classes. The old dominion of the Latin-English influence was approachable only with difficulty by the German influence before the War, was monopolized during the War by the Allies, and now remains closed to German culture. Exceptions obviously do exist; but German culture and German science have their sphere of influence in South America primarily in German circles. And in these circles the greatest political controversies reign. The relationships of the fatherland, both factions and war, here find a heightened life.

There is no question of a unified end—conscious policy or

pressure for expansion. Culturally and politically, Germany lost ground more and more; and the Tannenberg's dreams of an American Germany lie beside the idea of a Great Germany in the grave of the World War.

The German occupies the worst position in South America. He has not the glamour and prestige of Great Britain on his side, its wealth of capital and that of the United States; nor has he the cultural influence and family ties of the Latins. On the contrary, he still labours under the burden of the War psychology, and he has to rely solely on his own diligence and ability.

. . . .

Such is the wording of the proposals and declarations of the wooers. Different, fundamentally different, but always with the same aim which Lastarria defined over sixty years ago: "America knows Europe, studies it unceasingly, follows it step by step, and imitates it as its model; but Europe does not know America, and rather disdains it and looks away from it. . . . *A single European interest, the industrial interest, is the one which pays attention to America.*"[63]

The wooers are unanimous on one point alone: in understanding and combating the successful rival—the United States.[64]

2. THE UNITED STATES

For the moment let us imagine ourselves in the period of transition in America extending from the eighteenth to the nineteenth century; let us recall the time-spirit of that wonderful epoch. It was a period of political concentration in North America, "at the end of the eighteenth century, while at the same time in the old world the custom was to speculate on the spirit of rationalism and to make champagne-speeches upon the possibility and desirability of a union which would at the beginning embrace Europe and later the entire world."[1]

This was an age of revolutions against European states when

the new world was maturing, a time of wars and adventures and national heroes; when ideas of freedom and idealistic sacrifice were in the air; it was the American echo of the French Revolution.

New states were founded, organized, and built up. The beginning of the nineteenth century was first of all a period of creation. The Western world was really becoming a new world. It decided to be distinct from the old one. The exodus to America was in itself a protest against Europe and its prevailing conditions. The spirit desired nothing in common with Europe; it wanted to isolate itself and become independent; to build a new structure on a new soil, and to avoid any danger of interference from the old world.

In their emancipation from the old world, the thirteen original states naturally began to consider their distant neighbours in the Western hemisphere. Their mode of thinking was approximately as follows: As a result of a parallel development of the American countries from relatively sparsely populated colonies to free states, unburdened by historical or racial prejudices, the Western world, compared with Europe, was a new and isolated phenomena, and therefore formed a common basis for the common interests of the young states. There could be no strife among them as was the case in Europe. Proximity of interests seemed to be natural and desirable.[2]

The attitude is best expressed in the famous letter of Maia to Jefferson: "Nature in making us inhabitants of the same continent has united us in a common lot, in bonds of common patriotism." The following reasons for community of interests were always advanced: the geographical closeness, their common principle of governmental structure (anti-monarchical and republican), similar foreign policies (European danger), similarity of origins, as European colonies and the faith in the common future of the countries of the new world, which the history has soon disturbed.

Alexander Hamilton was the spiritual representative of this *continental* current of thought. "He bade his fellow-citizens to think continentally."[3] As one of his most acute biographers remarked, "Hamilton's love for his country was always greater than his love for his countrymen,"[4] and this love Hamilton extended to the whole continent, just as Henry Clay, who as early as January 29, 1816, asserted in the House of Representatives that the United States may openly have to "take part with the patriots of South America"; who spoke of the area "from Hudson to the Cape Horn" as if it were a homogeneous territory. The idea of an American policy uniting the efforts of the peoples of the United States and of Central and South America in order to build up a "great American settlement, superior to the control of all transatlantic affairs or influence, and able to dictate the terms of a connection between the old and the new world," had been pointed out by Alexander Hamilton as one of the greatest possible matters of the young United States, "bound together in a strict and indissoluble union."[5] "The interests of the states, in Hamilton's view, were not in Europe, but only in America. With the future of that continent their destiny was bound up."[6]

Bryce asks the question: "Is there, in fact, such a thing as that which the word Pan-Americanism is intended to describe, or does the expression denote an aspiration rather than a fact?"[7] At that time, the first quarter of the nineteenth century, common sense was alive on the whole of America. In that historical period it was proper to think in terms of continents.[8]

The continental idea in America is comparable to Napoleon's mode of thinking and his practical attempt in Europe; for Napoleon's continental system was an effort to unite the continent of Europe against England.[9]

The ideas of customs union of Frederick List were suggested by the continentalism of the new world as well as by Napoleon's European system.

Economic motives and visions are not strange to continentalism. Henry Clay gives utterance of that with rare frankness which is something typical for the arguments of that time. "It is in our power to create a system of which we shall be the centre, and in which all South America will act with the United States. In respect to commerce, we should be benefited. . . . We should become a centre of a system which should constitute the rallying bond of human wisdom against all the despotisms of the old world."[10]

From continentalism sprang the Monroe Doctrine, the will to erect a political wall separating the old world from the new, to become isolated behind it, and at the same time to guard distant Western neighbours against common enemies. This was a warning to Europe.

In this sense was the Monroe Doctrine understood in South America. The Peruvian Maurtua calls the doctrine "a Pan-American Declaration"; the Argentine Carlos Calvo conceives of the doctrine as "a declaration of complete American independence"; and Carlos Arenari Loaza emphasizes the Pan-American character of the declaration.

This is the light in which the declaration was regarded in the United States, for it was nothing else but official proclamation of ideas which were already current. One of the most important documents in the understanding of the Monroe Doctrine is the letter of ex-President Jefferson written October 24, 1823, to President Monroe. There Jefferson declares that "America North and South has a set of interests distinct from those of Europe and peculiarly her own."

The Monroe Doctrine was an official declaration of ambitions and opinions of the continentalism. The difference of opinion as to the rôle of England and the policy of Canning, as well as South American interpretation of the importance of these factors, are of no significance in our present discussion. Canning myth or Monroe myth—the doctrine was the high-water mark of continental thought, and as such it holds that place of honour in history, disregarding its subsequent interpretations and applications. The manifesto of Monroe in defending America against the encroachments of the foreigners formulated the negative side of the continental programme. In its positive aspect no successful practical attempt has ever been constructed or even clearly expressed.

The Panama Congress of 1826 (*infra*) marked the historical

close of continentalism. The first attempt at "a Continental Congress" was a fiasco. Indeed, an invitation to attend the Congress was sent to the United States, and it was accepted after a troubled delay. Official representatives were finally delegated—but they never arrived.

There were reasons for such a sluggish attitude. The United States was now busy at home; it was necessary to continue the building of the country, and her real interest[11] for her far-away neighbours, the brothers on the other continent, was still undeveloped. So the Latin-American family in South America was left to itself.

Then followed the expansion of the United States—the Mexican War, and "the ideals, the lofty purposes, the broad and generous sympathies of Henry Clay seemed for the time being to have perished. A new chapter in history was, however, about to be opened."[12]

With the Panama Canal continentalism was also geographically obliterated. The unity of the American continent had not only been physically broken, but politically there arose a sharp line of demarkation between the United States and its sphere of interest on the one hand and South America on the other. Everything "north of Panama" is severed from South America, and bears the mark of belonging either officially or unofficially to or being dependent on the new imperium. Only now and then do the old continental ideas rise to the surface. Sometimes they appear in a strange and comic guise—as, for instance, in a pamphlet published by a certain Robert E. Beasley, A "Citizen of Riovista, California."[13]

The World War fanned the spark into flame. The non-participation of the United States during the first period of the War and the new economic situation seemed to create a new continental sentiment, which, however, was not disturbed by the subsequent entry of the United States into the conflict. On the contrary, the United States was followed by several of the American countries.

At this time both continents believed for the time being in

the old continentalism of the early nineteenth century, preached the unity of America,[14] and failed to note that for the continent of the south the United States has become the chief buyer, purveyor, and financier; but that for the United States, South America is at present only one of several great economic divisions. For during the War all quarters of the globe depended on the United States. Europe was no longer held in respect, the contradictory agitation of the belligerent parties being in part responsible for the change of heart.

The idealistic speeches and the Wilsonism of the first War period prepared a favourable sentiment and atmosphere. There was even talk of "el nuevo panamericanismo" (Quesada). The World War effecting emancipation of Europe sponsored and brought a new vigour to the old continentalism; it had united the two American continents temporarily with economical and financial bonds. This change of sentiment is to be noticed in North as well as in South America. "If there is a silver lining to the war cloud, it is the development of Pan-American solidarity. No historical event since the declaration of the Monroe Doctrine in 1823 has done more to awaken the Governments and people of both North and South America to a true appreciation of their common interests. Never before have the people and principles in each and all of the American nations said so many sympathetic and kind things to each other as they are now doing."[15]

An Argentine writer corroborates. Ernesto J. J. Bott declares that the European War has put into motion various influences which manifest themselves in the strong sentiment favouring the revival of the old continental idea, thus bringing the movement one step nearer to the realization of "political unification of the continent." "The existence of a continental sociological unity as the result of primary social and natural conditions is, possibly, an undisputed reality. Organization of the political union based upon a sociological unity is a possibility."[16]

This new-old spirit radiates from the address of the Hon. William G. McAdoo, Secretary of the Treasury of the

United States, at the First Financial Pan-American Conference in 1915.

"It is not from selfish motive or sordid desire for material gain that this conference draws its inspiration. It has a deeper and a finer meaning. We meet for the purpose of considering how and in what manner the great Republics of the Western Hemisphere, representing as they do common ideal of liberty, justice, and self-government, and dedicated as they are to the highest and best interest of humanity, may, through common action and interest, not only conserve their material welfare, but become a more homogeneous and powerful moral force for the preservation of peace and the good of humanity."[17]

And—as in the beginning of the nineteenth century—the American continent came to be considered as a unified power with regard to Europe.

"So long as we are in large part financially dependent upon the nations of Europe for our internal development and economic stability, so are we exposed to the hazards of their internal strife and external wars. This seems to be the opportune time for the development of the spirit, at least, of continental solidarity."[18]

At this moment continentalism received at least a temporary economic basis. "European dislocation produced a corresponding dislocation in America. The sources of European capital were blocked instantaneously. The normal flow of imports and exports between America and Europe was completely changed; exchange experienced tremendous fluctuations; banking systems were disorganized, and it was necessary to devise adjustments which, if they did not correct the situation completely, at least might relieve it until the end of the War. When the closeness of the economic ties of the world were felt in such a sharp manner, it was realized immediately that it was important to unite the forces that still remained outside of the conflict and combine them for a common purpose in an astmosphere of serenity, to keep from the American continent the most serious consequences of the European cataclysm. Then, for the first time, it was seen very clearly that the economic solidarity of America was something very real, whatever might be the political conditions on the continent, something that should be preserved, studied, and organized in such a way that it would not only make America safe, so far as possible, from painful repercussions like that of 1914, but would also make it a storehouse of vital reserves from which, in case of necessity, aid might be given to peoples less fortunate than those on this side of the Atlantic."[19] That a unity of interests for the two continents existed at the time was asserted by Percy A. Martin, who, however, did not distinguish between Pan-Americanism and Continentalism. "Pan-Americanism has ceased to be a mere rallying-point, a diplomatic shibboleth. Under the stress of war it became a dynamic force."[20]

The secretary-general of this financial conference was justified in stating that "this Financial Conference marks an epoch in the relations between the United States and the countries of Central and South America. In one sense, the questions discussed were of a material character, but it is through the spirit of co-operation developed in the solution of these material problems that the foundations are laid for that closer relationship and spirit of unity which means so much to the nations of the American Continent, and without which they cannot hope to fulfil the world mission which they are called upon to perform."[21]

This "epoch," however, was not of long duration. The end of the War, the new world position of the United States, the rapidly growing alarm of the "Peligro Yanqui"—all this accelerated the breakdown of the continental spirit. The realization of continentalism could not be effected in spite of the existence of a ready apparatus in the form of official Pan-Americanism which had been active since the 'nineties. The motivation of continentalism lost its power with the changes in the basic factors: the revolution in transportation destroyed the geographical argument, history removed the political motive, the common past is a historical memory, and no one gives credence any longer to a common future.[22] The World War temporarily brought these motives into play again, causing continentalism to flare up.

The beginning of official Pan-Americanism[23] meant that the United States arranged itself among the seducers and was beginning an active courtship. As a child of the beginning of nineteenth century, continentalism was the product of the political movements of the time and the stormy confusion of ideas then current. The new Pan-Americanism, though officially a legitimate child of twenty-one states, is in fact an offspring of the United States only, while the other twenty states merely refrained from protest by tacit adoption of the child. Pan-Americanism inherited its theoretical programme from continentalism. Its practical aims were suggested by the economic growth of the United States.

The United States has always kept aloof from the desires and attempts of Latin-American countries to organize a union after the Panama Congress. At present, after the United States has successfully solved her internal economic problems, Pan-Americanism was brought to the surface.

The high lights in the economic development of the United States after the Civil War are well known. In industry the nation was becoming mature. Growing industrialization called for new markets. The eagle was ready to fly and took wing southward.

When the interest in Latin America was waxing in the 'eighties of the nineteenth century, it became necessary to consider the strong competition of Europe, and especially that of Great Britain, in Latin America. The position of the United States in the rivalry was not very favourable. Europe had several distinct advantages: geographically she was nearer than South America, traditionally she had a better knowledge of the markets, and her financial position was powerful. Yet in spite of these disadvantages the United States, goaded on by the pressure of expanding industry, entered the fight for South American markets; for in the 'eighties, according to a writer several decades after, "the manufacturing industries of the United States have developed and are developing at such a rate that the Americans are not afraid to meet the European rivals in almost any branch of trade."[24]

In 1880, upon the suggestion of Hinton Rower Helper, David Davis, representative from Illinois, moved in Congress that a conference of all American states be held.[25] One can find various projects advanced in this connection in the current literature (Ward, Douglas, and others). James G. Blaine, who as Secretary of State seemed to recall the words of Emerson, that "the world is founded on thoughts and ideas, not on cotton and iron," attempted to find the thoughts and ideas underlying cotton and iron.

Blaine, the father of official Pan-Americanism, was not an ordinary appearance.[26] There exists a peculiar similarity of opinion between Blaine and Henry Clay on many problems, in spite of the different epochs during which each of them was active. Not only did they agree on the tariff, as Blaine's biographer[27] remarks, but also in their outlook toward the entire American continent, the expansion of the United States and the Panama Canal.[28]

The programme of the conference was directed mainly toward the solution of economic problems. Concrete problems before the convention were mainly: Formation of an American customs union, adoption of a uniform system of customs regulations, adoption of a uniform system of weights, measures, etc., adoption of a common silver coin. In the recommendations one can find the projected construction of an intercontinental railway, the establishment of an international American bank.

The customs union scheme was clearly influenced by the German Zollverein and the consequent establishment of the German Empire. The influence which emanated from Germany becomes often clearer when we note that the first plan of such a conference was proposed by Frederick List. His letter of May 9, 1835, contains the suggestion that an international commercial conference be convoked by President Jackson.

List bases his proposal on the example of Europe, where, "Twenty-one German States, without being bound by ties of national feeling, have organized a Zollverein only on the strength of treaties. It is maintained that Austria, Switzerland, and Belgium are negotiating to join this customs union."[29]

The official argument favouring Pan-Americanism in the 'eighties sound continentalistic indeed; this programme corresponds to the programme of the Panama Congress. Blaine's ideas are practically those of Henry Clay; but the position of the United States in world economy underwent a considerable change, which introduced new motives for the restoration of the old concept, and explain the economic background of the movement. Economic motives were so important that the United States sent an invitation to the Brazilian Empire, although she had continually emphasized the republican character of the new world. The formal history of the conference is well known. The invitations to the Governments were sent, dated November 29, 1881, but the new Secretary of State, "Mr. Frelinghuysen, in the name of the President, practically withdrew the invitation on January 9, 1882, six weeks after it was sent out, when some of the Governments invited had already signified their acceptance of it."[30] William E. Curtis, the prospective director of the "Commercial Bureau of the American Republics," was delegated head of a commission to visit the independent Latin-American states with the view toward popularizing the idea of a conference. The commission was recalled before accomplishing its task, because of the presidential elections in the United States. Only as late as 1888, when Blaine for the second time became Secretary of State, did Congress reconsider acting upon Blaine's proposal, and on the resolution of May 24th the plan was accepted. The conference proposed herein has become a reality.[31]

It was virtually a *Brautschau.* The reception accorded the delegates glittered with courtesies. Everything in the country worth seeing was exhibited for their admiring eyes. In a word, United States was courting Latin America.

Meanwhile Europe—although previously not extremely anxious about the Panama Congress—now became jealously aroused,[32] although at first without reason, because the immediate results of the conference were quite meagre, "the United States had not yet sufficient economic means to undertake such ambitious projects. American industry, unequal even to the needs of the home market, was able to export only a very limited number of commodities, in a desultory manner at that. The South American republics were stocked with European capital, English for the most part; as a result, there set in natural commercial currents to pay for the interest upon their borrowings. Being itself dependent upon Europe for the capital required for its own development, the United States could not supplant her in the rôle of stockholder for these countries. Furthermore, the want of direct communications (they were almost non-existent) by land and by sea between the two Americas constituted a serious obstacle, while the fact that a number of agricultural products exported from the temperate lands of South America happened to be of the same kind as those exported from the United States only curtailed the possibilities of mutual relations. The only lasting result of the conference, therefore, was the creation of the International Union of the American Republics, through the agency of which has been preserved the custom of calling together Pan-American conferences."[33]

"In fact, the only positive and practical result was the formation of an international office of American Republics in Washington supported by government contributions; all this seemed to have the characteristics of an academic *balon d'essai*."[34]

The programme of the Second Conference in Mexico, 1901, was much more modest. No economic questions were to be discussed; mainly technical problems and of international law were to be considered by the conference. Sentiment immediately after the Spanish-American War was unfavourable for a new demonstration of brotherhood. The continued expansion of the United States in Latin America had aroused old suspicions again. Now the United States adopted the usual strategy of a seducer: visits and speeches, attempts to adjust themselves to the habits and tastes of the courted, and steps toward a conciliation for past breaches. Here the rôle of Elihu Root is not to be underestimated, although at the same time one should be cautious of such opinions as Joaquim Nabuco presents, that "if Blaine moulded the group of united American Nations, it was Root who put in it life and movement."[35]

The Third Conference in Rio de Janeiro, 1906, proceeded under the same auspices and along similar lines. The discussions were mainly of a legal nature. The following and fourth conference in Buenos Aires, 1910, was to a greater degree dedicated to economic and cultural problems of minor importance and to practical problems of commercial intercourse.

The World War, however, interrupts this series of conferences. The awakened continentalism could not rest easily within the ramifications of official Pan-Americanism. Even the financial conference which took place in Washington during the War was much richer in ideas than all other Pan-American conferences. The restoration of normal conditions after the War brought with it a renewal of Pan-American conferences. The fifth conference in 1923 in Santiago de Chile resembles that in Buenos Aires. However, behind the scenes one can notice a sort of palace insurrection.

The sixth conference of 1928, which was held in Havana, was of greater importance. Here the delegates deliberated over the question of reorganizing the union, thus furthering the revolt begun in previous conferences. The Havana programme is typical of the union's new form of evolution. It contained topics mainly concerned with problems of intercourse and intellectual co-operation; while a very small part of the programme was given to consideration of important economic problems, and political questions were excluded entirely.

When one compares the economic problems discussed in

Havana with those adopted in Washington, the decadence of the movement becomes evident. Even those resolutions adopted at the conference never became realities. This is true of both those of prime and secondary importance—as, for instance, the resolution concerning the Pan-American bank, of the proposal of a Pan-American Coffee Congress, or the adopted suggestion for the erection of a monument to Henry Clay.

What is the true significance of Pan-Americanism? In 1913 Enock believed that, "Due partly to the work of the (Pan-American) Union it is that the trade of the United States with Latin America is increasing in a rapid ratio."[36] Does this casual relationship exist in reality? Would not trade reach the same figure without Pan-Americanism? Of course these questions defy positive answers. Psychologically, however, Pan-Americanism was scarcely of important benefit to the United States.

Blaine's intention was to enter the competition in South American markets under the guise of Pan-Americanism. (It is to be noted that the United States'—not Pan-American—propaganda in South America was and is quite modest.[37]) The success was achieved through the sheer growth and power of the industry of the United States.

The country itself has undergone many changes during the forty years since the inauguration of official Pan-Americanism. The Spanish-American War was the turning-point in the recent history of the United States. Archibald C. Coolidge tells of a foreign ambassador who, after a short absence from this country during the War, felt upon his return that he was coming into a new and different country. Still greater was the change and transformation caused by the World War. The psychological and political atmosphere, with the exception of the War years, had been not favourable toward American attempts to gain goodwill in Latin America. Besides, there was no such thing as a Pan-American ideology in political and economic literature of the United States.[38] The great programme of Pan-Americanism remained unaccomplished both politically and economically. The central economic problems placed before the conference of 1889 wandered through decades from one conference to another, remaining unsolved. Neither the customs union nor the currency union nor the continental bank was ever realized. Only the trans-continental railroad project seems to have approached completion.[39]

And yet neither Hispano-Americanism nor Latin-Americanism can be compared in its practical results to official Pan-Americanism, in spite of the latter's barrenness. At least an organization was created. This organization, though it might not have been or even may not now be agreeable to all parties concerned, is already existent for several decades. It has rendered and at present still renders certain practical services in the field of co-operation among the twenty-one states. It sponsors intercourse among its members. In a word, the organization has become a customary institution.

However, taken as a whole, the programmes and work of the six conferences reveal a distinct decline in ideological content, and consequently the progress of practical achievements consists chiefly in the solution of minor and frequently occurring problems. A pronounced adversary of Pan-Americanism characterizes this evolution as a "downfall from the skies to the earth." With regard to the activity of the conference, he declares that "it (Pan-Americanism) had left the eternal heights of the Bolivarian eagle and plunged instead into the juridical and commercial jungle."[40]

There is no definition of Pan-Americanism, nor can there be. It is a matter of political slogan, and as such it contains no concrete meaning of its own. Its meaning is being constantly changed according to the tastes of those employing the slogan.[41] "Pan-Americanism may be defined as a tendency displayed by independent nations of America to associate together"[42]; but this attempt can hardly be considered as a definition.

Pan-Americanism is pronouncedly a realistic movement, even though it admits of certain sentimental deviations among its exponents. This movement takes no part of its content from the Knight of La Mancha, but owes something to Sancho Pansa. It is promoted, managed, and exploited by the United States, although the movement grants various advantages to the other participants. It is an expression of the economic pressure and seek for leadership of the United States. The official domicile of the Pan-American Union is Washington, its president is the Secretary of State, and its director-general is a citizen of the United States. "Yanqui centrista"—thus is the Pan-American Union styled by a Spanish writer.

The movement leads a double life. It talks much about Pan-America, but its life depends upon North America; it is a Pan-American illusion.

The activity of the union, very modest at the beginning, expanded very considerably, thus giving the organization the characteristics of a statistical bureau or chamber of commerce[43]—particularly the latter. This transformation in its present form, gradual as it was, had already begun at the second conference in Mexico. Giving sustenance to the Pan-American Union has been and is possible only through a careful avoidance of questions of political complication.[44] Otherwise this organization, devoid of a strong framework, would have broken down long ago. What then unites the States? Is it merely the fortuitous circumstance that the two continents bear the same name? If not, what is its logical foundation? What really is the community of interests? The twenty states could obtain in the nineteenth century from Europe all what the United States offered. The economic motive of the movement was in the United States.

The United States had a secret desire to organize, with the help of the Pan-Americanism, a huge holding corporation in which the different Latin-American countries could play the rôle of subsidiaries. Such a scheme would resemble recent developments within the British Empire; for what is the United Kingdom if not Great Britain, Inc., with dominions as subsidiaries? And are not the politically independent states of Central America and the Caribbean truly economic subsidiaries of the United States?

Thus the last trace of continentalism has dissolved and disappeared in the realities of official Pan-Americanism. And even though the modern exponent is trying to resuscitate the old continentalism, as Waldo Frank attempts to do, and to find "the lost America," yet the material bonds of union remain the same in spite of such prophetic utterances: "Our business with South America will rest on a sound basis when it represents negotiations, not between strangers but between brothers,"[45] or as J. Fred Rippy declares: "The United States now needs raw material for growing industries, markets for manufactured products, fields for investment of surplus capital."[46]

The difference between continentalism and official Pan-Americanism is not to be mistaken. Continentalism was an idealistic movement of the first quarter of the nineteenth century, with indefinite aims mainly of a political nature. The movement was a direct descendant of the spirit of the French Revolution as transplanted on American soil; was bound up with the epoch of struggles for freedom and with the romantic tendencies of its contemporary literature. The leaders of that time liked to regard themselves and the American peoples in the setting of Greek and Roman antiquity, a background of heroic images, names, and deeds. This young and romantic generation were consciously and passionately enacting epic history, and figured themselves in the ancient group of heroes and martyrs.

Quite different, however, is official Pan-Americanism. The movement is not political; its product is in organization. It is not idealistic, but utilitarian; not romantic, but realistic, in spite of the unrestrained lyricism that blossoms at the openings and closings of the conferences. Continentalism was born in the romantic atmosphere and sentiment which prevailed simultaneously in that epoch in the North and the South. It had no economic background in either of the Americas. Official Pan-Americanism sprang from the needs of the new-born industry of the United States. Successful entrepreneurs and mature economic realists took the initiative. Blaine conceived Pan-Americanism as an economic instrument which he adorned with the plumage of continentalism, thus attempting to rival the ideological frescos of Latin and Hispano-Americanism. This striving of official Pan-Americanism for an attractive ideological content in the United States corresponds to the lyricism rife in Latin America.

The difference consists in that official Pan-Americanism developed into a complex apparatus. It is becoming an organization and an organizing power. Its first steps were slow and uncertain. It was groping for the right path. It was crippled by the Spanish-American War. The impression of the United States as an oppressor of Spain, and the dubious, in that time, liberty of Cuba, could not be easily dissipated in spite of Elihu Root's attempts at conciliation. Slowly the machine proceeded at its work nevertheless, and a series of Inter-American conferences were called. They were constant attempts to broaden the scope of the Union's activities, and consequently painstaking reorganization was being undertaken, until "from a restricted commercial information bureau under the supervision of one government, it has evolved into a general administrative secretariat under the guidance and direction of the governments of all of the twenty-one republics of the new world."[47]

The World War again restricted the activity of the Union. The main activity was transferred to the financial conference mentioned above. Indeed, it is significant that the continentalism which flared for the short period during the War found no use for the facilities offered by the official organization. After the World War, the Pan-American Union went ahead at full speed.

To some extent the seducer can indeed rejoice in the results of his courtship, though the United States may be proud indeed of the organization built up, but not of the gains achieved through it.[48] The organization required much patience and hardship—yet it was worth while. It has nothing in common with continentalism, it is no longer a means of economic exploitation by the United States, but it is an organization for work, an agency as intended at first, endowed and adorned with all the *paraphernalia* of diplomatic splendour.

However, its actual developed technique and organization have diminished its importance in so far as specific interests of the United States are concerned.

Official Pan-Americanism, not being sufficiently elastic, is of no political value to the United States. It does not and cannot distinguish among its members. Being a corporate body of twenty-one states, the Union cannot possibly represent the policy of the United States, and is unable to treat with the countries individually corresponding to the interests of the United States. This lack of ability is in the nature of things without remedy. Pan-Americanism is no longer a cloak for the business policy of the United States.[49] It served the interests of the United States only indirectly in its amassing information in Washington and its close contact with Capitol, not only territorially but through regular co-operation with Government agencies. The technique of this instrumentality is what the United States may best utilize, and in it lies at the same time much of the binding force of the Union.

The ideological void of Pan-Americanism has been filled by the complexities of organization, the minutiæ of routine, and the extension of international co-operation in the collection of facts and diplomatical actions. In the practical realism of this policy lies the power of its mechanism, and the inertia of the movement keeps the United States and the Latin-American countries united in this system of co-operation.

The history of the Americas records nine Inter-American conferences until 1889, and eighty-two conferences have been held since that time. Of these eighty-two, seventy-eight were held in the twentieth century and forty-three convened since the World War. The machine is accelerating its speed. Correspondingly the different countries are becoming more and more firmly enmeshed in the web of Pan-Americanism, where Manuel Ugarte would give the role of spider to the United States. "Pan-Americanism is not yet a reality," says Usher.[50] One is obliged, however, to omit the word "yet" in order that the statement may be correct, because "We have no actual evidence of a desire on the part of the American peoples to make it real."[51]

"The policy of Pan-Americanism is practical. Pan-American spirit is ideal."[52] This declaration of Lansing is one-half true, for this ideal, this Pan-American spirit which was identical with continentalism, is now dead.

Thus official Pan-Americanism has become a useful organization which renders considerable service in the dissemination of information, culture, and jurisprudence. A body it is, but without a soul.[53]

> Dann eben wo Begriffe fehlen
> Da stellt ein Wort zur rechter Zeit sich ein.

(*b*) THE COURTED

What is the attitude of the courted toward the proposals of the seducers?

The attitude is not constant. It varies according to the country and the epoch. We can find countries with permanent and faithful sympathies and orientations; others which are fickle and vacillating. The former are consciously designing with a definite aim, while the latter are continually floundering in confusion. The great countries belong to the first group—Brazil and Argentina; to the second belong the remaining countries except Chile, which in the twentieth century is migrating from the second to the first group.

Of course, this demarcation denotes only nebulous tendencies and genial attitudes. One may find frequent exceptions in several countries and several epochs. But characteristic of the history of *Brazil* is *the continental tendency of inclining toward the United States; of Argentina, the anti-continental sympathy for Europe; of the remaining South American countries, uncertain groping and changing affections*. This uneasiness is greatest in the Pacific section, reaching its highest mark in Colombia and Venezuela; is almost absent in Paraguay and Bolivia, the two countries of the interior of the continent, who have no contact with the ocean.

At the beginning of the nineteenth century common sense dominated in South America. Continentalism, which we studied in the United States, was the main and perhaps the only current in South America. At that time, in the opinions of the leaders, only *one continent* existed. This idea was also strong in South America. The first naturalization papers issued in 1811 in Buenos Aires referred to *citizens of America*.[1] Moreno, Monteagudo, San Martin, Arguero, O'Higgins, were championing a union and close alliance with North America.

Besides, personal contact existing between the leaders of the two continents is greater than is commonly supposed. The relations between Francisco de Miranda and Alexander Hamilton are extremely interesting. The success of the United States inspired Miranda with the hope of freeing his own country from Spanish control. He confided in his friends in the United States, particularly in Alexander Hamilton, "upon whom he fixed his eyes as a coadjutor in the great purpose of his life."[2] This Venezuelan hero, while in Paris in 1797, dreamed of a "United States of South America."

We have seen how this continentalism has found its end on the part of the United States at the time of the Panama Congress; it was no more alive in South America at that time.

Brazil was the only country which remained faithful to continentalism during its entire history. The fact is known that prior to the gaining of independence Brazilian students held a conference with Jefferson in Paris in 1787. Jefferson weighed the advantages of an alliance with the Southern Continent and aroused the spirit of his young friends.[3] One of these young men, a Brazilian student named Maia, a member of a company of conspirators who were plotting for the independence of Brazil, in appealing to Jefferson for help, struck the keynote of Pan-Americanism. The United States should be their natural friend, said Maia, "because in making us inhabitants of the same continent it has in some manner united us in bonds of common patriotism."

In the first quarter of the nineteenth century the continental plan was openly discussed several times in Brazil.

"The idea of Pan-Americanism was first suggested in Brazil in 1817 by Cruz Cabuga, plenipotentiary of the Pernambucan Government in the United States. In 1819 another Brazilian, Rodrigo Pinto Guedes, presented to the Minister of War and Foreign Affairs of Brazil the idea that the only means Brazil possessed of safeguarding herself in the presence of the threats of Europe was an alliance with her neighbours to the north and south, by means of what he called an American League. In 1819 the Brazilian Government, endeavouring to carry out this suggestion, sent the following instruction to its political agent in Buenos Aires:

"After you have constantly reminded them that the interests of the kingdom are identical with those of the other States of this hemisphere, and that they should participate in our destinies, you will promise on behalf of his royal highness the solemn recognition of the political independence of those governments, and you will explain the priceless benefits that may result from their forming a confederation of offensive and defensive treaty with Brazil, in order that, with the other governments of Spanish America, they may bring to naught the crafty wiles of European politics."[4]

The issuance of Monroe's declaration brought once more into discussion the continental orientation of Brazil.

"In less than two months after the reading of President Monroe's message the Brazilian Government issued instructions to its representative, Rebello, at Washington to propose to the United States an offensive and defensive alliance on the basis of the newly enunciated Monroe Doctrine, acting on the principle 'that it was not in accordance with reason, justice, and right that sacrifices, such as those which the United States undertook to make for the other American nations, should be accepted gratuitously."[5]

Brazil has not participated in Latin-American congresses and attempts at union. The historical peculiarities of her position, such as the monarchial form of government, the family ties with the Austrian Royal family, the differences in origin and language, the boundary questions with several neighbours, and the slavery question—all this that "in Peru as in Chile, in Nueva Granada as in regions of La Plata, brought against Brazil the same accusations of desertion from the American principles."[6]

Like the United States, Brazil lost interest in these problems in the following decades. However, she participated in official Pan-Americanism like the others. At the end of the nineteenth century there arose a renaissance of Brazilian continental thought, whose ideology was familiar to the great Brazilian statesmen of that time. Joaquim Nabuco contributed much in order to effect the *rapprochement* of the two countries. He was one of the most influential diplomats at Washington. His wish was "to create a common American public opinion," and he employed the word "American" in the continental sense.[7] Being a friend of Elihu Root, he was nevertheless the initiator of the address to President McKinley concerning the Monroe Doctrine, which has a pronouncedly continental point of view.

Continentalism became during this time an inclination toward co-operation with the United States, and the same Joaquim Nabuco declared: "In Brazil, I must say, the leading statesmen were never afraid of associating with this country."[8]

The Brazilian Bismarck, Baron Rio Branco, was an exponent of the same policy of friendship. His opening address at the Third Conference in Rio de Janeiro (where Elihu Root was assisting) was a strong demonstration.

The awakening of continentalism during the War resulted in the corresponding argument favouring Brazil's participation in the War. On May 22, 1917, President Wenceslão Braz, in a special message to Congress, suggested that "the Brazilian nation, through its legislative organ . . . adopt the attitude that one of the belligerents (the United States) forms an integral part of the American continent, and to this belligerent we are bound by a traditional friendship and by a similarity of political opinion in the defence of the vital interests of America and the principles accepted by international law."[9] This continental idea was once more emphasized in the circular directed to all other countries. The conclusion is especially interesting, for Brazil uses the opportunity to clarify her attitude towards the Monroe Doctrine in the well-known continental meaning. "If hitherto the relative lack of reciprocity on the part of the American republics has withdrawn from the Monroe Doctrine its true character, permitting a scarcely well-founded interpretation of the prerogatives of their sovereignty, present events, by placing Brazil, even now, at the side of the United States, in the critical moment of the world's history, continue to give our foreign policy a practical form of continental solidarity—a policy, indeed, which was that of the old regime on every occasion on which any of the other friendly sister nations of the American continent were in jeopardy."[10]

Thus Brazil always remains faithful to the continental idea, and, on the other hand, indifferent towards proposals from Europe and South America. Brazil, which once ruled its mother country, which gave refuge to the Portuguese Court, refuses to accept even Lusitanian offers for union. Brazil possesses the largest German population in South America, but Germany was not able to influence it culturally, politically, or economically. France dominates culturally, Italy through immigration, England through her investments, and the United States through her trade. But not one of these seducers could become a political attraction for Brazil. Brazil—a continent in itself like the United States—never forsakes her continental attitude and policy.

We seldom find in Brazilian literature followers of the unionist movement. One of the few exceptions was Manoel

Oliveira de Lima, but even he was chiefly a platonist and not an orthodox follower of this political philosophy.

In this country one rarely finds cries against the "Peligro Yanqui" which are so frequent in Latin America. Brazil alone does not shrink from the danger, and cannot consider it as a menace at all because of her great distance from the United States and her own vast extension and power. Even the anger against the policy of the United States towards Central America and the Caribbean is not at all so violent in Portuguese America as in Spanish America. The fact that Brazil's attitude toward the United States is more friendly than any other Spanish-American country has been noted by many writers of the United States.[11] "The history of the diplomatic relations between the two countries bears frequent witness to this sentiment of cordiality and mutual esteem."[12]

Entirely different is the attitude of Argentina. Her conduct and political thought are consequent pronouncedly anti-continental. Argentina has not the same consanguineous sentiment toward the Americas. She emphasizes her European orientation. The Argentine is proud, and, as national sociology itself declares, arrogant. He is proud that "in a third of Argentine territory is concentrated a half of the economic strength of South America."[13] Thus we can find throughout the entire history of official Argentina a great lack of interest towards the unionist movement. In the undercurrent of her literature there was more or less of an interest in this school of thought; however, the government was always against it. Even prior to the Panama Congress, Buenos Aires was "opposed to the idea of an establishment of a certain authority presiding over a confederation of the American states."[14]

President Rivadavia, in 1825, refused, in the name of Argentina, "the invitation of Colombia, for the programme of the Congress seemed to him to be hostile towards the European nations," and he considered the trade and relation with them of advantage to the provinces of Rio de Prata.[15]

Argentina denied even the existence of a justification for a union in South America. An official note of the Government on November 10, 1862, declared that "America, consisting of independent nations with their own individual needs and means, cannot form a political union. Nature and deeds divided the continent, and diplomatic efforts are sterile." And the Chancellor Elizalde added the following supplement: "No one European element is antagonistic to the American element; more ties, more interest, more harmony exist between the American nations and the several European than among the American nations themselves."[16]

President Mitre formulated the same opinion more sharply in his historical letter of March 24, 1865, to Domingo F. Sarmiento, who without authorization had participated in the Congress at Lima in 1864: "It is time to abandon the childish lie that we are brothers."[17]

Calderon characterizes this policy as "policy opposed to everything exclusively American, to geographical or ethnical reason."[18] In the year 1889, "faithful to her traditions, Argentina once more defended European influence against the project of a continental federation."[19]

Sáenz Peña openly argued in favour of this European tendency of Argentina.[20] He emphasized the economic motives of this policy very early at the First Pan-American Conference which he attended as representative of Argentine.[21]

While official Argentina is always rejecting proposals of union, politely referring to her intimacy with Europe, and is proud of her successes at the present time,[22] a great part of her literature corroborates this point of view and insists that Hispano-American homogeneity does not exist. Thus Carlos O. Bunge preaches: "Hispano-America is not one country, but a combination of countries of different climates; it is not one nation, but a group of similar nations."[23]

Argentina is opposed to the United States because of competition in agricultural products, and is antagonistic to South American union because she feels herself to be European and not American. Argentina favours Europe and everything

European. She flirts with Spain, France, Italy, and friendly with Germany,[24] and encourages the advances of English capital. Argentina is as anti-continental towards America as she is friendly towards her European suitors, without undertaking a definite choice among them. In the last decade there were many symptoms indicating the possibility and probability of a change in Argentina's point of view, but Argentina is looking for hegemony and not for a union.

The remaining South American countries do not manifest a pronounced inclination towards a certain seducer, but fear is uppermost—fear of the friends as well as enemies. Continentalism also prevailed in these countries at the beginning of the nineteenth century, and there it also ended with the Panama Congress. The ruling desire of this part of South America was and is a Latin-American, or at least a Hispanic-American Union. The weaker and more threatened countries on the Pacific and in the north took the initiative. Chile, Peru, Venezuela, and especially Colombia were the centres of this movement. Here contact with Central America is greater, and the situation therefore more imperilling. These countries are weaker and smaller and feel themselves within the enemies' power. Every advance made by a foreign power—even France and Spain—causes anxiety to these countries, who feel that they may be next to suffer intrusion. Unity was temporary here. In the war for independence Colombian and Chilean, Peruvian and Argentine, fought together. At that time they were looking for aid from different sources, and were to a certain extent receiving this help. Miranda, as ambassador of the revolution, visited London, Paris, St. Petersburg, Constantinople, and New York. Generally, however, they considered Europe as an enemy; they were later separated from her by the wall of the Monroe Doctrine.

During the succeeding decades they noted that the United States also had a craving for power and expansion. They have now recognized that the only aid is self-defence. In this common fear lies a partial explanation of the political history of these regions of South America in the nineteenth and even the twentieth century. They were afraid to lose their political independence, their economic autonomy, their native culture. They feared Spain, Europe, the United States, and each other.

The idea of union was stimulating, and influenced the conduct of these States, which always pursued defensive aims. This unionist tendency was always suggested by their historical leitmotiv of fear. They were not able to exercise a free choice, and show favour towards any one suitor; they have been and are forced into politics; they are seeking help and aid from one against another; they are attempting to find safety in the family circle, but they have no peace even at home. These fear sentiments were always the soul of the political liberation of these countries of South America.

The dangers against which they jousted were not mere windmills. But disregarding the few exceptions, all the suggested means and programmes of self-defence were theoretical, rhetorical, or lyric. The history of these attempts is a chronological list of powerless (often brilliant) congresses, and a flow of an ever-repeated unoriginal literature of war and discontent, projects of union, speeches, addresses, newspaper articles, poems—how little is the progress in this field! In reading a publication on the projects of union, one cannot at first understand whether it is of the present or a former century.

The investigation of these ideas in South America leads us into a labyrinth, where the thread of Ariadne is the cry of a union.

The Mexican Government published in 1919 an interesting collection of these attempts, congresses, and projects, under the title, *El ideal Latino-Americano*[25]—a pitiful picture of futile attempts. Once foreign danger reared its head, there began foment for a union, speeches, articles, declarations; the danger once passed, the resolutions remained unratified, and each country became preoccupied with domestic affairs. Carranza says: "We ought to be united as well as we were in the time of conflict." He has forgotten, meanwhile, that even at the time of the struggle for independence a universal union could not be attained. Only partial alliances, local unions, chiefly personal alliances, organized *ad hoc* with limited specific aims—the situation was *societas unius rei.* The propaganda and attempts were not retarded. From 1797 until the Lima Congress (1865) there were forty-three literary projects in this field, and this figure is surely not a grand total. Who was not obsessed with this problem? Generals, presidents, journalists, South Americans, Frenchmen, Germans, Spaniards, and even an Irishman.[26] Literature constructs only broad and vague programmes. It is in an idealistic drunkenness, having been moved by the epic of the struggle for independence.

It was an interesting period. Nations were formed and split up. The Spanish colonies, divided in their helpless and inexperienced struggle for independence, were looking for the rehabilitation of the lost unity. There were suggested projects of association with Spain, with France, with the whole Pyrenean Peninsula, but not one with the United States. It is not necessary to study the contents of all these projects.[27] Even the wordings are often similar. One of the more interesting is that of Pedro Felix Vicuña (1837), who believed that "the only salvation for the Hispanic-American Republics" is "a general congress of them all," and wished "to secure the internal peace of each republic, and to regulate the differences among them that must be the authority of a Great American Congress." The economic element is strong in this project.

Similar is the *Memoria sobre la conveniencia y objetos de un congreso general americano*, presented by J. H. Alberdi (1848). In this work we are not able to recognize the future famous author of the *Estudios Economicos*. He preaches, but with reservations, "a continental commercial union," and considers the formation of a custom union based upon the German model, but without the co-operation of the United States. Alberdi is still under the spell of Bolivar's epic, and preaches Bolivar's ideas of a "Holy alliance of American Republics against the Holy alliance of the European military monarchies."

While Alberdi is opposed to co-operation with the United States, other writers were at the time beginning to realize—to use a modern expression—the "Peligro Yanqui." The rapid development of the United States, her activity in Mexico, territorial expansion on the northern continent, instilled fear into the South American countries.

The number of the projects grew larger in the middle of the century, and the North American Danger became the *punctum saliens* of the literature.

In a Memoria presented by Juan Manuel Carrasco Albano in Santiago (1855), the author explains his project through the necessity of defending the Spanish race in America against the North American Confederation, and he develops the usual programme.

At about the same time the above-mentioned pamphlet by Francisco Bilbao appeared, a result of a conference of South Americans in Paris. Dreamer and conspirator, the Saint-Simonian Bilbao is faithful to himself. A wealth of great ideas and an unimportant practical programme, lyricism, pathos, and the absence of a realistic attitude may be noted therein. Its title is, *Iniciativa de la America. Idea de un congreso Federal de las Republicas*, but in the text the word "Federal" is transformed into "normal (?)."

The outcome of his proclamation is a bold statement of the "Peligro Yanqui": "Walker is the invader, Walker is the conqueror, Walker is the United States." "We know that Russia is an absolute barbaria, but the United States, forgetting the traditions of Washington and Jefferson, is the demagogue barbaria." He desires to "unify the soul of America . . . unify the thought, unify the heart, unify the will of America."

"But Bolivar was erroneous in all of his presumptions concerning the real enemy," declares another propagandist, José Maria Samper (1859). "He supposed that all danger will come from Europe. Bolivar never thought that the ferments of the future conflicts were lying in the same continent." He presents as an enemy all not Spanish countries in America, and vents his hatred on "the Empire of Brazil and the Conqueror Republic of the United States." In his desire to be entirely cut off from the enemies, he even refuses the name America, and prefers to baptize the United Spanish America with the name "Colombia."

This movement reaches its theoretical high point in the *Bases de Union Americana*, a result of the work of the Sociedad de Union Americana de Santiago de Chile (1867). In this publication there are harboured no illusions concerning the former mistakes and disappointments. They wish to rouse the movement to new life. They believe in an American Union as a "Common Fatherland." After the usual lyrical outbursts on the homogeneity of the countries, there followed an appeal to concerted action and a concrete programme.

"What are we looking for? A united representation of all our republics, in order that in the scales of international law they will counterbalance the great powers."[28]

Literature at the end of the 'sixties suffered a marked decline. An anonymous writer in Guayaquil preached a "South American Alliance,"[29] and ornaments his plan with quotations from Tacitus and Olmedo; a certain Abraham Konig refers to Greek models;[30] M. Martinez claims that the "great idea of an American union is dreaming a humble dream"[31]—but it was, to be sure, not a peaceful dream.

Practical attempts followed. In the beginning they were for the most part opposed to Europe, and later to the United States. Their character and course corresponded to that of their literature: great ideas, brilliant rhetoric, inactive pathos, and lack of organization, official brotherhood, and internal distrust.

The Panama Congress was a great event in this wearisome series of powerless attempts undertaken by an acephalous organization.[32] This Congress, ebullient with romantic enthusiasm, was nevertheless from the very beginning pursued by bad luck. The adviser of Bolivar and the spiritual father of the Congress, Doctor Bernardo Monteagudo, "a valiant genius, who lived only in order to improvise systems and construct brilliant Utopias,"[33] was killed in a street in Lima, and the Congress lost its foremost advocate. The leader of the movement, Bolivar, was said to have nourished secret desires for becoming the king of the united countries. The means of communication at that time were such that, following a description by Monteagudo, in the south of Ecuador, one could not know what happened in the north, except indirectly by way of England or the United States. The technical accomplishments of the Congress rendered its work difficult: the delegates could not find the necessary repose at that time in a town suffering from war, pestilence, and misery.

But Bolivar wanted to conquer all obstacles, and this "magnificent hero of an Iliad transformed himself into a director of a Congress of peoples."[34] The territory of his domination was too narrow for him; he was striving for a union of the continent.[35] Bolivar was consequently a follower of the unionist idea.

In writing to the Government concerning the campaign in Venezuela in 1813, he said: "Only an intimate and fraternal union of the sons of the New World and an unalterable harmony in the operation of their respective Governments will be able to make them formidable to our enemies and respectable in the sight of other nations." On September 6, 1815, he wrote from Jamaica, where he was in exile, his famous Prophetic Letter which is inspired by the same idea: "The consolidation of the New World into a single nation with a single bond uniting all its parts is a grand conception. Since the different parts have the same language, customs, and religion, they ought to be confederated into a single State; but this is not possible, because differences of climate, diverse conditions, opposing interests, and dissimilar characteristics divide America. How beautiful it would be if the Isthmus of Panama should become for us what the Isthmus of Corinth was for the Greeks! Would to God that we may have the fortune some day of holding there some august congress of the representatives of our republics, kingdoms, and empires of America, to deliberate upon the high interests of peace and of war not only between the American nations, but between them and the rest of the globe." Three years later he wrote to Pueyrredon, dictator of the United Provinces of Rio de la Plata:

"When more favourable circumstances afford us more frequent communications and closer relations, we shall hasten, with the liveliest interest, to set on foot, on our part, the American covenant which by forming one political body of all our republics shall present America to the world with an aspect of majesty and greatness without parallel among the ancient nations. America, thus united, will be able to call herself the queen of nations, the mother of republics."[36]

The danger of the Holy Alliance was the principal cause of the Congress.[37] The answer of the United States to this peril was the proclamation of the Monroe Doctrine in 1823. Bolivar attempted in 1822 to form a federation with defensive aims.[38]

On December 7, 1824, Bolivar sent a new invitation to the Congress. He referred to his former invitation, explained the aims and purposes, and ended with the words: "The day when our plenipotentiaries will exchange their credentials will be an immortal epoch in the diplomatic history of America. After a hundred centuries, when posterity will investigate the origin of our public life and remember the treaties, which are consolidating its destiny, posterity will register with respect the minutes of the Isthmus; she will find here the programme of the first alliances, which will bear the mark of our relations with the entire world."[39]

The aim of the Congress was the planning of the defence against Spain, the protection of peace and harmony among the members,[40] and the special elaboration of a concrete programme for these purposes.[41]

The impression of this Congress on its contemporaries was tremendous. The Press of that time attempted to comprehend the historical importance of the event. The *Gaceta Extraordinaria del Istmo* reported on June 22, 1826, the "Installation of the Great American Congress," and exclaimed: "The day can be called the day of America!"[42]

But the representatives had doubts; they were not clear about the purely defensive or offensive character of the Union, about the attitude towards Brazil, Santo Domingo, and the United States; about the form of the organization—permanent united executive power or one supreme military chief; possibility of negotiations with European envoys towards problems of Cuba and Porto Rico,[43] and many other perplexities.

We already mentioned that, in spite of Bolivar's opposition[44] and the obstacles in the United States, the continental idea was victorious. The United States was invited and accepted the invitation, but her representatives did not appear. Europeans (England and Netherlands) attended this Congress, but no one from the United States and no one from the greater part of Latin America. Only a part of the Congress convened. When it adjourned South America parted from the United States for a long time without even saying "good-bye." Centrifugal forces were too strong in both Americas.

The results of this Congress wrought a "Treaty of Union, League and permanent Confederation" among Colombia, Centro America, Peru, Estados Unidos of Mexico. This treaty is a treasure for the student of the history of international law; it is simultaneously a treaty of "eternal peace," restriction of armaments, a mutual guarantee and alliance with a body of "Asamblea general de plenipotenciarios de las Potencias Confederadas." The treaty was ratified only by Colombia, despite the strong unity of opinion and sentiment at the Congress.

All subsequent attempts in this direction suffered the same fate. Extended solemn preparations, pathetic addresses, immense festivals, idealistic speeches had no practical effect. One of the weaknesses of these attempts was their continued foundation on historical reminiscences: they were conferences of revolted Spanish colonies united by former origin and actual danger. The important position of the most threatened Latin brothers of North America could not add vigour to the conferences.

Yet we ought not to underestimate the importance of the

Panama Congress. The above-mentioned invitation of Bolivar, in which he becomes prophetic both in form and content, is the most noteworthy characteristic of the historical significance of this Congress. But Bolivar himself understood that the union could not be constructed suddenly: "This union will not appear through divine wonders, but as the result of well-directed efforts."[45]

A period of quietness followed the Panama Congress. Of course, we can find in practice as well as in literature reminiscences and projects. Mexico took the leadership and sent out invitations to a congress in 1831. Peru and Colombia also competed in the distribution of new invitations. The former undertook the rôle of protector of the oppressed brothers in Central America. One "memoria" follows another, diplomatic correspondence, and more voyages. Diplomats bridled the old horse once more and mounted for another conference.

Only three political congresses took place: the American Congress in Lima (1848), the Continental Congress in Santiago de Chile (1856), and the American Congress in Lima (1865). These congresses resembled the Panama Congress, but did not possess its spirit. At these meetings delegates from the Pacific coast were in attendance, and at times Bolivia and Venezuela were present. A representative from Argentina attended (in 1865) the Lima Congress, but the Government refused his authorization (*supra*). Resolutions on customs union were adopted, political treaties discussed and prepared, and brotherhood and homogeneity was emphasized. The Argentine Government protested even against this *agitacion americana*. But the results, disregarding local temporary alliances, were unimportant. The accomplishment of a large programme could not even be attempted. In comparison with the aims, the effects were ridiculous. For instance, the agreements of "continental convention" of the Santiago Congress received ratification only by Chile and Ecuador. On the other hand, through the intercession of Colombia a *rapprochement* with Central America and the Antilles took place which again infected the Southern

Continent with fear, and the countries of the northern and Pacific coast became alienated from the large states on the Atlantic coast, where the union propagandists became considered as "inhabitants of another planet."[46]

Thus this movement ceased without obtaining "the particular physiognomy" which Peru desired for this continent. "The American fraternity is a lie" is an expression of Eduardo Prado, which may well be applied to these attempts.

In the second half of the 'sixties, universal continentalism, as well as specific Latin-American continentalism, became a thing of the past. War engaged the entire attention—the Paraguayan War, Chile against Bolivia and Peru, and quarrels between Argentina and Brazil.

From time to time efforts were again exerted, but the movement had no longer any spirit. The people demanded peace after the perturbations of the middle of the century, as they did after the weariness and exhaustion which followed the Panama Congress. They were threatened actually by repeated attacks.

The beginning of the 'eighties brought a new movement to the surface. As formerly, the two greatest South American countries remained indifferent. On the Pacific coast the states were no longer interested in politics, but were becoming engaged in more practical fields. In Lima a congress of "American" jurists (1877) and a sanitary congress (1888) was convened; in Rio de Janeiro (1887) a sanitary conference of the states of La Plata and of Brazil was convoked; and in Montevideo (1889) the International South American Law Congress was called. Even Central America held aloof from their Southern neighbours. A separate Central American Congress in 1888 was held in San José, Costa Rica. A breach between the continental Latin-American and South American family seemed to be evident. Everyone was going his own way.

Like the repeated congresses, the new unionist projects were disappearing from the political policies. In Buenos Aires (in 1880) we note a discussion about the project of a congress whose aim was "to unify the social interests of the continent.[47]

It was during these quiet days that the bomb of Blaine's plan was exploded. We have previously investigated the motives of his activity and his aims. But the idealistic glamour of the proposed Pan-Americanism was attractive to the South American; it seemed like his own thoughts, his illusion and previously futile effort. The not entirely forgotten reminiscences of the former epic seemed to take new life. Brothers! Union! A United Continent! The words were old, and were merely translated into a new tongue. The circumstances, however, had changed in the meantime.

Blaine's plan gave new impetus to the idea of a union. His action was, as we know, delayed, and Colombia made an attempt to take the initiative. In 1886, at a meeting of the Hispano-American envoys in Paris, the Minister of Colombia announced the intention of his Government to organize a new congress in Panama; but once more the project of a congress and of a league miscarried.[48] Thus after a stormy history the continental idea, the passion of Latin America for union, became transformed into practical and official Pan-Americanism.

Distrust and fear dominated Central America. The small countries in South America were also of these sentiments. The large states continued their traditional policy: Brazil—continental, *pro* the United States; Argentina—anti-continental, *pro* Europe. But all the states had participated at the conference.

The conference of 1889 could not accomplish its great programme; but it led the movement on to a quiet and practical road; it created an organization. The Pan-American machine began its steps slowly.

Disregarding Pan-Americanism, Central America and South America held family meetings from time to time without the United States. Official Pan-Americanism became a business covenant for the United States. It was an *Ersatz* for continentalism, a substitute for the numerous dreams of the American intelligentsia. The new century opened a new chapter in the history of this movement. The Spanish-American War was the turning-point.

. . . .

The close of the war with the United States was for Spain the beginning of a peaceful suit for the heart of Spanish America. We have already studied this movement and have seen how Spain sought to quarrel with the United States, France, and Italy on different fronts. We saw how strenuous and extended were her efforts to regain the sympathy of the former colonies and place herself again in the affections of her estranged daughters. South America's attitude was for a long time indifferent towards these offers. While Spain, the oppressor, still had a foothold on American soil, reconciliation remained impossible. The traditional hate could not disappear.[49] The first attempts at *rapprochement* by Spain met a strong alignment of opposition, the leader in which was Cuba, the "ever faithful" island, which still had fresh in her memory the Spanish rule, and was proud of its new American independence.

The attitude of the Spanish-American "children" can be best characterized by the answer given by the Cuban leader, Máximo Gómez, in 1889 to the Spanish appeal to fight together against the United States: "The Cubans and Spaniards can never live in peace on the soil of Cuba. You represent to Cuba an old discredited monarchy, and we are fighting for an American principle, that of Bolivar and Washington."[50]

Cuban literature contributes an impassioned and sweeping criticism of Hispano-Americanism. Dr. Fernando Ortíz opens this campaign with a series of publications[51] and his long polemical discussion against the Spanish leader, Rafael Altamira. He bitterly attacks Hispano-Americanism, representing it as an attempt at a "Re-Hispanization" of the former colonies, but the Latin Americans are far from agreeable with these attempts: "It is not convenient to be passive subjects of this attempt" (p. 9); he denies the existence of a Spanish race; he does not find a cultural union. He understands that the "Spanish

Americanists" were seeking new routes for Spain in America, but he refuses to understand a corresponding movement on the American side; that would be American quixoticism.

Ortíz explains the Oviedo programme, and finds in it the striving for a market, for commercial expansion, imperialism, international Utopia, idealized egoism.[52] He understands the motives of the movement on the Spanish side and invites the American people to resist this new penetration.[53] Sometimes Ortíz fulminates innately in his tirade against the Oviedo movement. He advises Spanish Americanists not to waste time in trying to spread their propaganda.[54]

Indeed, sentiment was against the Spanish. The list of the members of the Hispano-American Congress of 1900 in Madrid show clearly that the Spaniards were in their own society; Hispano-Americans did not collaborate. But the possibility of a reconciliation was not always refused: "Union is not possible with the Spain of to-day; it will be with the future Spain."[55]

The renaissance in Spain did not go unnoticed. The same Fernando Ortíz admits in 1910 the successes and the intense work of Spain; he hopes that, freed from the imperialistic tendencies, the spirit of Spain will regain a glorious life.[56] The Spanish renaissance softened the hearts of the former colonies towards their mother-country. Spain's soaring progress impressed them forcibly. Even Fernando Ortíz is no longer an enemy; he concurs in an intellectual union; he follows the moderate Hispano-Americanism of Posado; he even finds "a common spirit among all Spanish-speaking peoples," and salutes the attempts to strengthen this spirit.[57] Ortíz tends more and more towards Hispano-Americanism as a cultural but not a racial movement, and agrees with its definition as rendered by a Spanish writer, Benjamin Jarnes, who appeals to "the present, and not to the past."[58]

The miraculous happened. The enemy became friend, devotee, ally. Spanish neo-Imperialism gained foothold on the other side of the Atlantic. The familiar reconciliation was accomplished. The movement now had two sources, Spain and America. The two streams flow into one another. "A young, tolerant, liberal Spain" finds "sincere and fresh love" in America.[59]

"Soy un hijo de América, soy un nieto de España," is the poetical formula of Rubén Darío.[60] Calderon considers "an ideal association of the Iberians separated by the Atlantic."[61] Spanish America now supplies the movement with its most ardent and energetic figure, Manuel Ugarte.

The War brought new economic successes to Spain and heightened her position in America. The origin of Hispano-Americanism in Spain was a result of the United States' victory in the Spanish-American War; its development in the twentieth century was in part caused by the economic success of the United States and her changed world position.

The facts are known. We are already familiar with the growth of the United States' trade and investments. We must understand the psychological impression of this penetration in Latin America. The new United States—the former brother and companion—has become the political world power, the greatest financial power of the earth. The former debtor is dictating financial conditions to Europe. Wilson took leadership in the Peace Treaty, Dawes in the new economic arrangement, and Young in the reparations problem. Not only Germany but entire Europe was conquered by the entrance of the United States in the War.

Latin-American countries saw themselves delivered to their great neighbour in the north, and the incidental emancipation from Europe intensified their dependence. Although we must surely agree with J. Fred Rippey that "this fear of aggression from the United States is as old as the Spanish-American nations themselves,"[62] that does not change the fact that recent conditions have increased this fear many-fold.

The old danger has assumed new proportions. The cry of "Peligro Yanqui" has grown louder. This danger, in the opinion of Latin America, is now universal for the continent, for Europe as well as for the entire world, but especially for Spanish America.

Now the single incentive for openly recognized or tacitly adopted union is this danger; it became the new axis of politics south of the Rio Grande. Even poets of different political character (for poems and politics cannot be separated in Latin America) agree on this problem. Inconstant Latinists, like Rubén Darío, who "vive de amor de América y de pasión de España," but have their *querida* in Paris; pronounced Latinists like José Maria Heredia, Hispanists like José Santos Chocano, who often has continental visions and forecasts the centre of the world in Amazonas[63]—all became united in their hate for the United States.

This hate has new forces in Europe. In Spain Araquistain preaches the Peligro as the "Imperio Yanqui," which is only nominally a republic, and prophesies its transformation into a conquering monarchy in the Roman style.[64] "The Spanish ideal ought to be exactly the antithesis of the Yanqui ideal."[65] Spaniards prefer the aloof Latin-Americanism of France, because it is not so aggressive as the policy of the United States.[66]

Clarence H. Haring confirms that "Anti-American propaganda in part also derives its inspiration from Europe, especially from France and Spain. There is no doubt that Spain and the Spaniards constitute our bitterest and most active foe in Latin America. Spain is keenly desirous to recover her former ascendancy among the younger American communities which she herself established four centuries ago. Her ambitions are political, to create a Pan-Hispanic entente in which she will be *primus inter pares*; they are also intellectual, social, and scientific, to develop an Hispanic cultural union which will compete with and supersede the Pan-American Union in course of evolution to-day. Her ultimate goal is by these means to recover the position she once held as a great world power. But there also exists a Pan-Latin ideal, for which France especially is sponsor."[67] Haring emphasizes: "The idea that the United

States is imperialistic, and American capital therefore dangerous, is of course ably promoted by our European rivals in Chile, *sub rosa* by the British, French, and Germans, more openly by the ubiquitous Spaniard."[68]

On the entire American continent, where the Anglo-Saxons are not dominant, one can hear cries against the "Peligro Yanqui." Central America and Mexico have always been chief instigators of this movement; the Antilles, the states on the Pacific coast of South America, Chile and Argentina, Bolivia—with the exception of Brazil—everywhere the problem is discussed, propagated, and considered. Suddenly a real common sentiment originated in Spanish America. The "Hymn of hate" and "Isthmus of Panama" provided the leitmotiv, and became national songs.

The Venezuelan Blanco Fombona seems to define the sentiment of all in his cry: "The Yankees, the Yankees, here are the enemies of our soul, our civilization, our character, and our independence."[69] The Peruvian Calderon agrees with him: "The Anglo-Saxons are conquering America commercially and economically, but the traditions, the ideals, and the *soul* of these republics are hostile to them."[70] The Colombian Reyes, with the flexibility of an ex-president, mentions the existence of "doubts and fears entertained in Latin America in regard to the United States."[71] The Argentine Moreno Quintana accuses the United States of being an "imperialistic democracy based on the supremacy of the dollar."[72] Writers recall the history of the territorial expansion of the United States and the conquest of Spanish states,[73] and speak of a kind of Spanish Irredenta in North America. They appeal for counsel to the writings of the brilliant Brazilian Eduardo Prado,[74] in order to find for Brazil also the purposes to join this movement. The Iberian current of thought also has a "Peligro Yanqui" as one of its sources.[75]

The first fiddle in this orchestra is Manuel Ugarte, the wandering Jew of the unionist movement.[76] Faithful to the traditional European orientation of Argentina, he emphasizes the family ties, the gratitude, past friendship with Europe, common opposition towards the United States. His opinions may be outlined as follows: We owe a debt of gratitude to Spain for our civilization, the Hispanic spirit with which she endowed us; to France for our spiritual wealth, which animates our cultural life; to England, who loaned us generously of her gold; to Germany, who supplied us with manufactured goods; to Italy, who gave us the labour of her sons. But our sole ties with the United States are of fear and suspicion.[77]

It is sufficient to recall Ugarte's famous "open letter" to the President of the United States (1913), in which he states that the United States is "the most unpopular nation among us."[78] He emphasizes the "cry of the peoples," and asks a change in the conquistador policy of the United States.

He desires for his fatherland—and this is contrary to Argentine traditions—"a policy of consideration for the sister-republics";[79] he emphasizes, also untraditionally, that "Latin America has solidarity";[80] and he presents an extended conception of the "Great Fatherland," which, resorting once more to the words of Rubén Darío, is that America which "still prays to Jesus Christ and speaks Spanish."

The whole apparatus of Hispanic-American and Latin-American propaganda finds an animated reception now, and echoes and invitations. South American propagandists are also beginning to travel, to speak, to write, to preach, to form associations, hold festivals, submit addresses, organize conferences. Everywhere we can find the same figures of the anti-Yanqui movement. Several of them are serious and sincere, several vulgar and ridiculous, all pathetic and none concrete.

Their trumpeting is disturbed by the pessimistic moans of sociological trends. On all American soil south of the Rio Grande and north of Cape Horn there resounds a peculiar cacophony raised by the war-cries of the anti-Yankee nationalism and the deep pessimism of a few scholars.

This pessimism is not a new phenomenon in South America.[81] The intellectual father of this current (is there any limit to the progeny we may ascribe to his fatherhood?) was Bolivar. This "thinker of the Revolution" (so styled by Calderon), who gave the republic of Bolivia his name, constitution, and President, who liberated five states, who organized the Panama Congress, whom America frequently compares with Napoleon—this hero, who reproduced ancient history in word and deed, was the first and perhaps the deepest pessimist of Latin America. Calderon surely exaggerates in stating that "in Bolivar's writings are to be found the best programmes of political and social reform for America; he was the first sociologist of these romantic democracies."[82] But the origin of the South America's pessimism belongs to him.

He lost faith in America; he saw its future as dark. In America "treaties are pieces of paper, constitutions—books, elections—fights, liberty—anarchy, and the life a trouble."[83]

The pessimism of Bolivar was a result of disappointment of this unsated fighter. In contrast, the pessimism of Alberdi (modern literature exploits largely the negative elements of his opinions) is a criticism of the sound intellect of an historically trained scholar.

This pessimism is a universal phenomenon for all America which is not Anglo-Saxon. In Brazil and the Antilles, on the Pacific and on the Atlantic coast, in Mexico and in Central America, in Bolivia and in Paraguay, one can find similar complaints. The "sick continent," the "ill people," are not merely titles of books. This pessimism is homogeneous even in its content. Disregarding the particular style of the writer and the expression of his personality, in every book one can change the names of the countries and the specific data without disturbing the general thesis. The Europeanized Argentina suffers from the same "malady" as Bolivia, Venezuela, or Chile. It depends upon the personal taste of the writer, which point is to be emphasized; but the general symptoms remain the same. Bunge, Ingenieros, Calderon, Bomfim, Monteiro Lobato, Blanco Fombona, Arguedas, point out the same symptoms and concur in their investigation of South America's melancholia.

One reads these books with suppressed sentiments. Many of the writers brilliantly paint frightful pictures, which are pronouncedly Latin in character. How sorrowful is this continent! Where is the Latin affirmation of life?

In Calderon's book one cannot miss these sharp notes of disappointment. "Nothing could be more monotonous than Paraguayan life" (p. 197); Chile: "a false democracy governed by absolute overlords" (p. 165); in Argentina, Rivadavia wished to transform "a Spanish province into a European nation" (p. 137); Colombia is always "the land of eloquence and Jacobinism, extravagant and excessive as the tropics themselves" (p. 212); "Bolivia has also had its tyrants, figures of tragicomedy, vulgar and gloomy" (p. 126); in a chapter entitled, "About Blood in our History,"[84] Arguedas has penned expressions even more bitter concerning his own fatherland, Bolivia.

Where are we virtually? In Grand Guignol? In a museum of frights? Is this the continent of the future?

The chief characteristic of the continental malady is the perennial contrast between theory and practice, ideas and their fulfilment, the eternal dualism between idealism and realism. The usual Don Quixote–Sancho Panza contrast is weak alongside of the Ariel of South America and the Caliban of the United States, as portrayed by Rodó. Latin America holds herself aloof from the Anglo-Saxon Caliban; she is jealous of her individualism in "heart" and "soul." She must, however, confess: "In the conquest of hostile circumstances the Saxon acquires a sense of realism; while the Iberian, under a fiery sun, becomes in Spain, as in America, a hunter of chimeras."[85] The chimeras are often built not upon the present, or the future, but upon the past. Archibald C. Coolidge notes that in the United States: "Many a traveller has been struck by the fact that in a new American town the patriotic citizen will more often talk about the future than about the present."[86] South America is still gadding *about* and living *in* the past, in that romantic epoch of her struggle for independence which she remembers with pride. She tries to enact ancient history in the twentieth century, forgetting that we already possess the radio and the airplane. (Is Calderon's book not a stirring example of this kind of thinking?) A sense of the reality of the present is sadly lacking.

The continent is considered the most favoured in its natural riches, but the constituent countries are poor. Specialists estimate that the continent is able to hold and provide for hundreds and hundreds of millions, and yet the population is small. Immense desert regions still exist. Agriculture is primitive; industry is in an embryonic stage; trade is dominated by the colonial *venda*, and governmental finances, woefully disorganized, are supported by foreign loans.

"South America is occupied by poor people, inhabitants of a rich soil, contrary to Europe, where for the most part rich people populate poor soil."[87] "Two-thirds of the *wealth* of South America is expended for the production of *liberty*, *glory*, and *national honour*; the result of the art of this production is that all these four things are not existing in South America."[88]

It is then not to be wondered at that "the poverty in South America is not an occasional crisis. It is a fact of centuries."[89] The crisis is permanent. Alberdi published books on the crisis of 1860, 1861, 1866. Finally he was forced to write a new book bearing the title *Permanent Crisis of the Argentine Republic*, for contemporary history is merely a "series of crises," or a "chronic crisis with interruptions of health."[90]

South America is continually suffering from parasitism. Formerly the crime of the mother-countries, it is now due to the governmental system.[91] Although free politically, the republics are colonies in an intellectual and moral sense. Everything is mere acceptance and imitation. The constitutions are for the most part copies of that of the United States. The countries accepted them like ready-made clothes without having been measured or fitted.[92] Eduardo Prado shows great acerbity in his opinion of their ready adoption of the Constitution of the

United States.[93] The leap from a colony to a democratic republic was too great; South America received her independence too soon. Calderon expresses the opinion of the American élite of that time: "The American monarchy would have entered into the group of Occidental nations, and the Monroe Doctrine would not have isolated her politically from the Europe that sent her men, money, and ideas."[94]

"The founders of South American independence understood that only a strong Government could save the new nations from demagogy, anarchy, warfare between military chiefs, and untimely provincial ambitions. They wanted autonomy without licence, monarchy without despotism, and political solidity without Spanish suzerainty.

"Despite this conviction on the part of the revolutionaries, South America saw the birth of the Republic."[95]

Laws and principles were adopted without the comprehension that the "proclamation of these political and economic freedoms is not a creation of them.[96] Anarchy may be said to dominate on the continent even when its character is often different. For instance, "in Colombia men have fought for ideas; anarchy there has a religious character."[97]

The conception of "nation" is too weak, too limited, too local. Every part of every country is a fatherland to itself. In domestic policy *Caciquism* is dominant in a system which transforms parliamentarism into friction.[98] No one attacked the *Caciquism* of this "Confederation of clans" more strenuously than Carlos O. Bunge; no one investigated and analysed more thoroughly the personal motives of this social phenomenon.[99] This *Caciquism* gave birth to the many permanent dictators and revolutions, the rule of "Generals and doctors," the eternal divorcement between written constitutions and political life. "The Government in South America is an administration of employees, protected by other employees, the army. A group of mandarins rule,"[100] or, as Alberdi once expressed it: 'Sultans do not exist in South America, but democrats more despotic than they."[101] Sarmiento compared Argentine in his

Facundo with "la Tartaria." Their imitations of parliamentarism and federalism are caricatures.[102] Strong conservative classes do not survive as well as an aristocracy either of birth or spirit. "Every large South American city pretends to be a petit-Paris."[103] But virtually "in the cities, despite the invasion of cosmopolitanism, the old life persists, silent and monotonous, flowing past the ancient landmarks."[104] And the interior? It is silently awaiting a description of its tragedy. Among the intellectual classes dilettantism prevails. There is a lack of specialization, a continuation of the "almacen" system. The same "generals and doctors" making politics are the lawyers, physicians, architects, professors, employers, and, of course, the poets. Improvising replaces scientific preparation in all walks of life. There is an over-production of *littérateurs* and a lack of specialists. And even the literature is considered only as a recreational pastime.[105]

Those great accomplishments with which we may credit the continent are chiefly the work of a few outstanding individuals: there are no "schools." The universal pessimism has even cast its shadow over religion, for the people have been criticized as being too religious, but not moral enough.

But we do not want to enlarge this sorrowful picture. The pessimist draws its details in all fields of life, society and culture, art and technology. The pessimism is intensified by invidious comparison with the United States. One recalls that the St. Marcos University in Lima was in existence long before John Harvard considered the organization of a college in Cambridge, and that at the time, when the early New England settlers began "to consider establishing a colony in Massachusetts, the Portuguese had already built dozens of sugar factories in Pernambuco."[106]

"When Emerson visited England fifty years ago he declared that the heart of the Britannic race was in the United States, and that the "mother island," exhausted, would some day, like many parents, be satisfied with the vigour which she had bestowed upon her own children. In speaking of Spain and

Portugal, might not Argentines, Brazilians, and Chilians employ the same proud language?"[107]

The conclusions are clear. "Without population, without wealth, without industry, without national and racial patriotism, how can the Hispanic-American people organize a league for defence against the United States, against her hegemony, and her imperialistic appetite?"[108]

The so-called brotherhood of the people is a figment. "American fraternity is a lie. Consider the Iberian nations of America. More hate, more quarrels among them than among the nations of Europe."[109] Eduardo Prado and Francisco Bulnes develop with great dexterity this thesis, and present a review of inter-American relations from this point of view.[110] The consciousness that Europe is also threatened, and that she cannot help, serves only to add another cloud of gloom. What is Europe? "A mosaic of religions and races" (Calderon). "Paris to-day seems to be a suburb of New York" (Araquistain).

The question which naturally suggests itself is: "Shall we see the Anglo-Saxons dominate over the Latins of America? If this happens, it will be a defeat of the Latin spirit,"[111] the prophecy: *Finis Latinorum.*[112]

The extreme pessimist (significantly a Mexican) makes the final prognosis. "Militaristically, industrially, financially, and from other points of view, we are disarmed against the power of the United States."[113] And in the year 1980 (?), is his opinion, the greater part of Latin America will no longer be independent.

There is something coquettishly playful and inventive in all these complex diagnoses and classifications of the continent's infirmities; something of the *malade imaginaire* suggesting his own illnesses, and of the hypochondriac. And no doubt there is an element resembling the voluptuous passion of the self-infliction of pain in the descriptions of the national temperament as ***pereza*** and ***arroganza***, in all the humiliations of their fatherland.[114] This pessimism is itself a product of the criticized "illness," and suffers from its symptoms. The pessimists morosely point at the shadows and ignore the progress. They are indicating only at one aspect of the continent of contrasts.

They are talking about imported, adopted literature, and neglect the admirable literary development of Brazil. Mitre in Argentina and José Verissimo in Brazil even denied the existence of a national literature. They are talking about the poor local newspaper of four pages, cheaply printed on bad paper, and of worse content; but on the coast, on the façade of the continent, especially on the Atlantic, there are newspapers surpassing even the European, and in content often superior to many North American papers. The same is true in many other fields.

The pessimists are looking for the causes of the malady. They accuse their mother-countries, their history, the negro, the Mulatto, the "Yanquis." They find causes in the spirit of the peoples, in the racial problems, in the constitutions. However, we shall return to a diagnosis of the malady in a subsequent chapter (V, *a*).

It must be emphasized that pessimism has a certain positive checking influence on South American nationalism; it forces romantic nationalism to reckon with facts; it encourages the realistic approach. Pessimism contributed to the concentration of effort; acrid criticism prepared the ground for work. Pessimism was and is the moving power of the mobilization of forces in South America which has already begun.

The World War destroyed the old international system. The entire world is seeking to find a new equilibrium between the old and the new. After the process of dissolution, there begins a long process of integration and concentration.

"During the last few years a spirit of rebellious self-determination has seized upon hitherto inert subject-races: Nationalist Turkey has turned against European exploitation; Nationalist Egypt has won independence; Indian Nationalism has assumed monumental importance; Nationalist Persia and Afghanistan have cast off British shackles; Filipinos have become more insistent in their pleas for independence."[115]

And also in South America, where the "Peligro Yanqui" has been newly rediscovered, we can note new sustained attempts to counterbalance the power of the United States and to restore an equilibrium, which in reality never existed. How can the defence be organized? The danger having come to be considered mainly as political, political means of resistance are to be adopted: alliances and federations. "The history of our ephemeral unions is a history of foreign aggressions,"[116] is the opinion of one pessimist. Another confirms: "Should not a common danger, such as the Yankee peril in Panama and Central America, impel nations toward federation and unity? . . . Latin America cannot continue to live divided, while *her enemies are building up vast* federations and enormous empires."[117] There is, afoot an unmistakable defensive movement, seeking allies, mobilization, and concentration against the "Peligro Yanqui." The following opinion is typical of this sort of cry for help: "We wish Hispanic solidarity against Yankee Pan-Americanism; in America we count in this solidarity Brazil, speaking Portuguese, and in Europe, Spain and Portugual."[118] In Mexico Porfirio Diaz advocated an international covenant with Japan against the United States.[119] Manuel Ugarte attempted a renaissance of this idea. "Only a fusion of complementary interests can give to America a definite independence against the vigilant imperialism," wrote Calderon prior to the War.[120]

The efforts have taken various courses. The programme-maximum requires a universal union (with or without Central America, and with or without Brazil); the programme-minimum considers an American League a parallel to the League of Nations; the realists prefer concrete local alliances and federations. We may baptize this movement as Latin-American Continentalism, differing from the universal continentalism of one hundred years ago in that to-day none of these writers in Latin America desire political association with the United States. European sympathy is growing correspondingly. The proposals of the seducers are being listened to. Latin America is looking toward the League of Nations or Europe for help against the

United States. The fountain-head of this propaganda has not shifted in North America. It is still Mexico. Contrary to former traditions, however, the "principal focus in South America of the movement for a literary and intellectual *rapprochement* of Latin-American peoples is Buenos Aires,"[121] which at the same time is the vortex of the anti-United States propaganda.

The centre of the unionist champions have migrated from the Pacific to the Atlantic coast without entering beyond the boundaries of Brazil. *Brazil remains unchanged and indifferent to the new projects.* But the greatest South American adversary of the unionist idea has become a friend to it, for Argentina is joining in the chorus with the slogan: "The Andes between the Nations ought to disappear," the same Argentina of which General Olañeta wrote in a letter to Bolivar: "Argentina has expired a long time ago so far as a great American project is concerned."[122]

This change of the Argentine traditional policy arises from her new young imperialism. It must also be considered that Argentina feels very keenly the influence of the United States' competition in agricultural products; here lies the economic background of her anti-Yankee sentiment.

The strong Argentine nationalism, emphasized by all observers,[123] and the economic progress of the country are the moving powers of her expansion, which has already penetrated into continguous regions. "The dominating idea of the Government (Argentine) during the last years of the World War, under a president presumably pro-German in personal sympathies, seemed to be one of antagonism to the influence of the United States. Argentine diplomacy was apparently aimed to isolate this country, and possibly Brazil, from the rest of the American republics, and afford the Argentine president an opportunity to assert a dominant influence in the direction of Latin-American affairs."[124] This antagonism extends to her single rival in South America—Brazil. Argentina senses that she will be blocked in her expansion by the United States and Brazil. It is in this manner that the common theory of a "Greater Argentina" developed into a striving for a hegemony in the Spanish-American family.

Argentina attempted in former times to assume the rôle of a protector of the "brothers" in America. The Argentine Drago doctrine was a parallel to the Monroe Doctrine. Now Buenos Aires has begun to build the negative and positive programme for Spanish America, that movement against the United States which is seeking union and favours Europe.

"The great Fatherland" of Manuel Ugarte begins at the boundaries of the United States and ends on the Tierra del Fuego. This is the land of Latin culture, the territory of the "Great Fatherland." The striving for hegemony has been proclaimed openly. "If in any part of the world the advent of these great transformations of human society may be hoped to be approaching, it is on the American continent, and if any country can initiate on it the great liberating crusade against old prejudices, it is the Argentine Republic."[125] The argument, which can be found in the writings of Alejandro E. Bunge[126] and others, is most sharply formulated by José Ingenieros. The objective of his fulminations is always Brazil. He attempts to paint Argentine imperialism as peaceful, and suggests that his country adopt the position of tutor to the others. He denies the rights and capacity of Brazil and Chile to this position. His objections to Chile are based upon her small area and the gravitation of her interest toward the Pacific. However, he recognizes that the spirit there is pronouncedly militaristic and imperialistic. Although he realizes that Brazil is larger, more populated than Argentina, and concentrates her attention on the Atlantic, Ingenieros states that Brazil's disqualifications are her unfavourable climatic and racial conditions. After such neat elimination his conclusion is that Argentina and only Argentina is able to undertake South American leadership.[127] This dream of hegemony provided the incentive for Argentina's unionist movement. The words of Mitre are forgotten.

The economic aspirations are formulated by Francisco Seeber (although in the sense of a not industrial state): "The initiative should be taken by Argentina, which, with wheat and flour, meat, wool, and hides, can give most of the neighbouring countries very powerful assistance in the development of mining industries and the exploitation of tropical products, and thus augment her own riches and well-being. Argentina, preponderant in her productions, with the progressive development of her natural industries, which before long will be only cattle-raising and agriculture, and which will very soon acquire enormous and surprising proportions, has to place herself at the head of this movement of South American confraternity, which ought to be converted into practical facts."[128]

There are no illusions in South America about the difficulties which beset the path of the union and even of local alliances. "It is perhaps easier to create new republics in America than to organize the existing confederations," Calderon once said. The new movement attempts to abandon the beautiful Utopia of a continental union, and, striving for a rapid mobilization of the forces, to begin with local alliances.

One of the first practical steps was the so-called ABC liaison, a treaty between Argentina, Brazil, and Chile. The aims of this treaty are not entirely clear even at present. Officially the agreement promulgated "rules for proceedings to facilitate the friendly solution of questions that were formerly excluded from arbitration," provided a permanent commission, and other similar stipulations. But what are its real aims? Clemenceau, agreeing with the current opinion, considered it as a contracted hegemony of three against an eventual monopolization of these states by a single foreign country.[129] From this point of view the treaty is only an extension of the old relations existing between Argentina and Chile, now including Brazil.

Hiram Bingham considers this treaty as "a kind of triple alliance, with a definite object of opposing the encroachments of the United States."[130] This opinion is dominant in South America also. The ABC treaty is an "equilibrium between Latins and Anglo-Saxons."[131] A counterpart to the ABC treaty was the mysterious Caracas Congress of 1911, a truly "Bolivian" assembly. "The object of this Congress was to reconstitute Greater Colombia with the three republics which formerly were part of it—Venezuela, New Granada, and Ecuador."[132]

In the history of independent South America, the twentieth century first introduces projects of a general change in the political alignment. The motivation of this change is the realization that it is impossible to unite the *whole* of Spanish America or Latin America; and the same difficulties are encountered by any attempt to a Spanish-American union of the southern continent.

Thus originated the programme of federations, which constituted an attempt to rationalize the political division of the continent. The upshot of this current is that "Hispano-Americans are living divorced from geography";[133] the geography must be repaired. This idea is explained from the standpoint of Hispanism by Malagrida, of Latinism by Calderon. Credit for this belongs in a large measure to Archibald C. Coolidge, who in his well-known book first developed the plan of new groupings in Latin America. His outline corresponds in its main points to that of other authors. Coolidge's wish is to repair history. "Latin America would then consist of a few large states, each of sufficient importance to claim a dignified place in the modern world, and to be safe against aggressions on the part of any outside power. It is one of the clearest proofs of the political backwardness of the Latin-American people, as well as an unfortunate inheritance of Spanish temperament, that where there are so many essential similarities between them they persist in political divisions which are but historical accidents."[134]

Calderon formulates: "We should have not the vague union of which all the Utopian professors since Bolivar have spoken, but a definite grouping and confederation of people united by real economic, geographical, and political ties."[135]

"If the unity of the continent by means of a vast federation in the Anglo-Saxon manner seems impossible, it is none the less necessary to group the Latin-American nations in a durable fashion, according to their affinities."[136] The proposals of Coolidge, Malagrida, and Calderon are more or less identical. Coolidge strikes only the idea, Malagrida attempts to give it foundation, and Calderon sketches the political elements in play. The new conception may be said to have been brought about through a division of labour between writers from the United States, Spain, and South America.

Calderon's plan considered entire Latin America and organized the confederation of La Plata (Argentina, Uruguay, Paraguay), of the Pacific (Peru, Bolivia, Chile), of Great Colombia (Ecuador, Nueva Granada, Venezuela), of Brazil, of Mexico, and of the Antilles. Malagrida was more violent and dismembered several republics, basing his divisions on economic geography. (His arguments are often very cogent.)

Although no official practical attempts have ever taken suggestions from these plans, the influence of the new programme is not to be underestimated. It seems that a permanent basis has prepared for work in this direction.

Both currents—unionist and federationist—have the European sympathies. The pro-Latinist Calderon intends that "only the federation of all the Latin republics under the pressure of Europe—that is to say, of England, France, and Italy, who have important markets in America—might save the nations of the Pacific, just as a century ago Great Britain was able to defend the autonomy of these peoples against the mystic projects of the Holy Alliance."[137] Calderon constructed (prior to the War) ferine fantasies about the expulsion of the Latins from Europe by the Teutons and Slavs, and their welcome to a new home in Latin America, so that in the years to come Buenos Aires or Rio de Janeiro may be the new Rome or Paris.[138]

Malagrida, who is under strong German influence in his thinking, develops a characteristically complex and bloated German theory of three steps: local nationalism, American nationalism, and Spanish super-nationalism. Even Ugarte wavers between the "Great Fatherland" in America or in Europe.[139]

As at the beginning of the nineteenth century, Latin America looked to the United States as ally and defender against Europe, to several European states as protectors against Spain, now in the twentieth century she is trying to organize a common defensive front through union. The difference is that to-day she is seeking in Europe help against the United States, help from a companion in a common danger.

Latin America is thus predisposed to listen attentively to the proposals of these European seducers. From European influence she "hoped to obtain not only culture, but also the consecration of political independence." She "begged the old world for emigrants, for capital, and for princes—against the United States."[140]

Political flirtation with Europe is carried on mainly through Buenos Aires. The old lasting contact with Spain, France, and Italy, Argentina's traditional affection for Europe, and common sentiment against the United States, make Buenos Aires the point of confluence of all these national currents. While Great Argentina, dreaming of hegemony, considers the proposals of Europe favourable, the smaller states are even easier to persuade.

"Pan-Hispanic propaganda, active in Buenos Aires, finds a repercussion in Montevideo, where the Spanish colony is numerous and influential."[141] As the imaginative Minister of Foreign Affairs in Blanco Fombona's "El hombre de oro" said: "In order to defend us against the United States, we must create interests and relations with Europe and South America." Manuel Ugarte expresses the same wish: "But it is from a combined group of nations, without exception, that we may hope for that influence which shall balance or regulate events in the New World."[142]

The strategic position of Pan-Hispanism is now clearly more favourable. It regained the sympathy of the former colonies; they are now looking for Spanish favour. Spanish America, fearing lest Europe remain tranquil in the face of the threatening danger of Yankee imperialism, suggests concerted propaganda by France, Spain, Italy, and Portugal.[143] In this manner European Pan-Latinism finds allies on the other side of the Atlantic.[144]

Even the League of Nations is important in the process of mobilization against the "Peligro Yanqui": "From a legal standpoint, the relationships of Latin America to the United States have been revolutionized by the League of Nations."[145] Substantial assurance lies in the fact that the League Covenant guarantees territorial integrity. "Under League procedure, a Latin-American state is entitled to invoke at once the protection of the Council of the League of Nations, should the United States intervene within its territory."[146] "Geneva offers forum for Latin-American states," more attractive than the Pan-American conferences. "At Geneva some Latin-American states feel that they have a position of real equality which they have not found at Washington." . . . "These criticisms of the United States may be repeated annually at Geneva, but it is difficult to answer them effectively, since there is no representative of the United States to reply."[147] Europe, of course, endeavours to win Latin America to the League of Nations, and places generously at her disposition offices and dignities which make deep impression on the representatives from the smaller states.[148] The large states are not entirely with the League. The withdrawal of Brazil, in spite of her official excuse, was consistent with her traditionally American continental policy. Argentina keeps its reserved position, but indications are becoming more and more evident that Argentina is on the way back to the League, especially after the retirement of Brazil and the new possibility of becoming the Spanish-American leader at Geneva. On the other hand, her struggle for South America at Geneva is facilitated by the absence of her most formidable rival, the United States. The League of Nations is strengthening South America's ties with Europe.[149]

A ceaseless opposition to official Pan-Americanism is growing. Spanish America participates in Pan-Americanism, but places neither her faith nor her affection in it. A revolt against it is drawing near. Frequent are the speeches about the dead body, useless principle, dangerous system.[150] The revolt is even starting in the "Hofburg" of the organization—the Pan-American Union. The attack is internal and external. One demands the replacement of Pan-American congresses by racial[151] conventions, another considers the present conferences as of a "congress of mice presided by a cat,"[152] or a "meeting of opposed brothers";[153] the organization in Washington is the "Ministry of Colonies";[154] it is no more than a "Pan-Yankee policy";[155] it is the "manifestation of North American imperialism."[156] Latin-American wishes are to stand aloof. The Latin countries are not inviting foreigners in "family quarrels."[157] Moreno Quintana suggests a Latin-American League.[158]

In 1895 there was already a new attempt at an Hispano-American Congress.[159] In 1914 there was proposed the foundation of an "American House" in Paris, a suggestion which was repeated once more in 1917, entitled "a scheme for creating in Paris an association *similar to the Washington Pan-American Union,*" under the auspices of all nations which colonized America"; similar offices in the most important metropolis of Europe were to be founded.[160]

Reyes considered the Ibero-American Union in Madrid a future parallel to the union in Washington.[161] France pretends to weep over deceased Pan-Americanism and hastens to bury it.[162]

A project is in discussion to co-ordinate the Latin-American diplomatic activities in the various capitals and to organize local congresses in each.[163] An attempt was made to transform the North Pan-American Scientific Congress at Lima, 1924, into a purely Latin-American occasion. The Panama Congress of 1926 in commemoration of the First Congress of 1826 impressed Clarence H. Haring as follows: "In reality a purely Latin-American gathering, the United States being tolerated because of its bigness and the political and economic power it wielded, but rather as a spectator than as a participant."[164]

Opposition is no longer silent, no longer concealed, but is

officially enunciated in the union itself. The attempts to extend the programme through a discussion of the Monroe Doctrine were not successful in Buenos Aires (Fourth conference), but the two Congresses following the War witnessed the distinctly growing opposition. Public opinion in the United States must recognize that the "very lack of unity at Havana may be another indication that Pan-Americanism is weakening, in favour of special alignments between certain Latin-American states or between such states and European countries such as France and Spain."[165]

. . . . .

Thus in the courtship of South America the wily seducers and the wary courted have taken new positions.

South America, though she still performs her habitual courtesies to her most dangerous wooer, the United States, would in reality prefer to keep at a safer distance. She is timid of his approach. Meanwhile, feeling more tender toward his European rivals, she is strategically accepting their advances, thereby assuring herself of helpers in time of distress.

And just as the rivals had attempted in the past to win South America by high-sounding suggestions and emissaries, South America welcomes these advances and flirts with each in turn.

Hispanism, Latinism, and all the rest are catchwords which have been employed in the service of political schemes, and as such have rallied the people against a common enemy. These factions are no longer diverse, dissentient, but are confederating to oppose the United States.

Thus the European rivals unexpectedly find themselves on common ground with South America. The countries of both continents are presenting a united front against inroads by the North American aggressor.

Brazil is not joined with them.

CHAPTER III

THE "PELIGRO YANQUI"

The "Peligro Yanqui" is a part of the much-discussed world problem of the "American Danger"; it is merely a local appearance of a world phenomenon; it is the specific name for this peril in Latin America.

Each great nation has her day of world power. That day is often accompanied by the proclamation of a new danger. Was not a French danger broadcast in Europe at the time of Napoleon, and was not Napoleon fighting against the British danger? Further, we need only recall German peril, the Russian, the Yellow. The period after the War was one of wide propagandizing of the American danger.

The American danger is not a recent menace. Although it loomed up more formidable during the War and was intensified by the War, it is not to be regarded as a product of the War. This danger was often spoken of during the nineteenth century. In the twentieth century the anxiety over the impending peril became greater, and continually occupied the attention of the leading statesmen of Europe.

"In 1902 Mr. Luzzatti proposed to convene a European customs conference with the view of studying a policy of common defence against the United States."[1] In the year 1906 Professor v. Schulze-Gaevernitz emphasized that the greatest danger to the world position of Great Britain was the growth of the United States. The Western Empire was "*the* granary of the world; now they are becoming *the* industrial state, to-morrow *the* clearing-house of the world."[2] That was a clear prediction of the actual world position of the United States.

Professor Parker T. Moon refers to "The fear that had once led the German Emperor to talk of the "American Peril" along with the "Yellow Peril"; the nightmare vision of Baron Sonnino, that astute Italian Foreign Minister who feared the United

States would establish a *pax Americana* in quarrelsome Europe; the apprehension expressed in his Memoirs by Count Serge Witte, the famous Russian statesman, that the United States would enthrone itself on the debris of Europe."[3]

This danger was also a pre-War product in South America. The war with Mexico elicited the proclamation of this danger, disregarding the sporadic aggression in earlier times. A book by J. M. Torres-Guicedo, published in 1865 in Paris, gives attention to this problem in connection with the Destiny Manifesto.[4] A peculiar pamphlet by Justo Arteaga Alemparte (1866) studies the same subject.[5]

Official Pan-Americanism caused a flood of "danger literature," in which Europe endeavoured to explain the degree of the danger to Latin America. The character and style of these publications recalls, in spite of the difference in time, European sentiments during the Panama Congress. Bingham quotes a French writer, Maurice de Waleffe, writing on *The Fair Land of Central America*, who begins his book with this startling announcement of a discovery he has made: "The United States had made up its mind to conquer South America. Washington aspires to become the capital of an enormous empire, comprising, with the exception of Canada, the whole of the New World. Eighty million Yankees want to annex, not only forty million Spanish Americans, but such mines, forests, and agricultural riches as can be found nowhere else on the face of the globe."[6] A scarcely known work by Furey-Chatelain is typical of this literature. The aim of the publication is to outline the "annexationist" tendencies of the United States. The Monroe Doctrine combined with Pan-Americanism presents, in his opinion, a danger for Europe and for America.[7] He paints a broad picture of the future, of an "America for Americans"—that is, a federation of the three Americas under the tutelage of the United States. He sees a decline of Europe, and especially of England; he sees United States first in world trade, New York the first harbour in the world, and the financial centre of the entire America. Is not a prophecy fulfilled?[8] English writers note, of course, in another manner, the same phenomenon. "A strong American element is at work at the present time in acquiring railway interests in the River Plate republics, and if successful the conservative and passive British control may be exchanged for the American "trust methods," in which condition some South American and British journalists see an undesirable element."[9]

Blanco Fombona distinguishes between the "distrust borne against the United States" in the years 1845–50 and the fear at the beginning of the twentieth century,[10] which the World War augmented.

The "Peligro Yanqui" originated in Europe. From this continent it was drawn to America, found following in the North as well as in the South, was transferred to Europe, found here once more fertile soil, and after these boomerang-like migrations became *communis opinio* of our time. Europe discovered this danger; literature in the United States endeavoured to demonstrate that the danger was real; Latin America agreed and accepted the situation as described by writers in the United States. And thus it was that one more product made in the United States found its way to the world market.[11]

In the United States this anti-imperialistic movement was caused by internal political dissension.

"Memories of the 1900 democratic campaign against American imperialism, of the criticisms of the 'Dollar Diplomacy' of Secretary Knox, of the Harding charges against the Wilson policies in Haiti—all of these and many more bear heavily upon the official spokesman. The continuous criticisms of the liberal press are always in his mind."[12] The foreign countries drew from these discussions new proof for the existence of the danger. "Political imperialism" and "Dollar Diplomacy" became common phrases in liberal writings.

We can understand the psychology of political writers and speakers wielding these phrases, for it is attraction to paint such a picture of the expansion of the United States based on "Dollar Diplomacy."

The opposition to the Peligro became an hysterical cry. We have become acquainted with the leaders of this movement in Latin America in a previous chapter (Chapter II, *b*). They are not only pure theoreticians, but passionate propagandists, trying to defend themselves against the "Peligro Yanqui" by union. They symbolize union in their permanent crusades through Latin and Latin-American countries.

The home of these propagandists is in Europe—Paris or Madrid. Here we can find the elegant Calderon, the temperamental Ugarte, the learned Carlos Pereira, the former superhomo Blanco Fombona. Voluntarily or forcibly they are all emigrants. They have lost touch with their native soil, and have been influenced unconsciously by the sentiments of their adopted country, where they found new stimulus for their ideas. We cannot deny the size and the importance of this movement. Nevertheless, the movement does not seem to have taken root in the masses of South America. The positive current—Hispano-Americanism—may, under propitious circumstances, develop into a popular movement. The negative current—anti-Yankeeism—is a literary occupation for the intellectuals.

What is the content of the American danger? We cannot find a clear answer in literature, but more or less intemperate descriptions of the geographical and economic expansion of the United States; enthusiasm or hatred for the machine age; mass production and standardization, hailing it as highly civilized or damning it as barbarous; vague prophecies of the future and dim adumbrations of the past; but never a clear conception. The danger became discovered mainly in "American imperialism." But this expression is misused too often to be clear. The United States' imperialism has not found an ideologist yet, as the British have in Seely, the Germans in Paul Rohrbach, and the French in Rambaud. Compared with them, Reid, it must be admitted, is inferior.[13] Theodore Roosevelt was virtually his own ideologist.

The usual description of this danger came to be formulated as follows: "Investment of foreign capital easily leads to economic absorption, and economic absorption to political control."[14]

A summary of all the aspects of this phenomenon brings us to the conclusion that the danger is the *intention of the United States to conquer economically, and consequently culturally and politically, the entire world* (in the case of the "Peligro Yanqui," South America). It is a matter of common opinion that the United States' imperialism is mainly of an economic nature, and that its political and cultural aims are of a supplementary character; that the financial capital of the United States is well on the way to a conquest of the world.

The main cause of this movement is, of course, the immense financial power of the United States which she gained by her favourable position during the War. It was forgotten that this power saved Europe from anarchy. Europe itself was not afraid to accept and invite the capital of the United States for many purposes; for Europe and the United States knew their own economic history, and remembered that even English economic power needed, during the seventeenth and eighteenth centuries, help from Dutch capital, just as did the railroads in the United States and the mining industry in Rhenish Westphalia. In the nineteenth century England was the workshop of the world, but where is the British danger to-day? The industrialization of several countries, the United States, for instance, was effected by the use of English capital, machines, and methods.

The modern movement can be understood only in connection with the world situation after the War. It was a time when the dollar virtually ruled the world. Exaggerations like the "Stock Exchange of Paris became entirely vassal of Wall Street"[15] became popular.

But the minds of Europe became more peaceful and saw that Europe was not yet Americanized either economically or politically. The hue and cry raised over the conquest of Europe by the United States died down and a cultural fight against Americanization was proclaimed.

"These European fears are natural enough, but—like nightmares—they are chimerical. Like all nightmares, they leave certain realities out of consideration. One of these realities is that though American finance in post-War years gained great influence in the world, it by no means enjoyed an irresistible power to dominate either its own Government or European nations: it could make terms before extending loans, but it could not play the master as England had done in Egypt, or France in Morocco and Tunis, or Japan in Korea. Another reality is European civilization. European nations are too highly industrialized and too highly conscious of nationality to be easily or permanently dominated by a nation of kindred civilization."[16] Of course, the sentiment of Europe, which feels itself in an advanced age, are comprehensible.

Investments are usually more alarming than the trade. ("The lender attaches himself more permanently on to the borrower than the buyer does to the seller."[17]) Active industrial investments and the trade, connected with the activity of the "Big Thirty," are clearly of primary importance, while passive investments, the savings of the people, are welcomed. It is false that the United States trade conquered the world; it is an optical illusion. It is true, however, that the "Big Thirty" are endeavouring to become the leaders in their own branches of industry over the entire globe. Just as Europe by means of her coal, iron, and railroads obtained the world supremacy, so petroleum and motor-cars are attaining a new world position for the United States. The economic expansion of the United States is a child of necessity; it is not of conscious desire for power. It is not an organized advance, but expansion caused by the irresistible internal pressure of mass-production, which in striving for rationalization is compelled to take into account the entire world. It is a *perpetuum mobile*: industry must increase production in order to sell more cheaply, and it must sell more in order to produce more. Expansion abroad constitutes the organization of a means of marketing domestic overproduction and of securing raw materials for domestic economy. Imagine the automobile industry in the United States without export. Would the world buy cars more cheaply if the export from the United States, now 12 per cent. of the production, were stopped? In this respect one can speak of automobile imperialism, sewing-machine imperialism, razor-blade imperialism, and so forth. In order to conquer foreign countries or penetrate into them economically, there is no plan, agreement, or alliance either between the sewing-machine industry and the General Motors Corporation, or between the Standard Oil Company and the International Telephone and Telegraph, with or without the knowledge of the Government. Even the "Big Thirty" in their expansion no longer belong to a national economy. Is it possible seriously to believe that the centre of gravity of the material interests of a world concern lies in its own country? Such as Krueger and Toll in Sweden? The "Big Thirty" are no longer national, nor even international. They are anational. The universality of their economic motives is, theoretically, as cosmopolitan as a radical communistic labour organization.[18]

And "Americanization"? It is indeed a fact that thousands ride in autos made in the United States, use her machinery, street cars, telephones, telegraph, radios, razor-blades, typewriters, sewing-machines, and—so all along the line of mass-production. But does this Americanization constitute "economic estrangement"? or is it the victory of the more progressive mass-production—rationalization? And the great advantage especially to Latin America consists in having adopted this Americanization, its newest methods, directly from the United States; for the American *is* the pioneer in the technique of mass-production; that is the line in which he excels because he understands how to produce less expensively and to create a demand for his goods. That is the mission of the United States—to bring the modern achievements of mass-production to the farthest corners of the world. This imperialism is, to quote Spengler, "pure civilization."[19] And that must be learned from the United States, must be used and adapted in the interest of cheap mass-production, of the industrialization, and in the interest also of consumption and higher material standards of living for people in general. Acceptance of this materialistic Americanism is a rational economic act, which from this point of view can only be welcomed.

Thus Sombart understood Americanization to be a victory of economic progressive methods of production. "By the sweat of your brow shall ye labour in the American manner!" "That is, you must rationalize labour profitably, put into practice the economic principle which exists still yet in economic text-books only."[20]

But material uniformity has as a result a cultural uniformity, the anti-Yankees declare, in referring to the non-existence of a real culture in the United States. They are in fear of "quantity civilization," using an expression of Paul Valéry's. "From Frisco to Boston, from Chicago to New Orleans, the same thinking and the same power of mechanical culture."[21] However, is this standardization of life not a world phenomenon, which is not specifically applicable to the United States alone? Is it not a *testimonium paupertatis* to fear a "non-existent" culture? Was it not a great historical mission of the United States to give Europe the material power to save her and her culture from chaos? Generalizations, in this respect, are vulgarizations, like the opinion, for instance, that Latin America possesses only fighting generals and natural wealth.

The United States began her life by endeavouring to satisfy her material needs. Even after satisfying the fundamental wants, her material desires were not stated, but lead her on the path of transition to modern mass-production. What this country, from its secured material foundation, can deliver to humanity in the field of culture and arts—this question will be answered in the future.

The economic penetration of the United States is characteristically a matter of business and not of politics. The essential quality of this "imperialism" is business; the methods of its foreign policy are business-like. Their very character was emphasized already by Frederick List in his discussion of the United States' foreign policy. "When we judge this conduct by principles, there is nothing but contradiction; but when we look at the aim of the country, there is nothing but conformity. Her aim was always and ever to raise her manufactures and commerce."[22] One of the first formulations of this principle is in Washington's Farewell Address. The United States tried for decades to buy Cuba, bought Alaska from Russia, the Philippines from Spain, the Virgin Islands from Denmark, bought the foreign obligations of Santo Domingo; Louisiana was purchased from France and Florida from Spain; and Texas alone was incorporated as a result of the Mexican War. Where else in the world has there ever been such a trafficking in lands? The Yankee values above all a precise documentary statement and recognition of his rights by the contracting governments. Is not the incorporation of the Platt Amendment in the Cuban constitution a typically commerical treaty?

The United States does not crave colonies. She does not want to possess a new Ireland and have to recall in bitter circumstances the famous words of Turgot: "Colonies are like fruits which cling to the tree only till they ripen," words confirmed by the history of the United States itself. Even Manuel Ugarte does not fear a military conquest by the United States.

The foreign policy of the United States adopts the policy of an honest merchant. Is not the liquidation of the World War under the United States' influence a striking example of this business psychology: "A committee of bankers who with cold calculation understood to prescribe the fate of 500 millions of people, set aside old animosities, and undertook the programme in their agenda in the face of a sentimental world of bleeding civilized nations; this aim was something new to Europe's way of thinking, and for a time the Yankee motto 'business policy' might well be the leading theme of all editorial articles and essays; policies were formulated as if the history of the world were a balance sheet in dollars and cents."[23] The main characteristic of the imperialism of the United States is that it is *non-political* and strictly business-like; its secondary feature is its *impersonality*.

These times have passed into history when the North American promoter with small means, great energy and initiative came to foreign countries. The expansion of the United States has become a mechanical business just like every other business. Interest and rents are produced annually in great quantities, which mechanically and almost automatically, according to certain rules of average investment risk, etc., are invested not abroad, but in foreign securities, that is, *in domestic securities which replace foreign ones*. This is the height of impersonality of relationship between debtor and creditor, between the financed and the financier.[24]

Compare this system with the English, where the control rests mostly with the financier; or with the German, where capital never goes abroad alone, but always accompanied by men.

This peculiarity of the investment organization is unknown to the Peligro writers; in this system of securities substitution lies a certain diminution of the influence of the United States' capital. Is Canada politically or culturally dominated by the United States, in spite of the large investments, geographical vicinity, community of language?

The direct industrial investments of the United States could be compared with the triumphal march of the Swedish match syndicate, Krueger and Toll, who with few exceptions have virtually conquered the world production and world market.[25] Even in the United States it possesses a dominant position.

That is the ideal of great corporations of the United States, which are unconsciously forced to strike the same position in their own fields. Only few United States' groups possess the financial power of the Swedish concern; no one of them lent so much money to foreign governments as the Swedish. Nobody is talking about Swedish imperialism, and what is the qualitative difference between the expansion and influence abroad of, for instance, International Telephone and Telegraph and Krueger and Toll?

It is primarily a business policy without ulterior motives or supplementary purposes; it is "business for business' sake," like "art for art's sake."

These general considerations are at the same time a refutation of the "Peligro Yanqui" for South America, in spite of certain definite peculiarities in the situation. We must, of course, differentiate between Spanish-speaking peoples and Brazil, between the Northern coast and the remainder of the continent.

If we mean by "Peligro Yanqui" economic Americanization, the extension of money economy and modern capitalism in undeveloped countries, the farewell to the primitive and inorganic forms of economic life—in a word, economic progress—this "danger" exists, especially for the Latin countries of the Northern continent—Mexico, Central America, and the Antilles. Here lies the focus of the Peligro; here are the wells of lubricating oil; here is sugar; the banana; here is the centre of the propaganda, for it is here that the process of expansion is taking large forms. The penetration of the United States is one of the stages of economic progress of these countries; it is the victory of the economic principle of cheaper, more modern, more progressive methods of production. Even the authors of the well-known anti-imperialistic series are forced to admit this.

Mr. Melvin M. Knight sees a "real Yankee peril" for Santo Domingo, and considers it as "the economic process of Americanization."[26] The peril exists only for those old economic forms which should be replaced. For the same reason, it could be said (and it was a popular opinion in Japan) that Europeanization was dangerous to Japan.

Miss Margaret A. March, whose book on Bolivia is one of the same series, is disappointed, and declares: "The North American imperialism is, in Bolivia, not a matter of present time."[27] Even the third and best investigation of the series, that on Cuba, does not give conclusions at variance to these. (See Chapter IV.) Americanization is inevitable if these countries have the will to economic progress.

Latin America is disappointed that "experts from the United States have performed such (financial) services for Colombia, Cuba, Guatemala, Honduras, Panama, and Peru, with the co-operation" of the United States Government. Bolivia, Chile, Dominican Republic, Ecuador, Mexico, and Paraguay have employed experts "without assistance of the Government of the United States." Haiti has an American financial adviser.[28] It is true now that the United States practises financial sanitation as a business almost all over the world. She is a financial doctor through whose acquired relations, knowledge, and study American business as a whole will, of course, profit. But has not the Bank of England invited a Harvard Professor as financial adviser?

Paul M. Warburg pointed out in his speech at the First Pan-American Financial Conference in Washington, 1915: "The chief lesson which all American nations will have to learn from last year's experience is that it is unwise for the world to place its financial dependence upon any single nation; and those who can afford to do so, as, for instance, the United States, should from this time on adopt a policy of greater reliance upon their own resources. Those countries which cannot rely exclusively upon their own resources should adopt a policy of dividing the risks of financial dependence as evenly and widely as they possibly can."[29]

This distribution of lenders still prevails in South America, existing even in most threatened Colombia and Venezuela, and "their creditor nations are geographically, politically, and economically separated from one another."[30] That is an historical fact in South America, while in the Latin countries of the Northern Continent history did not admit this distribution.

In spite of wartime success of the United States in South America, its general influence and importance are (as we saw in Chapter I) behind Europe's. The optical illusion of monopolization by the United States is not a new phenomenon. Professor Viallate, who studied the American danger in 1907, prior to the War, was also very much disappointed.[31]

The cultural danger for South America does not exist. The question of the great poet

> Serémos entregados a los bárbaros fieros?
> Tantos millones de hombres hablarémos inglés?

is already answered by an astute observer from the United States: "As the people all speak the same tongue, and that a great European one, Spanish, which has a glorious literary heritage, they will be slow to abandon it for English, in spite of all efforts of the schools."[32]

"It is not probable that American friendship will lead Mexico and Argentina to forget that Spain was their mother-country, any more than there is an immediate prospect that the literary and æsthetic standards of New York will supplant those of Paris, Rio de Janeiro, or Buenos Aires."[33] The resistance against the United States' influence stimulated a re-crudescence of national Spanish culture, especially even in Cuba and Porto Rico. The immigrants in the United States who have sought and found there a new country are quickly assimilated. The supposed struggle abroad between the national culture influence and the influence of the United States does not exist. The United States has created elementary, material mass culture, and had developed in this field a genius, power, and energy never before seen; but spiritual articles are not produced in wholesale quantities, and, besides, give no promise of great profit, so that the North American *homo economicus* would hardly dedicate his energies to such as these. The danger of such competition does not exist.

One of the best known and most talented anti-Yankee writers, Louis Araquistain, who paints the Yankee danger very black, has to admit the following: "No matter what the ultimate fate of Porto Rico may be, I believe it will preserve its cultural personality by means of the Spanish language. The Press, which comprises good periodicals and modern dailies, constantly publishes works by Spanish authors, although the regular collaboration is furnished by North American literary agencies, which with the telegraph agencies are another instrument of Americanization.

"The booksellers sell Spanish books and periodicals almost exclusively, not in great quantities, but in larger proportion than any of the independent republics. In general *the plane of Spanish culture in Porto Rico is quite high, and shows a tendency to rise.*"[34] Where, then, is the menace of the United States to the native culture?

We must understand that the entire character of the United States' expansion is indifferent to cultural victory. Neither the Western Union nor All American Cables is interested in the language used in cablegrams; nor is the I.T.T. anxious about the language of telephone conversations; nor the General Motors Company about the nationality of the passengers in their motor-cars.

The psychology of the "Peligro Yanqui" movement is clear. The modern American danger is a child of the world economic situation of the War and post-War period. The modern "Peligro Yanqui" was aroused by many specific psychological factors in America. Besides the gloomy power of the "Colossus in the North," South America awoke one day to find that all that is new and modern is coming from the North: the automobile, the radio, the tramways, the moving pictures, light and power, etc. They saw that in time the United States would become the greatest customer, supplier, and financier. The immensity of her operations, the newly erected skyscrapers, the pressure of the "Big Thirty"—all these influenced their imagination. And that is important. The United States are a new figure in their economic life. Bingham relates that in the year 1911, "One looks in vain for an American bank or agency of any well-known Wall Street house. American financial institutions are like the American merchant steamers—conspicuous by their absence. The Anglo-Saxons that you see briskly walking along the side-walks are not Americans, but clean-shaven, red-cheeked, vigorous Britishers."[35] And now South America believes that she is to be delivered to these "hombres de ojos sajonos y alma bárbara" (Rubén Darío). The rapid tempo caused fright,[36] and thus the "Peligro Yanqui" became one of the leading characters of the "Drama of Hispano-America."

The influence of Great Britain, which almost monopolized the economic life of South America for many decades, was an habitually accepted fact. "The Englishman is our acquaintance, quasi friend"[37] of old times. But the Yankee was regarded as a new interloper, a new financial power, a new business giant, the danger of Europe, the oppressor of Latin America! The propagandists were quick to shout from the house-tops: "Peligro Yanqui." But if even Manuel Ugarte, by the will of fate, should ever become a leader of a government, even he would open the door to the foreign capital and invite the United States' co-operation.

The anti-Yankee movement in South America is not due to economic penetration; it is not a cultural danger (who believes seriously in it?), but mere political atmosphere. The "Peligro Yanqui" in Spanish America is a *psychological phenomenon*, continually incited and nourished by the propaganda in Europe and North America on the one hand, and by the foreign policy of the United States toward Latin America on the other. The conditions in Latin countries in North America, darkly painted by travelling and writing anti-Yankees, coloured by European propaganda, and exaggerated by the anti-imperialists of the United States, is one of the causes of these sentiments. The feeling gained currency that Latin America exists now on the Southern continent only; in the North the Yankees are dominating and ruling.[38]

But South America has no geographical connection with the United States; the United States does not possess political privileges there; there is no American Navy, and the visits of battleships are only international amenities. A great deal of the continent is of a different mode of importance than Central America and the Antilles. "It is the political suspicion which many Latin Americans entertain of their Northern neighbours, and which Europeans will always be ready to keep alive, that is perhaps the greatest bar to closer connections."[39]

The axis of the United States' policy toward Latin America has been the Monroe Doctrine for more than one hundred years. Throughout history this clear and simple statement became a labyrinth of myths and legends,[40] a "servant for all." Almost every President and Secretary of State gave to this Doctrine a personal note, according to his own interpretations. The Monroe Doctrine of 1823 was a distinct warning for Europe: "You have nothing to do on our hemisphere." Though it was not intended as such, it subsequently became a defensive declaration in favour of Latin America. During the century this Janus turned his second face toward Latin America. Roosevelt developed this side theoretically and practically in his "big stick" policy; and even when Roosevelt was not urging on this policy, Latin America understood it as a continuation of the Destiny Manifesto, of the famous words by Secretary Richard Olney. There were attempts to mitigate the ill-feeling of Latin America—Elihu Root, Woodrow Wilson (especially in his Mobile speech), Warren Harding (in his address at the dedication of Bolivar's statue in New York), but always with only temporary success.

The Monroe Doctrine is a permanent source of friction and conflict. It no longer corresponds to interrelations in the new world, nor to the League of Nations.[41] It is the cause of ceaseless quarrels with Latin America (even Brazil is not excluded from these), and internal conflict in the United States between trade and foreign policy,[42] between the Government and the intelligentsia.

But public opinion in the United States is not aware of all these things. Officially the United States is not informed about the anti-Yankee movement. The official optimism dominates. Charles E. Hughes believes that in spite of "all that is the subject of criticism, proposals, and discussions, I think that it is fair to say that our relations with these countries are better than they have been for many years."[43] Even most critical Hiram Bingham assures us that "South America is ready to take American goods in very large quantities as soon as we are ready to take time to give attention to her needs."[44] The Federal Frade Commission declares that the United States' "investments are regarded with great favour by the South American Governments."[45] Another writer thinks that "notwithstanding the effort of many European writers to persuade themselves and their constituencies that the United States and Latin America are farther apart in every way than Latin America and Europe, and that all the methods invoked to remove the distance partake of artificial stimulation, something like an American consciousness and a sense of confraternity does, after all, animate the republics in the Western Hemisphere."[46] The Director-General of the Pan-American Union declares that Yankees are always "welcome guests" in Latin America,[47] which must be understood surely as only a diplomatic formality.

It is comprehensible that the flexibility of the policy of the United States and the indefiniteness of the Monroe Doctrine has made a great impression upon America South of Panama. "The statesmen of the South refuse to believe in the friendship of the Yankees. Which is the truth: the imperialistic declaration of Mr. Olney or the idealism of Mr. Root?"[48] The ex-President of Honduras, Policarpo Bonella, declares: "Latin America has lost faith in platforms and the speeches of candidates, in proclamations of aspirants for power, because those promises nearly in every case are not fulfilled. It has lost faith in Presidents' messages and speeches, because they regularly say the contrary of what they think."[49]

What are the wishes of Latin America in this respect? They agree with the formula of Calvin Coolidge: "We are thoroughly committed to the principle that they are better fitted to govern themselves than anyone else is to govern them. We do not claim immediate perfection, but we do expect continual progress. Our history reveals that in such expectation we have not been disappointed. It is better for the people to make their own mistakes than to have someone else make their mistakes for them."[50]

"The republics of America are no longer children in the great family of nations";[51] they require "co-operation and not patronizing tutelage."[52] South America is not satisfied even for the rest of Latin America that the money-lender be "the judge of his own case."[53] They demand a practical application of the Pan-American speeches.

And Manuel Ugarte is speaking virtually for the entire Latin-American continent when he explains the "cry of the people."[54] When even in the United States many authorities agree that "the Monroe Doctrine is dead, and has been dead for many years,"[55] that it is an "obsolete shibboleth," and that "international trade is largely a matter of sentiment, and the Monroe Doctrine does not sell any American-made goods,"[56] when from all sides the intellectual class of the United States is suggesting a new programme, distrust in Latin America becomes comprehensible. The atmosphere has been poisoned.

Even Brazil, where anti-Yankee sentiment does not exist, that vast South American empire, which invites the co-operation of the United States, takes her stand alongside of Spanish America in opposing the Monroe Doctrine, because of her traditional continentalism.

CHAPTER IV

AN EXPERIMENT

CUBA

The position of Cuba is peculiar in every sense. Geographically the island lies in the Mediterranean of the New World, ninety miles south of Florida; yet it must nevertheless be admitted that Herder's geographical theory of economic development contains much truth when applied to this case. For generations, possession of the island was highly prized by the United States. In the hands of a foreign power, the island would be a constant threat to the United States, because of its pre-eminently strategic position. For this reason the importance of Cuba to the United States is singular: the key to the Caribbean and the Mexican Gulf.[1]

During the entire nineteenth century the United States carried on diplomatic negotiations with a view toward either buying or acquiring control over the island for the purpose of shutting out rivals. The "British danger" was the primary consideration of United States' diplomatic policy here. Cuba, it was feared, might become the American Egypt, or, as Lathané calls it, a transatlantic Turkey, "trembling to its fall, but sustained by the jealousies of those who were eager to share the spoils."[2]

Politically, history put Cuba in exactly the same position that it occupies geographically, namely, under the influence of the United States. The island, politically a new state organism, was still a Spanish colony thirty years ago. It had no history of its own. Several parts of its political and economic structure are still depending on the Platt Amendment.

The economic attractiveness of Cuba is well known: holder of coffee supremacy for a long time in the past, still leading in sugar and famous for its tobacco. Economically, its ties with the United States are strong. The influence of the United

States is almost monopolistic in character. The figures for Cuban foreign trade appear as follows:[3]

TABLE 23

(IN U.S. DOLLARS)

	1927	1928
IMPORTATION		
Total	257,384,062	212,816,812
Of this from United States ..	159,055,695	122,432,278
EXPORTATION		
Total	322,704,591	278,069,669
Of this to United States	256,142,692	202,535,160

The investments of the United States in Cuba date back farther than in South America. Small entrepreneurs of almost negligible capital, but great energy, were the first business pioneers from the United States in Cuba. Only with the beginning of the twentieth century did the "Big Thirty" appear on the island. Their activity here bears striking resemblance to the investments and trade carried on by them in South America. The fact that small entrepreneurs began the penetration of the island makes the personal element in Cuba a more preponderant factor of United States influence than in South America. In their invasion of the Cuban market the "Big Thirty" was accompanied by many other firms of the United States. The United States combined in Cuba her specific methods of expansion with the European practices described in a previous chapter. Thus it is to-day that the United States supplies wellnigh all the needs of the Cuban market. On the strength of the Platt Amendment even the financial operations of the Cuban Government are practically controlled by the United States.

The investments of the United States in Cuba in 1928 are estimated to amount to $1,500,000,000, out of a total of $1,750,000,000 of foreign investments on the island.[4]

There exists between the two countries a tacit agreement on currency. United States currency is accepted in Cuba under the Cuban name. Besides, there is an informal co-operation between Cuban banks and the Federal Reserve System; and the Federal Reserve Bank of Atlanta, through its agency in Cuba, acts in a regulating capacity.

Rivalry of other nations for Cuba is entirely eradicated. Even with regard to tourist services and accommodations the single customers are from the United States.

In so far as spiritual Americanization is concerned, it seems that "the last daughter of Spain" could not offer the slightest resistance: Spanish culture was hated and a native culture had not been born.

Thus, the activities of the United States in Cuba are manifold and have developed without opposition. The United States is political guarantor and protector, customer, provider, financier, and partner—without competition. On this island the seducer has gained his point completely. Here he had the opportunity of achieving his secret desires.

One must admit that in the case of Cuba an especially concentrated "Peligro Yanqui" exists. The island, for our purposes, may be considered a laboratory, where a study of the influences of this peril on a former Spanish colony can be undertaken. The long duration of Cuban relations with her Yankee neighbours, extending over a period of thirty years (many of which were years of occupation or intervention by the United States), is a factor which strengthens the influence of the United States in Cuban affairs. And we must not forget that even prior to the liberation of Cuba from Spanish rule the influence of the United States was very potent. "Although we depended on Spain politically, we were economically a colony of the United States of the North."[5]

In investigating the nature of the "Peligro Yanqui" in Cuba, our study should be especially enlightening, because in the economic structure of this island we find many weaknesses of South America in a concentrated form. For economically Cuba is a typically mono-productive country: everything depends on sugar; moreover, Cuba is a land of only one market, its export depending entirely on its northern neighbour; the latifundio system prevails in Cuba; all this makes Cuba a classic example. Thus the characteristics of industrial fluctuations in the sugar industry during and after the World War were particularly pronounced both with regard to booms and depressions.

Cuba bears almost all the marks which can be construed as the most distinct expression of a "Peligro Yanqui" in a Latin-American country. The conditions for the development of this phenomenon here have been especially propitious, as if history intentionally created an artificial laboratory for the cultivation and study of this virus. Cuba is at the same time subject to the influence not only of world economic tendencies, but also local tendencies of the United States, besides being affected by the native course of events in sugar production.[6] Here one can sense distinctly the great waves of world economy, the reflex of United States' economic and political movements, together with Cuba's own peculiar economic rhythm. This mixture of influences makes Cuba an especially interesting and at the same time complicated, object for the study of the theory of economic crises.

. . . . .

It is not intended to represent Cuba as a paradise on earth. Yet, in spite of the apparent economic progress of the island,[7] you constantly hear people speak there about a crisis. It is true that Cuba's economic development has moved in paths that may be called anything but steady since the foundation of the republic. On the other hand, it must be remembered that the great economic success of this young country, its favourable position during the World War (when Cuba as a producer of sugar was one of the greatest profiteers of the War), and the famous "dance of the millions" since the War, have accustomed the psychology of the people to abnormal prosperity.

What is the situation in the island now, after thirty years of independence? In order to construct a clear picture of the varying and contradictory currents and orientations existing in the country on this subject, it may be well to divide opinion into three categories: (1) *The pessimistic current*, which holds that Cuba's economic (there in part also her political) independence cannot be maintained; and it is only a question of time before the formalities attendant upon the fact will be fulfilled;

(2) *The romantic current*, which ascribes the causes of the crisis to the sugar and agricultural problem, in connection with the investments of the United States, which fights for the re-establishment of the small landowners, and which sees in this a panacea for almost all existing ills;

(3) *The realistic current*, which stands calmly on the ground of existing facts and attempts a solution from the standpoint of the state and its entire economy. Just as the romantic idea lays its stress on the agrarian problem, so the realistic movement seeks the economic progress in advancing industrialization.

It is typical that the pessimistic movement is represented principally by North American authors. They study statistics, regard the island from their own shores, notice the increasing importance of the position occupied by the United States in its foreign trade, try to calculate the amount of their investments, and draw the conclusion: "Cuba is no more independent than Long Island."[8] Twenty pages farther on the authors think it over and declare: "Theoretically, Cuba is a sovereign state. Practically, the economic and political life of the island is dominated by New York and Washington. This method of control saves the cost of colonization, while it leaves the field open to Yankee interests."[9]

Leland H. Jenks is much more mature, better qualified, and more interesting; but his book has the *ad hoc* tendency of the series. He has, however, been able to gather a great many interesting facts, to study the situation thoroughly, and to work it out elegantly and animatedly.[10]

His ironical remarks about Yankee imperialism do not always prevent Jenks from being partially blinded by it. He is of the opinion that political annexation hardly comes into the question, but emphasizes the fact that "it has made of Cuba a great sugar plantation governed by privileged accountants and salesmen of securities. It has seriously raised the question whether a country can continue to be a great latifundio managed by absent proprietors."[11] He then asks ironically: "Can a country remain politically independent, being at the same time dominated economically from without?"[12] But he must admit that "the Yankee capital has contributed much to the material development of Cuba."[13]

The young Cuban author, Raul Maestri, represents a transition to the romantic idea.[14] (He has written a vivid, spirited booklet.) His pessimism is quite categorical: "The Cuban government is not the arbiter of Cuban economic life. More than that, the government finds itself pressed by Cuban economy."[15] And then follows the well-known strain: Cuba had a pronounced colonial economy completely depending on the United States; the enormous expansion of the sugar industry is also a consequence of the influence of North American capital, as is the sudden and rapid industrialization of the sugar business which was formerly on a more agricultural basis. And now the treatise approaches the romantic idea; the author admits that from an economic point of view the Yankees have done much, immense capital has been invested technically, modern giant plants have been installed, North American methods of mass-production have been extended to Cuba; but the industrial latifundio of sugar has complicated the social question; and for Maestri the present crisis presents the conflict of "The North American sugar economy of the island against the nationalism which has formed itself on the same."[16] But at this point the relation with the romanticists ceases, because of the apparent socialistic leanings of the author; for him the problem is only a school-example of the modern controversy between "economic nationalism" and "world market" against the odds of the dynamic impulse of anti-national economy.

To the pessimists, the crisis is therefore not a normal economic one as part of a world and local conditions, but a state and national crisis in consequence of the economic penetration of the United States, and the carrying off of the child Cuba by the ever-hungry wolf of Yankee imperialism. As for the future, the inevitable is to be expected.

It is noticeable that this pessimistic current of opinion originates principally with foreign investigators and such Cubans as are of socialistic inclination.

The romanticists are more interesting. Their principal leader is the well-known Cuban historian, Professor Ramiro Guerra y Sanchez, who understands how to combine erudition and knowledge with fascinating description. His work on sugar has become a classic, and belongs to the standard works, as does Lippmann's well-known *History of Sugar*.[17]

His principal idea is as follows: "The danger exists that the history of Cuba will be a repetition of all the development of the West Indies." In a masterly way he describes the social history of the little island of Barbados, and fears that the same fate awaits Cuba. He complains of "the rapid disappearance of the independent Cuban rural landowners, the constant decline in the standard of living of the rural population, and the enslaving development of the sugar latifundio."[18] He expatiates upon "displacement of the small landowner by the cheap labour of the slave,"[19] and goes on to say that "Cuba by herself would not have been able to extend the industry to a degree dangerous to the majority of the community."[20] And here already is a beginning of what must be called economic romanticism: "The latifundio is necessary in order that the mills may dominate the planter and exploit him, imposing on him such hard conditions as they please; that is to say, a few companies, forty or fifty at the most, subject hundreds of thousands of planters; *this is not necessary in order to plant cane and make sugar*" (italics are mine), but it is necessary in order to compete in the world market.

"Are there other bases, more just and more humane, on which production may be organized?"

This heartfelt cry is comprehensible, but it represents not an economic, but an ethical, point of view; and we have no desire to follow the author on this ground, because we must reckon with the facts of the actual epoch of capitalistic economy.

The latifundio wins, because it can and does produce cheaper, because it is in harmony with the mass-production of modern industrial methods; and the thought of preserving more expensive forms of production is Utopian.

It is the same storm that was conjured by the first railways—competition with the then existing means of transportation—the same consternation that followed the development of the English wool industry—the well-known period when, according to the expression of the economic romanticists of that time, "the sheep devoured the men," because then, too, one of the consequences of the acquisition of land was the disappearance of the independent small landowner; it is the same conflict that always and everywhere is waged against concentration of the industry by the leading representatives of antiquated methods of production.

But now Ramiro Guerra becomes still more violent: "The sugar latifundio concentrates (about 40 per cent.) enormous areas of the best land in the hands of a few persons or companies, perhaps not half a hundred, and, as necessary and inevitable consequence, attacks and destroys the small and medium property. . . . The latifundio process is one of revision of the secular historical work of the creation of the Cuban state" (p. 76). "The Colono system is a devilish invention" (p. 79).

The present condition is described as follows: "In the zones where it (latifundio) dominates it creates a society as simple as that of Barbados: high and low employees of the companies, labourers who receive a small daily wage paid weekly" (p. 79). [And how is it in other industries?] When latifundio is satisfied, "when it has sufficient cane assured, it is no longer interested in the land" (p. 82), and it pays only a very low price. Pages 92–93 give an interesting résumé of the accusation.

But Ramiro Guerra understands the economic necessity for the sugar industry to develop mass-production and reduce the cost of production; he also understands that it is a question of life, of existence, for the industry: "The latifundio is thus obliged by a superior force, which it cannot resist, to create unceasingly, to extend itself, to improve its machinery, to have a larger extraction, to seek new land without ever satisfying its land appetite, until unavoidably and fatally it occupies all the cultivable land of the country" (p. 109). But more sugar at less cost sooner or later will inevitably make of Cuba a new Barbados" (p. 121). [Here the author overlooks the fact that political, historical, and economic conditions in Cuba are entirely different.]

The author develops a campaign programme in favour of the small man, but realistic feeling obliges him to emphasize: "But the welfare of Cuba must not be an action against the sugar industry or against national or foreign capital" (p. 114). What enemy does Ramiro Guerra wish, then, to combat?

The campaign programme is divided into two parts:

(*a*) Associations of the planters for mutual assistance. This would be welcome, and the proposition might be further and more thoroughly developed; but it is, and will continue to be, only an effort to lessen the difficulties of this period of transition.

(*b*) State intervention, without which the author believes there is no prospect of success; such state intervention should relate to:

(1) No further extension of the latifundio; (2) No further importation of labourers; (3) Land owned by the cultivator. But if the author rightly describes the influence of the sugar

magnates, how can he hope to enforce points one and two? The State must act correctly from an *economic* point of view, without making production dearer; it is influenced also by economic interests. The answer to point three has already been given by a great Cuban, Dr. Gonzalez Lanuza, in his criticism of the similar law proposed in Congress by Wilfredo Fernandez.

The positive part of the programme: "A national fund for the help of the small proprietor" (p. 114), would be also welcome; but it is technically and financially difficult of realization, and even if realized would have little significance.

After the construction of this programme, Ramiro Guerra comprehends that by the enforcement of his propositions the sugar industry would be ruined; and he now essays a new programme to protect the industry from the consequences of his first programme, a typically mercantile system which would lead to an increase in the cost of production.[21]

The same agricultural romanticism is to be noticed in Vicente Pardo Suarez, who declares: "We need nothing except the defence and protection of agriculture, because this is the only thing that will save Cuba."[22]

The same point is sustained by Fernando Berenguer:[23] "The economic problem of Cuba . . . is agrarian" (p. 18). His proposition to help the small landowners sounds strange: the cash on hand in the banks should be used for this purpose (p. 80)—the best means for creating the worst crisis and financial panic; he is also a partisan of the law proposed by Wilfredo Fernandez.

To this current belong also the declarations of Dr. José Antonio Taboadela.[24] His economic ideals move in the sphere of the "isolated state" of Thünen, and are at the same time influenced by Malthus; he believes that the collective life should be exclusively Cuban with an exclusively Cuban population (opposed to every kind of immigration), with a tendency toward economic autarchy. His ideal is really: *omnia domi nascuntur*. He also expects a solution of the economic crisis through "home industries," through "manufacture of fans, mantillas, boxes, clothing, hats, and fancy goods" (p. 16).

A very bright book, written with distinct journalistic talent, by Luis Araquistain,[25] brings nothing new to our Cuban problems. A talented and interesting compilation of the works of Ramiro Guerra, it belongs to this movement, even though indications of the problem of industrialization occur here and there.

The realistic movement also starts from the realization of the complexity of the sugar question and the relation to the United States, which influence the whole economic life of Cuba; but it is not founded on the standpoint of social help for the small landowner, *colono*, worker, or manufacturer and merchant, etc., but sees the problem from the economic standpoint of the entire country.

The work of Professor I. C. Zamora, published in the first number (December 1929) of the new *Revista de la Universidad*, in Havana under the title of "The Tariff Union between Cuba and the United States," is outstanding in the economic literature of Cuba, because for the first time in Cuban literature a clear, thoroughly constructed problem of industrialization has been set up. It is short in form and expression.

Zamora's outstanding characteristic and at the same time chief merit is that he reckons with facts. Yes, Cuba is a monoproductive land; the United States is the only market for Cuba; the United States is in a position to produce an artificial crisis in Cuba through a tariff, and to starve the island and precipitate all the economic and social consequences connected therewith by closing its market to Cuban sugar.[26] This can be combated only by means of palliatives; sugar production or supply may be artificially influenced; agriculture should be stimulated to greater development; and the Cuban problem lies elsewhere, namely, in the question of the economic future of the island: back to agrarian romanticism,[27] or transform itself into a great industrial nation (p. 22).

In favour of industrialization are the favourable geographical location of Cuba, the existent intimate relations with the United States and knowledge of modern working methods there. But the difficulties must not be overlooked. Cuba has no moving power; she has not sufficient capital,[28] and young industries need much money for a long period of time, and are attended by greater risk; the buying power of the country is slight, and the foreign markets are closed to new industry ("and what advantage can we give to other peoples if the reciprocity treaty with the United States, which guarantees them a tariff margin, . . . eliminates all competition?" *ibid.*, p. 24); and the high protective tariff necessary for the development of the industry contains the danger of a tariff war and complications with the United States.

These difficulties can be eliminated—and here is the practical meaning of the work—only by a *direct understanding with the United States with this object: tariff union.* Thus the dreams of the Continentalists, the desires of Clay and Blaine, have come to the fore to-day, and in this special case the demands of life and the realities of economy are the background of these ideas.

The author is of the opinion that "this measure would be of advantage to the United States and a saving for us" (p. 27). The tariff union would be really the natural development of the existing relations, since the *tratado de reciprocidad* was also only a temporary measure (p. 37). Zamora does not ignore the difficulties of this programme; he tries to explain them and remove them, very skilfully and ingeniously (he overlooks one difficulty more: the prohibition law of the United States, which, under a tariff union, would have been extended to Cuba; but it is not our intention to enter into technicalities here).

Zamora sees the opposition of certain interests in the United States, tries to remove them and create compromises with the tact of a clever lawyer, seeks and finds probable partisan multitudes there for his programme, and believes that interests of the States and the majority of the people will emerge victorious and bring about the establishment of the tariff union.

Economic consequences of the tariff union: *passive*—removal of those uncertainties which produce crises and which result from changes in the United States' economic policies and the fluctuations of the sugar market, that is, creating a steady market for the principal product of Cuba; *active*—removal of the principal obstacles to the industrialization of the island, like moving power, capital, etc., etc.

The tariff union would mean for Cuba: Mass-production, standardization, highways, great purchasing power, protection of industry through the commun with the United States' tariff, finally, also protection of the workers through the commun with the United States' immigration policy.

We may consider also Alberto Llamar Schweyer[29] as a realist, who declares: "Like Spain, our northern neighbours exercise on our economic and social structure an inevitable influence, against which it *would be absurd to rebel*"[30] and further: "Thousands of Cubans live and prosper under the protection of northern capital, the great enterprise unites with that of our nation, surrounds it with northern interests, and these make it a part of their complicated economic scheme and come to identify its future with theirs."[31]

Earlier, Gonzalez Lanuza expressed clearly the realistic current in discussing the proposed law for the prohibition of the acquisition of land by foreigners in the Congressional Session of March 8, 1909, when he declared: "The Cuban needed capital; he did not have it; what did he want? To cultivate the land, to make it produce. He had no capital; how was he going to make Cuban land produce without the resources indispensable to the economic life of a people in modern times? If he seeks it (capital) from foreigners, it is necessary to obtain it under acceptable conditions."[32]

One can cite other expressions of the realistic current; but the object is not to formulate a review of opinions; and no one has propounded the principal problems of the country so keenly, and so clearly formulated and erected the guides for future development as Zamora.[33]

. . . . .

The apparent crisis in present trends of Cuban economy, though an echo of the period of deflation immediately following the War, a reaction from the "dance of the millions," are principally *birth-pains of the coming industrial state.*

Zamora has proven the presence, or at least the possibility, of conditions preliminary to this development, but has underestimated the capitalistic spirit, the urge toward enterprise.

For, even if the capital is present, the workmen ready, the markets demanding goods, still there must be the man who undertakes things, the *homo economicus*, with his enterprise and push, the capitalistic spirit (whom Werner Sombart has placed in the foreground of the doctrine of modern capitalism), in order that modern industrial structure may be created out of latent wealth through the application of capital and labour. Fortunately, it is not necessary to import this spirit into Cuba. Here one can find those forces which accelerate the transition of society to new economic forms, but which at the same time intensify the painfulness of the change.

"The race, imaginative and precocious, is fertile in poets, heroes, and orators."[34] But the Cuban possesses economic initiative and enterprise, and has shown equal talent and interest for the financial affairs.

The Cuban's principal or exclusive occupation is no longer politics, as is the case with the white population of many Latin-American countries. The "dance" has benefited the country, in that it has attracted the attention of the majority of the population to economic questions and induced part of the educated class to abandon politics and pay more attention to business.

The years of the "dance" correspond to the epoch of

post-War speculation all over the world. The only difference was that the profiteers, "Schieber" and "Barons van Sip" (considering these as historical), have not inherited in Cuba a land destroyed by the War, or with paper-money inflation. At the end of 1920 it was, as Jenks correctly remarks, "a typically tropical country exploited economically by the foreigner."[35]

Then came the credit inflation, not all from the United States, but caused primarily by Cuban establishments of credit. It has become the custom in every book on Cuba to give the biography and describe the success of the main figures in Cuban economic history. But who in the country is not familiar with the beginning of the rise of Frank H. Steinhart, who through friendship and work with North American military authorities has come to his present position and recognition by the Cuban people; or Horace Seymour Rubens, who through co-operation with Marti has lent great service to the country and is considered the father of the Cuban railways? But also the names of an unfortunate "Pote," W. A. Merchant, and many others, should be mentioned in this connection, as well as the names of prominent still existing firms and contractors. It must be stressed that they have also contributed to the development of the business spirit of the country. The personal element became especially strong in Cuba, where personal ability was often the only fortune the immigrant enterprisers brought with them, and its importance was even intensified by the permanent political and economic struggles and the speculative character of the sugar market. "The dance of the millions" was a pronounced national phenomenon, which brought individual potentialities to the surface. The "dance" has changed the appearance of the city, has influenced social life; "the *colono* became a business man".[36] The "dance" has contaminated the Cuban youth with ideas of earning, but has at the same time welded the workers into a class through imported ideas and growing industrialization of society.

This presence of the spirit of capitalism is one of the most important conditions preparatory to the coming industrialization of the land.

. . . . .

How deeply instilled is the "Peligro Yanqui" on the island? Politically Cuba has become and remains independent, supported by a guarantee of help and protection from the United States. The dispute about the legal status of the Cuban Government has at present a pronounced theoretical significance. That they call it semi-protectorate, limited sovereignty, masked protectorate, etc., does not affect the error of the statement by Nearing and Freeman, that "Cuba is no more independent than Long Island."

The correct definition would be as follows: Cuba is a sovereign state, which has ceded a certain part of its sovereign rights by treaty to another state (the treaty forming a part of its own constitution).[37]

Does the danger exist that the United States might want to terminate this state of affairs and absorb Cuba? Even those who paint gloom, or try to do so, do not consider this danger seriously.

Why should the Yankees do it? What would they gain by it? Imperialistic political appetites, as we have seen, are for the United States no categorical imperative. The political, strategic, and economic interests of the big neighbour are sufficiently safeguarded. Furthermore, his world power is at present so great that he is not threatened by any danger from other governments (especially since the opening of the Panama Canal).

Cuba, on the other hand—aside from the Platt Amendment—will be very careful not to oppose its largest customer, provider, and financier. Economic factors bind Cuba more intimately and strongly to the United States than does the Platt Amendment.

An annexation would certainly harm the position of the

United States on the whole American continent; its treaty signatures and its commercial value would certainly work negatively, and probably prove harmful to its economic outbursts.

This is understood in all America. A political writer on *The Yankees in Santo Domingo* declares plainly: "The fate of the Pan-American doctrine depends upon the attitude of the United States toward any nation forming part of the Pan-American Union; if any Spanish-American Republic were a victim of the violence of any of the most powerful nations on the continent, this would be sufficient to make the others consider themselves freed from obligation toward the Pan-American Union, whose sole object is mutual protection and defence of common interests."[38]

And the foreign policy of the United States must reckon with that and does so; it adopts the policy of an honest merchant, whose motives are far from any desire to apply force in his dealings. That the Americans evacuated after the first occupa tion has made an impression on the entire world: "It was a novelty for a great power to keep its word to a small country."[39]

Moreover, one must not underestimate the increasing international importance of Cuba. "Cuba has won for itself a place in the world, a place in the sun";[40] and this furnishes also a moral protection against the feared danger. The thirty years of political independence prove that the experiment of Cuban independence has been justified.

At the same time, it is to be expected that the United States will renounce the Platt Amendment, which has outlived its usefulness in its present form. Its provisions are assured through the economic power of the United States; and regarding its main points, the young state has already so much political experience and tradition, that it will not give up its sovereignty voluntarily to a third power or follow a burdensome economic policy. The lien of the United States on the harbour and coaling stations should be retained, but the right of intervention which disturbs Cuban national feeling (and the interpretation was sometimes pretty broad in practice) should be relinquished. The Platt Amendment, in its present form, is not in harmony with the sovereignty of the state; it was first thought of only as a provisional measure. The experiment of the Cuban state has been successful—the Platt Amendment must go. On this point the best minds of both nations agree. One can find a good analogy here between the Platt Amendment as applied to Cuba on the one hand and the Monroe Doctrine as applied to South America on the other.

. . . . .

Of what importance to Cuba is economic penetration by the United States? It was at an early date that capital from the United States first began to fructify the neighbouring island.

Materially the economic participation of the United States in Cuba was a great success, especially when compared with the Spanish economic system. Spain had neither the idea of Greek expansion nor the creation of military colonies like Rome.[41]

The so-called Americanization of the island is not a new phenomenon. We have seen above that already in the 'eighties the influence of the United States was powerful. But, of course, Americanization of the external life, the material culture, has really made its greatest progress in the last thirty years.

Americanization took the form mainly of acquisition of control over the Cuban sugar industry by corporations of the United States. On Cuban soil these concerns have transplanted their usual methods of mass-production and their drive toward the reduction of the costs of production. The sugar industry, the main wealth of the island and the centre of her economy, is peculiarly sensitive to cyclical fluctuations; this caused and called forth the concentration of capital and the transition to forms of production on a large scale. "The Cuban is lacking in the stabilizing advantages afforded by great corporations, which absorb the investments of many individuals, thus easily accumulating such enormous capital sums that they are *able to resist economic crises without difficulty*"[42] (italics mine). Only by the mass-production of mammoth corporations can the costs of production of sugar be lowered and the Cuban position in the world market maintained.

Due to the peculiar conditions in Cuba, industrialization and commercialization proceeded at a relatively rapid rate, while the "Big Thirty" easily penetrated into the country, acquiring a great part of the world's sugar production. Thus in the Cuban sugar industry we are confronted with a familiar situation: investments make possible the erection of new or the enlargement of old plants, and bring about the exportation of machinery and equipment from the United States to Cuba; and sugar produced with the aid of this imported capital is shipped back to the United States. In this way the United States has so increased her domestic sugar business as to extend over Cuba.

But what effects has this Americanization? Writers from the United States are proud to state that "Present-day Cuba is rapidly becoming Americanized. Thousands act, think, talk, and look like Americans, wear American clothes, ride in American autos, use American furniture and machinery, often send their children to American colleges, live for a time in the States themselves or expect to do so, and eat much American food";[43] this list may be supplemented by American railways, street cars, telephones, telegraph, radios, omnibuses, hotels, and numerous other commodities and services, all of which have been brought about by mass-production.

If this Americanization, this economic penetration, is causing a mechanization and uniformity of life, is this not a universal phenomenon of our stage of economic evolution? This tendency is all-pervasive. Sooner or later Cuba must learn the new economic methods from the United States. She must adopt and use them in the interest of cheap mass-production, of industrialization of the country, and for the improvement of the material standards of living of the people. Acceptance of this material Americanism is a rational economic act, which from this point of view can only be welcomed.

Zamora explains this by citing the example of the great Cuban newspapers, which are completely Americanized externally, and have become great mainly through the exemption of newsprint paper from import duties. "Have our dailies lost their Cuban character on that account? Certainly not. With the importation of paper and machinery, and with the exploitation of advertising in the American way, great, prosperous, and strong Cuban enterprises have been established, which give employment to Cuban workmen, Cuban intellectuals, Cuban owners, and Cuban families."

"What would our dailies be to-day were it not for incorporation into the North American newspaper system? They would be one of the poor four-page sheets, badly printed on poor paper, with two articles, three cables, and four advertisements, such as abound in Latin America and continental Europe."[44]

Viewing this situation and analysing it, the realists declare that in Cuba the domination of the United States' capital is already an existing economically inevitable fact; the tariff union could bring no surprise more in this relation. But they emphasize the innocuousness of importing this capital; for, since it is impossible to industrialize the country on a large scale and to relieve the present crisis without foreign capital and tariff union with the United States, and since the continuation of present conditions of maladjustment involves great social and economic dangers, they recognize that "association is our best defence,"[45] as Zamora expresses it; they place their trust in co-operation, making North American capital share as a partner in the economic fate of Cuba.

Especially in the sugar industry there is pressure toward the establishment of a tariff union with the United States. And this is obvious, because the interested corporations in the United States wish also to clear away all impediments or barriers between their domestic and foreign business fields. (In this connection it is interesting to note the attitude toward this question adopted by beet-sugar producers in the United States and the sugar industry in her outlying possessions.)

One of the best authorities on the Cuban sugar industry states: "We are the destroyers of world sugar prices because we produce in a disorderly manner and without a predetermined plan. Once in a while we break the market with one million tons of sugar more than is expected of us. Such a catastrophe would fall on our own head."[46] Cortina favours the promulgation of a definite agreement with the United States. Is this wish of rationalization not corresponding to the desires of the "Big Thirty" and their plans in other branches of the industry?

Does not the danger exist that the mechanization of life such as has resulted in the United States will corrode the culture of the island? The Cuban state, which existed before the nation, adopted Spanish culture (against which the island fought before its liberation with the aid of the United States) as protection against the eventual cultural encroachment of North Americanism. Cuba adopted the material code of life. But in the intellectual relation Cuba does not owe even her capitalistic spirit to her North American neighbour. "Yankee capital did not bring to Cuba the mercantile and industrial spirit.[47]"

Albert Llamer Schweyer affirms the rôle of "Hispanismus" in Cuban life: "North American culture, by its economic power, its extended capitalism, the streams of gold from the super-powerful neighbour, has moulded our economic life in the last twenty years. The Spanish influence, to which the Cuban is more susceptible than to the culture of any other race, imposes by its presence an actual character transcending generations of her sons; this force, which is Spanish culture, would cut strongly in its homogeneity and persistence."[48]

But even after exposure for thirty years to the "Peligro Yanqui," the former colony became a land with its own history and culture; it is not a mechanical extension of Wall Street, as Raul Maestri affirms; and even Jenks, greater partner of these ideas, admits: "Cuba has developed its own culture, which resists Americanization."[49]

The union of the individual elements into numerous powerful "Centros" (it is estimated that one-third of the population is thus associated) is ostensibly also a strong protective wall against Yankee influence. These organizations are reminiscent of the Polish economic associations and unions established in German Poland by the Poles during their economic and cultural struggles before the War, as described by Ludwig Bernhard. The difference is that here there is no conscious cultural struggle, and the "Centros," having existed for decades, have a firm footing in the country, and were not created for this purpose in the first place. And even if the spirit of the "Centros" is more Spanish than Cuban, they serve nevertheless as a defence against Americanization.

Besides, Cuba is no longer entirely a land of pronounced social contrasts, a land of two distinct classes only: "a handful of very rich and highly cultured people and the mass of poor people."[50] The post-War period with its rousing economic exhilaration and distress has created a national class of merchants, and has also given the labourer some importance in the country.

At the beginning of the development of the Cuban state one might perhaps have spoken of a possible danger, since in Cuba, according to the remark of Schweyer, "the state was born without the nation and the population was converted into a people."[51] The "Peligro Yanqui" has not disturbed this evolution.

In 1862 José A. Saco was fond of asking: "Is there patriotism in Cuba?" To-day the answer is so free from doubt that the question now only calls to mind an historical period of the past. Even Calderon must concede that Cuba "opposes the Anglo-Saxon invasion, being still thoroughly Spanish, her deliverance being a matter of yesterday; but America also by the mixture of the two races, the conquerors and the vanquished, by the usual Latin virtues and defects." He is mistaken in maintaining that "the United States offer peace at the cost of liberty." On the contrary, the alternatives, "independence or wealth, progress or tradition," do not exist, for there is but one course—interdependence, which is the goal of his programme. "Only great streams of immigration under benevolent tyrants strong enough to enforce a lasting peace, only a new orientation of national life, setting business and industry and rural life before politics, could save the country from the painful fate which seems to be hers."[52] Even the romantic current in Cuba would not accept these opinions.

But does Calderon not contradict his own declaration in the following? "The civilizing work of the United States has been admirable. Once Spain was defeated and her colony conquered, they transformed the educational system, the finances, and the hygiene of the island to prepare the people for a liberty they ignored. It was four years before they gave it; four years of pedagogy."[53]

Despite the alleged intense "Peligro Yanqui," the integration of the nation, the stabilization of the state, and the economic evolution of the country have been in constant progress. Cuba of 1900 and Cuba of 1930 are too different even to bear comparison. To-day the Cuban problem is not in struggle against the invader, not at all a question of resistance, but a matter of quiet, well-planned, object-conscious organization.

• • • • •

Ramiro Guerra sees Cuba of the future as similar to Barbados or Canada. Jorge Roa, believing Cuba's individual personality to be distinct, declares: "Neither England nor Haiti."[54] The peculiar geographical situation of Cuba has led to the belief that Cuba has a special mission to perform with regard to the future of Latin America. José F. Gomez hoped that Cuba would become the polar star of a Latin federation.[55]

Cuba is especially well-prepared to play an important rôle

because of her geographical position, her native initiative, financial capacity, and intimacy with the world's greatest money and capital market and with its methods, and because of the relations of blood and language with Latin-American countries. Cuba can be the bridge, the point of contact, between North and South America, the financial intermediary, which fructifies the South with the gold of the North; the Cuba of the future appears rather as *the Holland* of America. It is by no means an accident that the science of international law, which has flourished in Holland, has now attained special importance on the island of Cuba. The Cuban should take the initiative, should study the business possibilities in the West Indies and Central and South America.

Havana could eventually develop into a financial centre of the Western Hemisphere. As before the War everyone in search of money had to go to London, which was then the world's money market, so will Latin America, with its financial worries, make its pilgrimage to Havana, the entrance into the circle of finance. The key in the Cuban escutcheon should not only be an historical reminiscence but should become a new truth.[56]

Even if this material link between Anglo-Saxon and Latin America is only *pia desideria*, Cuba has without doubt already become the point at which two cultures meet and mix.

It is significant that José Marti, the greatest Cuban patriot and apostle of independence, was at the same time a convinced propagandist in favour of the industrialization of Cuba and co-operation with the United States.

This island was the birthplace of Neo-Hispano-Americanism, which is the movement favouring co-operation between the United States and Latin America. Calderon must even acknowledge that "some Cubans, satisfied with the material progress effected, would prefer annexation. Others, and among them one of the most remarkable writers of the country, Señor Jesus Castellanos, are never tired, remembering their happy intervention, of calling the United States 'the great sister

Republic'."[57] Parker T. Moon emphasizes that "the American method is more subtle, achieving as it does the desired financial economic domination, without political annexation, and often, as in the case of Cuba, without much impairing political self-government. As an attempt to reconcile business interests with political principles, it has its philosophical as well as practical attractions."[58] And Jenks is sullenly compelled to concede that it is not a question of condemned imperialism, but "we must see in the history of our enterprises in Cuba a new type of international relations."[59]

All of the orientations—the pessimistic, the romantic, and of course the realistic—recognize the economic successes of Cuba under the benediction of incoming foreign capital. While the pessimists emphasize the incomplete sovereignty of Cuba and point at the foreign impingement on the culture, and while the romanticists[60] are afraid of the social consequences of mass-production, the realists agree with Neo-Hispano-Americanism, in that the defence against the "Peligro Yanqui" lies in industrialization, and that cultural Hispanism (in this case Cubanism) and materialistic Americanism are complementary phenomena. This idea is represented by Eliseo Giberga. He declares: "The influence of Britannic America is quite widespread in the neighbouring Latin-American republic. In not a few fields of life have the Cubans benefited by this contact."[61]

"All, or almost all, admit the political hegemony of the United States resulting from the war of 1898 and sanctified by the permanent treaty of 1903. All recognize the great economic influence of the United States, here in the economic life of the country, their favourable situation with regard to commercial activity established by the present reciprocity treaty. No one considers re-establishing political relations between Cuba and Spain. There is no basis for economic influence by the former mother country. The economic influence of Spain in the colonial period was negligible, if existent at all."[62] Giberga does not see any opposition between Pan-Hispanism and Pan-Americanism. To the Latin-American countries he asserts that there is no difference because they are striving to foster trade relations with *all* foreign countries,[63] United States and Spain included.

A similar theory extended on investigation of Porto Rico is to be found in another publication of Giberga.[64] These ideas are followed through in the book by Santiago Magariño y Ramon Puigdollers. The authors maintain that both movements are complementary, and that Cuba, the point of contact of two cultures, is a conspicuous example of a "synthesis of both doctrines." The authors even go farther, saying that the two civilizations fructify each other. "The two Americas already begin to interpenetrate through the contact and intercourse of the principal races."[65] These opinions extend "also to other Hispano-American republics. We start with Cuba, because of her singular geographical position between the two continents, as a possible approach."[66]

Fernando Ortíz (see Chapter II), F. Carrera Justiz, Orestes Ferrara,[67] and others in Cuba are of the same opinion.

The Yankee phobia is at its weakest on this "Americanized" island; the denial of imperialistic exploitation by the United States originated in Cuba; and the movement toward union, with regard to Latin continental or local federation, is weakest on this island.[68]

Thus a strong national consciousness along with a pronounced predominance of Spanish-Cuban culture do not interfere with the development of those economic possibilities afforded by relations with the United States and the peculiar geographical situation of the island.

A union of currency is a fact only in Cuba, although it has been a constant problem in the programme of official Pan-Americanism during the past forty years. Is it not symbolic of Neo-Hispano-Americanism that the United States dollar in Cuba bears the name of peso, and that a Spanish word serves to designate a coin of the United States? The transportation problem which has beset Pan-Americanism is solved so far as Cuba is concerned. A tariff union is in the making. And thus an essential part of the current economic programme of the continent is here being accomplished. Is it not further significant that after thirty years of international commercial intercourse with the United States the question of tariff union first arose on Cuban soil?

The Cuban experiment illustrates neither idealistic continentalism nor official Pan-Americanism, but indicates the course of Neo-Hispano-Americanism in recent times. It points to the possibility of peaceful co-operation and mutual participation of two different worlds which are simultaneously competing in other Latin-American countries. These two cultures have learned mutual tolerance and understanding.

This synthesis and the realization that such co-operation is in the interests of economic progress, this realistic attitude toward fact forces itself upon the most persistent Latin-American adversaries of the United States. Thus Manuel Ugarte emphatically declares: "We wish to collaborate with them (United States) in the work of discovery and development of the riches of the continent."[69] In one of the most sharp enunciations on the subject we read: "we admire this great country, and we are far from believing that the people are responsible for the errors of a few of its public men in high office. We hope for justice and for a revival of Pan-American fraternity which will give peace, progress, and liberty to all the nations of this continent."[70]

Rafael Reyes, ex-President of Colombia, declares: "The doubts and suspicions prevailing in South America as to the policy and intentions of the United States toward the other republics must disappear to make way for a true union of the two Americas."[71] And the ex-President of Honduras, Policarpo Bonilla, invites the United States to carry into practice the Wilsonian doctrine (Mobile speech), "and then American capital, immigration, industries and commerce will be welcome again in the Latin-American countries."[72]

But on the whole such opinions are being propounded by lesser luminaries, namely, in Argentine by the imperialist

Francisco Seeber;[73] Ernesto J. J. Bott, who is friendly to the United States, and who speaks of the "fantasy of Yankee imperialism";[74] Enrique Gill, who regards the United States as a "business partner" and Spain as a "spiritual partner";[75] Ignacio Calderon[76] in Bolivia; in Chile Guillermo Subercaseaux,[77] and before him Malaquias Concha, who believed that help from the United States in the organization of a Latin-American union could be secured on purely economic grounds partly because of European competition.[78]

Similarly, a recent anti-Yankee, who sees in union the only way to deliverance, admits that there is even for a united Latin America no possibility of economic progress without the co-operation of the United States. "Confronted with a united America, the country of Washington will learn how to limit its ambition, and will also understand how to pursue a policy of collaboration in order to develop peace and the amicable exploitation of the country's riches."[79] Even in Mexico one finds approximately the same opinions expressed by Antonio Manero.[80]

. . . . .

Mariano Aramburu maintains that "Hispano-Americanism and Pan-Americanism are virtually in conflict in our American world."[81] In Cuba such a struggle is non-existent. Here the economic realities of everyday life are victorious. The eternal dualism of Spanish America—the wavering between Don Quixote and Sancho Panza—does not exist on this island. Ariel and Caliban live here in peace, building together a new future. The Latin culture and the material civilization of the United States mutually cultivate the fecundity of the natural resources.

Neo-Hispano-Americanism is a current of thought which, in the words of José Santo Chocano, would result in a bi-continental union wherein the Adam from the North meets Eve from the South. This is a thought to which even Rubén Darío has occasionally given his support.

Cuba is the birthplace of this realistic Neo-Hispano-Americanism, which acknowledges that in the year 1930 it is modern capitalism and not the conquistadores or bandeirantes that holds leadership in history and moulds economic progress; it also recognizes that the future lies in progressive industrialization, and that course is impossible without the co-operation of the United States. This island confirms the apt remark of Spengler,[82] that "he whose idealism is provincial, whose standards of life are those of bygone times, must abandon the hope of understanding history, living in it, and creating it." And here in the Cuban laboratory the lessons of history are evident and comprehensible.

CHAPTER V

THE FUTURE

(*a*) INDUSTRIALIZATION[1]

Everything in South America is virtually in the making: the race, the nation, the economy, the culture. Everything is still in flux—*παντα ρεῖ*. Development is not proceeding everywhere with design or symmetry. In some cities a few skyscrapers dominate the skyline and hold prominence above a surrounding level of smaller buildings; in other places foundations are only begun. And yet it is a general characteristic of the entire continent that everything is in a process of construction. In spite of different stages of development, there is practically no difference in tendency between Argentine and Ecuador, between Chile and Bolivia, between Matto Grosso and São Paulo. The Heraclitean whirl is actual in the economy of the continent: railroads, highways, public utilities, towns, villages, palaces, log cabins, factories—all in construction. Sometimes the process is slow, sometimes it advances hysterically fast, often uneconomically, and without plan; but on it goes. Crises occur, construction temporarily ceases, and then after an interval chimneys puff again, factory machines hum, and the work is resumed. The course of this general construction reflects the transitional epoch of South America's economic development. It makes a change in her economic forms.

The present period of transition accounts for the pessimism and for the "malady" of the continent. The "illness" springs from the very nature of the changes which South America is suffering. And in them is the cure to be found.

What is the nature of this "illness"? It is possible, after considering the facts, to co-ordinate all the symptoms and causes of the illness into a single explanation, without scattering attention on irrelevant details; the political superstructure does not correspond to the economic foundation. There developed a permanent friction between the written constitutions and the prevalent social conditions, between law and economy; a collision between theory and practice, between words and action, between content and form. "Le grand changement," as Montesquieu called it, that change of status from colony to republic (often modelled after the example of the United States), was too sudden. The ideas of the French Revolution did not find the propitious economic conditions in South America. It was wellnigh impossible to establish a model republic and to organize an ideal government on a continent that lacked the simplest means of communication. It was impossible to transfer there the atmosphere of the ancient Greeks and Romans, and the ideas of the encyclopedists on an eremite continent, for South America was excluded from the outside world during the colonial period.

The transplanted ideas did not blossom; the economic soil was not fertilized by centuries of history. "All the existing riches were going to the metropolis,"[2] because "the whole object of Spain's colonial policy was to extract gold and silver from America and to force Spanish manufacturers and products upon the country."[3]

Secluded Paraguay under the dictator Françia is a symbol of the entire continent during the first fifty years of political independence.

Thus South America came to lead a double life. There developed a permanent dualism of words and actions, between which the chasm was being constantly deepened by the obsession of the dominant classes, with brilliant theorizing and idealistic speculation. Rufino Blanco Fombona felt this dramatic situation most vividly, which he expressed in his own obituary: Here lies a "soul of the sixteenth century, and a man of the twentieth century."

Theory and practice on this continent were not duly divorced, but were of different centuries. In spite of new political forms, the ancient regime held sway over South America long after her liberation, for the configuration of actual forces did not correspond to the political structure which had been transplanted from elsewhere. The bourgeoisie, the support of a democratic republic, was non-existent on this continent.

In this lack of harmony lies the primary cause of the South American malady. And thus the much-discussed defects and failings of South American social life fit not into logical but into historical categories; they are products of the epoch and not inborn to the spirit of the people, their soul, or racial peculiarities. The philosophy of *mañana*, the nebulosity of *más o menos*, the literature as *recreo*, the *almacen* character of the intellectuals, these are historical descriptives. From this point of view it is instructive to review Dickens's *American Notes*, or *Martin Chuzzlewit*, or Brooks's *As the Others See Us*, and to compare these writings with modern descriptions of South America.[4] The differences are merely those of time and place, but the trends of development are markedly similar.

The period of construction referred to above is in fact a decisive struggle in which the organism is attempting to overcome internal antagonism. It consists of filling the hundred-year-old republican forms with economic substance; it is distinguished by convulsive efforts at relief from the remaining poisons of economic feudalism.

The modern era in South America is not only a transitional stage, but also a gradual demolition of forms which, though physically existing, have become inorganic. To use Sombart's striking words, "these agricultural people have succumbed to the outrageous desire of eating to the fill."[5]

This process is the start of industrialization on the continent. It is also a transformation of the social system and of the entire mode of life and its standards; it is a continued ingression of money economy; it is a capitulation of provincialism and local pride; it is a farewell to mediævalism.

The essential element in this transition is the adoption of money economy, which is being brought into South

American life through modern finance and technology. The progressive significance of money economy lies in the fact that it crushes the reign of rustic habit and intellectual narrowness. In this sense the greedy, self-seeking type of usurer, one of the first products of early money economy (like the Russian "Kulak" or the so-called "local banker"[6] in British India), constitutes a phenomenon which indicates economic progress. This is so because he represents the first stage of individual self-determination. This is why the owner of a *venda* in Brazil or the *almacenero* in Argentina are manifestations of economic progress.[7]

The greatest minds of the Americas foresaw this impending evolution and did their utmost to induce their fellow countrymen to enter the lists of enterprise.

As early as 1816, in a letter to Benjamin Austin from Monticello, Thomas Jefferson indicated the approach of a new era. "We must *now* place the manufacturer by the *side of the agriculturist*. Experience has now taught us that manufacturers are now as necessary to our independence as to our comfort."[8] (Italics his.) Ten years later Frederick List stated that "a merely agricultural people remains always poor,"[9] and he emphasized that the aim of the United States "was always and ever to raise her manufactures and commerce."[10]

Sarmiento and Alberdi considered applying this system of "American Political Economy" to South America. It is significant that these two political adversaries should unite on this programme; it is even more interesting because on the whole Alberdi adopted the European orientation, while Sarmiento regarded the United States as a model. In one of Sarmiento's books, written in 1845, which, like his *Facundo*, even at present sounds contemporary, we read the following appeal: "South America has remained backward and is going to lose her Providential mission to become a part of modern civilization.... Let us achieve the stage of development of the United States. Let us be America, like the sea is the Ocean. Let us be the United States."[11]

"How can *this* America follow the prosperous and free course of the *other*? To assimilate—this has been done with other European races, thus improving native blood through modern ideas, and putting an end to the Middle Ages."[12] But Sarmiento was aware of the pains which the transitional period would necessarily provoke. Similar is the counsel rendered by the much calmer Alberdi, who, however, lacks the ebullience of the great Gaucho. He believes that "In economic or political problems, the best example for America to follow is America herself. In economic problems North America is the perfect model for South America."[13] Alberdi, the former young dreamer, the conspirator, the Saint-Simonist, calls for practical work: "Without manufactures and without her own merchant marine South America is dependent upon industry and the merchant marine of Europe, the continent which transports in her own boats the products of the factories to the American consumers."[14]

Are these not the words of Jefferson? Is this not the "American Political Economy" of Frederick List? And, like Sarmiento, Alberdi is conscious of the nature of the South American illness, the causes of which he locates in the permanence of heroic wars and revolutions. As a remedy he summons the war heroes to becone plain citizens working for the acquisition of wealth, on which the power of the nation should be based.[15]

Alberdi's economic programme is industrialization. He is aware that this "chronic illness" requires chronic treatment.[16] The significance of Alberdi's and Sarmiento's activities can be compared with that of Joaquín Costa in Spain, whose aim was the Europeanization of his country. Their activities may further be compared with the revisionist branch of Russian Marxians, which saw the necessary and preliminary conditions of development in an advanced capitalism. These revisionists called upon the country to become "educated in the school of capitalism."

Neither in South America nor in Latin America has anyone

proclaimed the programme of industrialization more clearly than these two great Argentines. But this programme had not been realized at that time; and these were only words, soon to be forgotten. While the words of Joaquín Costa were at least heard and listened to, the Argentines never succeeded even in arousing the attention of their contemporaries. Of Sarmiento and Alberdi one may say the opposite of what Rufino Blanco Fombona wrote about himself: Living in the nineteenth century, they had ideas and desires of the twentieth.

It is not accidental that Sarmiento and Alberdi have suddenly come into the centre of modern young industrialism's interest in Argentina. It is in fact a true rediscovery of the economic literature of the middle of the last century, which assumes even greater significance because of the fact that the young, pessimistic generation, infected with the tragic dualism of South America, is able to explain its illness thereby and state its symptoms, but is unable to return to the advice and the programme of the great Argentines. It is rather an exception to the general rule that the Bolivian pessimist, Alcides Arguedas, suggesting a "National therapeutic," refers to the "iron surgeon" Joaquín Costa. But even in this case the Argentines are neglected.[17]

Even on the island of experiment, Cuba, it is difficult to trace continuous trends of thought with regard to industrialization. Programmes were being proclaimed and readily abandoned. On this island the national hero, Marti, developed a similar programme of industrialization. Fernando Ortíz's inimical attitude toward Hispanism was a result of his plan of industrialization. He calls attention to the paradox that the Spaniards intend to re-Hispanize America, while Spain herself ought to be Americanized.[18] "Europeanization for Spain is what Americanization is for Cuba."[19] [Is not the Americanization of economic methods the question of the day in Europe?]

South America after the War has become ready for a regenerative movement. This movement must and does find its inspiration in the writings of Sarmiento and Alberdi. The continent needs an intellectual leader and is waiting for "El que vendrá" (Rodó).[20] Industrialization is advancing. The conflict between the country and the town, farm and factory, has already appeared. The entire economic system, characterized by the extensive cultivation and colonial methods of commercial capitalism, must give way before the crushing advance of new forms. The period of storm and stress of young industrialism is in its first stage of development. Buenos Aires is no longer a "pretentious capital in a pastoral republic."[21]

The twentieth century has already seen the beginning of industrialization in several countries of the continent. The World War gave new vigour to this movement. Sudden changes in the habitual course of events have forced people to think, to work, and to enter upon new paths. New business possibilities and wartime business exhilaration have helped to multiply these attempts. Governments have learned that "the dominant motive of each nation has been to secure as large an amount as possible of economic independence." They all played the same horse, "industrialization."

As yet no study has been made of the influence of the World War upon the South American continent. Existing material and preliminary studies are not sufficient for a thorough investigation of the subject.[22]

During the War trade restrictions introduced by the Allies, inflated prices, and transportation difficulties caused the development of several new industries in South America. The course of development was similar everywhere. "Traditionally pastoral and agricultural, the Argentine Republic ignored her industry; the World War of 1914 has called industry into existence. Though hesitating during this period, industry through a powerful effort has, as much as possible, achieved success and was able to provide, in an improvised manner, for all the needs of the country, in spite of the large decrease of European imports."[23]

It is, of course, an exaggeration to say that "the time is possibly not distant when the industry of Argentina will become so powerful as to be able to provide its own markets and then to compete with the American and European products on the world market. The manufacturing countries will some day see a new industrial power emerge at their sides, whose existence they had not suspected."[24] Industrial psychology radiates from this statement.

How rapidly the new industrialism is gaining foothold in Argentina is shown by the following description of Souvaine:

> Taken by surprise and with modest means at its disposal, young industry began on a temporary scale. There were no modern factories: a back-yard dwelling or a barn and random machine; a handful of workers recruited, Lord knows where, and the owner at the same time; the technical manager organizes, Lord knows how, a factory; and the factory began to produce without the public suspecting its existence. Thus the capital and its suburbs were covered with a multitude of miniature enterprises, which enabled the population to get nourishment and clothing, and to live without the slightest privation during the period of the Great War. But everything in Argentina matures quickly. Evolution there proceeds at a rapid pace; soon industrial structures were erected, replacing the temporary installations; the best materials were imported from England and America to take the place of the antiquated machinery; engineers took over the technical management of the enterprises, while the owner supervises the commercial branch of the business, and thus quietly and imperceptibly the pastoral and agricultural Argentina has become an industrial power, to the great astonishment of the Argentine himself.[25]

Brazil presents the same picture:

> After the first shock Brazil started to work, to do for itself what it could in the development of its resources. It has accomplished much during the War. Vast stretches of land have been put under production. Great impetus has been given to the cattle industry. Brazil has increased its production in cotton, corn, and in other food products. Its cotton manufacturing industry has shown remarkable strides. . . .
>
> Brazil has probably attained a greater degree of economic independence during the War than almost any of the Pan-American countries; this on account of diversity of its resources. With the exception of coal, Brazil is abundantly supplied with practically all of the important natural resources.

> The development of Brazil's economic independence has been delayed by the War in so far as it has been unable to raise capital to develop those resources which would materially aid it in achieving its economic independence. In this connection may be mentioned the enormous iron-ore deposits in Brazil and the country's ambition to develop a steel industry sufficient to take care of its needs.[26]

Four years later the Department of Commerce, as a result of a new investigation, stated:

> Industrially, Brazil ranks first among the South American Republics. The country now produces most of the textiles, hats, shoes, clothing, tinware, enamelled ware, furniture, and many other items of domestic need, and has even gone into the production of pig-iron, although the coal supply is none too good. The assistance of the Government through a highly protective tariff and by means of special favours has been a decisive factor in the development of the country's manufactures, and as a continuation of the present policy for some years to come is prophesied, there seems to be no reason why further rapid progress should not be experienced. Manufacturing is to a great extent carried on along modern lines, although there are countless numbers of small shops using old-fashioned methods. Profits have on the average been large, many of the textile mills, for instance, having earned net incomes of 40 and 50 per cent. the last few years.[27]

The successes in several branches of industry are immense. "It is necessary to specially mention two branches of industry which achieved a considerable success during the last few years: these were the textile and shoe industries. For several years Brazil used to import English cotton products in large quantities. To-day Brazil's own production is sufficient not only to cover the needs of the country, but also leaves a surplus, which is being exported. In 1919 the value of cotton products sold abroad was £54,411.

"In 1913 Brazil imported shoes amounting to £161,642. In 1919 this import decreased to £7,452. One can say that Brazilian-made shoes replaced the foreign-made article. It is interesting that we even export a certain quantity of shoes; in 1919 we sent abroad shoes the value of which amounted to £1,065. Surely this is not an imposing figure. But there it is. Doubtless this trend is very significant to the development of our industry."[28]

A compilation of data of 1924 shows that the national production of Brazil covered 99·04 per cent. of shoe consumption, 90·6 per cent. of furniture used, and 86 per cent. of textiles consumed.[29]

In the same way Argentina has become emancipated with respect to leather products, Venezuela with regard to paper products. In other countries of South America industrial changes were proceeding along similar lines. There were, of course, differences in the rate of growth, the industries developed, and the extent of development. The tendency, however, remains the same everywhere. That Chile, Bolivia, Peru, and Uruguay also entered upon an era of industrial development can be seen from the report on the investigation of the Federal Trade Commission, which emphasizes the incipient competition of national industries with foreign countries, especially when aided by progressive protectionism.[30]

Industrialization forged ahead, accompanied by a growth of protectionist feeling. No studies exist on the history and characteristics of the tariff policies of the ten South American countries. Without these investigations, it is barely possible to know the exact character and significance of the tariffs. One is confronted with the problem as to whether the tariffs represent fiscalism or protectionism, or, what is more probable, a transition from pure fiscalism to protectionism, varying with the differences in economic development of the various countries. It may, however, be stated that in Brazil and Argentina the influence of the industrial class upon the tariff system has already reached considerable proportions.

The only review of the tariff systems prevailing in South America maintains that "the tariffs of South American countries are, in the main, revenue measures, although most of them have some protective features."[31] Protectionism in South America is intended not only to help the already existing industries, but also to promote the establishment of new industries. "By omitting duties most of the countries encourage the establishment of new industries and the building of railroads and public works."[32]

The Federal Trade Commission is much more decided in its opinions on the character of the tariffs. "No more misleading observation has been made about some Latin-American tariffs than that they are solely revenue tariffs, not enacted for the purpose of protecting national industries. It is true that in almost all the countries they are the chief source of government revenue, but it is indisputable, as statements of prominent South Americans in this report show, that one of the avowed objects of the tariff of Brazil, Uruguay, Argentina, Chile, and Peru is to foster and protect their nascent industries."[33]

In Argentina the tariff throughout the greatest part of the nineteenth century was mainly of a fiscal character, expressing free trade tendencies in principle. The 'eighties saw a change in attitude. Protective tendencies began to show their influence. In the post-War period protectionism was definitely established. The Brazilian tariff which is being considered as ultra-protectionist is in fact mainly of a fiscal nature.[34] One can hear in Brazil prudent voices propagating a moderately educational but not prohibitive tariff: "We ought to be protectionists, but with prudence."[35]

The disposition towards large-scale production develops clearly into a tendency towards concentration. There is also a lack of preliminary studies on the subject. This strong tendency toward large-scale production is to be noticed most clearly in Brazil. The shoe[36] and the match[37] industries there serve as examples.

The greatest success in large-scale production has been attained in textile manufacturing in Brazil. In 1929 this industry claimed 347 factories and employed 125,000 workers, produced commodities valued at 1,000,000 contas. Of these 347 factories, 97 are located in the State of São Paulo, and 91 in the State of Minas Geraes.[38]

Industrial centres are being built up. And São Paulo, which

is usually characterized as a coffee city, is more properly a Brazilian Manchester or Chemnitz, just as the State of São Paulo, disregarding coffee production, reminds one of Saxony. Because the problem of marketing the products has hardly arisen, the population being commodity-hungry and having increasing purchasing capacity, the question of the location of industrial units has also not assumed remarkable importance as yet. Location at present is merely a matter of accident. It is, however, to be regretted that no systematic planning is being undertaken. If cities like Bello Horizonte in Minas Geraes can be projected and built according to a previously accepted plan, the question of location of industries might be dealt with in the same manner.

This industrial development is not spread evenly over the entire continent, either in regard to time or degree of advancement. The continent is at present markedly heterogeneous economically, in spite of the many observers, scholars, and travellers who usually speak of the homogeneity of South America. They are in fact deceived by the unity of language, religion, and customs; they base their contention upon common history and common social ailments and phenomena. And often they erroneously conclude that the future of the several countries will also be similar.

Compared to the small continent of Europe, divided into many independent states, where the religion and nationality of each country accentuate the variety of the panorama; compared to vast Asia, where in this respect circumstances are much the same; to North America, where reign is divided between the Spanish and Anglo-Saxon elements; to Africa, where the language of the mother countries are used alongside of the native tongues, South America, like Australia, seems to present a perfect continental monism, resulting from the integration of Iberian language, religion, custom, and history.

This sort of thinking is constantly being politically exploited.[39] Even the cautious Bryce states: "But marked as are the differences between the various republics, they all have something in common, something that belongs to South America as opposed to Europe, or North America, or Australia."[40]

It is, however, necessary to state that the South American continent is virtually a museum of the variety of economic history. All the stages of economic evolution are existent there. They constantly interpenetrate, are in conflict, and influence one another.

Karl Bücher might find here interesting material for an eventual third volume of his *Origin of the National Economy*, and Bernhard Harms could find enough data here to substantiate his contention of the existence of world economy and its expansion. All of Bücher's stages of economic evolution are present here, being at the same time linked up with world economy. *Certanejo* is still in the rude state of natural economy, the small interior towns still possess the character of Bücher's second stage, while national economy predominates on the coast; but all are already integrated into world economy.

The economic evolution of the continent did not advance consistently through the same stages throughout the continent. All the phases of economic development appear simultaneously. They do not follow each other in a historical series. "Here in Spanish America it has been going on under the eyes of the civilized world in an age when everything is or can be known, and it has taken only a hundred years."[41] Where the llamas supplied transportation facilities yesterday, automobiles are in use to-day, and aircraft is introducing even faster means of communication. To-day—natural economy; to-morrow—modern capitalism.

The economic development of South America is far from being uniform; the continent is too large for such uniformity, and the climatic, geographical, and historical conditions of the various countries are too divergent. The continent nurses within its boundaries the vast enigma, Brazil, Europeanized Argentina, superficially Anglicized Chile, and cloister-like Peru, which is attempting to harmonize Spanish colonial methods with the modern urbanity of Lima. "Bolivia suggests the seventeenth century and Peru the eighteenth century, and even in energetic Chile there is an air of the older time and soothing sense of detachment. But here all is of the twentieth century with suggestions of the twenty-first."[42] Economic and social life is beginning its invasion of the interior of the continent, although there is still a great difference between the coast and the hinterland. The coast, especially on the Atlantic, is well settled. Pernambuco, Bahia, Rio de Janeiro, Santos, Montevideo, Buenos Aires, Valparaiso, Callao, all present an imposing façade of the continent in construction. But the spirit of modern life is already reaching *certanejo* in the farthest corner of Amazonas, and the Indian in the Bolivian Chaco.

As late as the nineteenth century the typical *fazendeiro* was accustomed to say proudly: "My house buys only salt, iron, powder, and lead—nothing else."[43] The motto *omnia domi nascuntur* still had a wide application. In the twentieth century even the humble *certanejo* is a cog in world economy, in spite of the many conditions of primitive economy which prevail in his life; rubber, cotton, sugar connect him, though indirectly, with the world markets. In the narrow scope of his activities world economy and natural economy operate side by side.

Between the two extremes of coast and desert lies the vast South American interior, varying greatly in its geographical and political complexion, quasi-modern as in Argentina, sorrowfully backward as in Matto Grosso.

There are certain types of evolution to be distinguished on this continent. The various lines and tendencies of this evolutionary process do not always correspond to political boundaries; they are not definite types; they do not suit each and every country; they may often be found together in one country.

One can find on this continent a prominent *European tendency* represented by Buenos Aires, with its striving, internally and externally, to imitate Paris, with its true and sham culture and snobbishness. "The city of Buenos Aires must be considered to-day as the most European of entire Spanish America."[44] "Buenos Aires is nearer to Paris than to Madrid."[45] It "is a large European city," confirms Clemenceau.[46] The same European character is visible in Cordoba and Tucuman, which, outside of their economic importance, are on the road to becoming the centre of culture, like Salamanca and Coimbra, like Heidelberg and Oxford, like Harvard and Columbia.

Typical of this tendency is Chile, with its mountains and lakes, its fruit and garden cultivations, its landscapes resembling those of Italy and Switzerland, which, like Argentine, organized its army according to German patterns, but its navy on English standards. It has developed its trade under the English, German, and North American leadership, and strives to play the rôle of the Englishman in South America. In South America the most urbanized state is Argentina, one-third of whose population dwells in the cities.[47] The Brazilian, on the contrary, is primarily "a man of the country." Even Lima is illustrative of this tendency, although Peru as a whole is not. This city in which European urbanization is forging successfully ahead resembles simultaneously Rothenburg and Hildesheim, Lourdes and Escoral.[48] A French writer, in order to emphasize Argentina's advanced status, declared: "Having left the metro in Paris, the traveller finds it in Buenos Aires."[49] This European trait especially characterizes the AC states.

Parallel to this tendency there developed a drift toward the adoption of the *North American way* of life with its tempo, uniformity, mass-production, standardization, struggle for existence, emphasis on superlatives, and money-making point of view.

Representative of this tendency is São Paulo, a city of a million inhabitants, grown from a small town within a period of twenty to twenty-five years, and which resembles Chicago or San Francisco, where the construction of a new building is begun every hour. To this type of city belong Rosario in Argentina and many other rapidly expanded South American towns. Of the same character is the progress of settlement in Rio Grande do Sul, where every ninety days a new colony is established. Undoubtedly this development has not yet reached as high a degree of North Americanization as in the United States (one often encounters amazing contrasts, such as a skyscraper standing beside a barn), but the tendency is beyond dispute.

In Brazil this tendency still has to contend with the *colonial mode of life*, as in Rio de Janeiro, where, in spite of American and European influence, there still remain the original and autochthonous characteristics of the country. The city presents a farrago of European, North American, Negro, and Indian ideas, cultures, tastes, and traditions—seeds which in Brazil's fecund soil and under her tropical sun grew into something rich and strange.

"If Paris has to have its Haussmann, the prefect of the Seine, so Rio must have its Pereira Passos."[50] The modern Rio de Janeiro with approximately two million inhabitants, and numerous skyscrapers, is not a typically North American city. It emulates neither New York nor Paris, in spite of the strong French influence throughout Brazil, which is even more pronounced than in Argentina. Rio de Janeiro is and remains Rio. It is neither a copy of Europe nor of the United States of America. To its kind belong Bahia, Brazil's Rome, and Recife, Brazil's Venice. Everything in this land is in *statu nascendi.*[51] Countries in the northern part of the continent, namely Colombia and Venezuela, are also to be classed with that group of states where the emphasis upon Americanization is unmistakable.

Industrialism is extending its sphere of activity and influence toward the interior. Each new railroad and highway draws new areas into the whirl of industrial life, awakens new forces which spur on further progress, and serves as an agency for the extension of money economy over the hitherto backward provinces. It is a process requiring decades for its completion, which cannot proceed with a uniform rate in the various countries. It is a process in which modern capitalism must first conquer the coast and then slowly colonize the interior.

The fundamental conditions essential to industrialization vary with the character of the country. They vary because of the differences in the sources of energy: the oil resources, lumber, and electric power, not to mention coal. Besides, the amount of natural riches and their accessibility are not uniform in many countries and provinces. These conditioning elements must be taken into account in any study of the process of industrialization.

Natural riches are to be found everywhere, whether one speaks of the land of the endless pampas, the country of ten thousand silver mines (Bolivia), or the land where "the beggar is sitting on a hill of gold" (as Humboldt calls Peru).[52] "Unexploited wealth abounds in America. Forests of rubber, as in the African Congo; mines of gold and diamonds, which recall the treasures of the Transvaal and the Klondyke; rivers which flow over beds of auriferous sand, like the Pactolus of ancient legend; coffee, cocoa, and wheat, whose abundance is such that these products are enough to glut the markets of the world."[53]

One must not forget that "the physical features of South America are on a more gigantic scale than North America. Its mountains as a rule are higher, its rivers broader and deeper, its forests more impenetrable";[54] though over-optimistically it has been stated "that the Republic of Argentine could support 100,000,000 inhabitants without recurring to chemical fertilization."[55] Volumes have been written about the natural riches of Brazil. One of the official publications in the United States emphasized that "about 48 per cent. of Brazil's total area, approximately 988,000,000 acres, is covered by forests. The forest reserves of this country are varied and principally unlimited."[56]

"Brazil has great mineral wealth. The State of Minas Geraes ("General Mines") owes its name to the variety and abundance of useful and valuable minerals. The plateau of south-eastern

Brazil consists of deeply eroded horizontal strata, bordered on the east by crystalline metamorphic rocks of the Serro do Mar. Age has weathered the surface layers. Deposits of manganese and iron lie almost exposed at the surface. Coal measures are exposed in Rio Grande do Sul and Santa Catharina. Diamonds are washed out of the blue clay of disintegrated ancient lavas. Gold and silver are mined. Monazite sands and mica are produced in appreciable quantities. Petroleum has been developed to a small degree. Tungsten, copper, nickel, lead, platinum, salt, and a score of other minerals lie accessible to exploitation."[57]

The general economic foundation of Chile, Peru, and Bolivia consists of mineral riches.[58]

Chile is supposed to possess:

	Millions of Tons
Nitrate	2,000
Copper (mines investigated) ..	3,000
Iron (mines investigated) ..	2,500
Coal (mines investigated) ..	2,000

Gold, silver, and copper are being exploited everywhere, from Guayaquil to Patagonia; besides, Peru possesses petrol, and in diminishing importance lead, mercury, nickel, bismuth, and borax. Bolivia is able to produce tin in considerable quantities, and in Chile nitrate is the chief constituent of her riches. Besides, Chile has begun to produce hard coal, manganese, and sulphur.[59]

The domestic market is potentially immense, for the present market is, in fact, almost always hungry. Even the elementary material needs of the masses are not as yet satisfied. That is why colonial markets are always growing much more rapidly than European markets. The gradual establishment of money economy adds a fresh impetus to the creation of new markets, which automatically expand through the opening of new areas and through the growth of industrialization. The uniformity of satisfying economic wants in the United States finds its parallel in South America in the uniformity of unsatisfied material wants.

The labour problem varies in its intensity and extent in the different countries. On the whole, however, Alberdi's principle remains true: "in America, to govern means to populate." Immigration into this continent is in its infancy as yet. The immigration policy of the United States has simplified the problem for South America because the flow of immigrants is now automatically directed towards the south. However, until the present time, there was no mass-immigration similar to that in the United States. The governments of South America are already initiating a regulated immigration policy. Several of them are even introducing restrictions modelled after those of the United States, which, however, are economically unjustified at present.

The exploitation of natural riches, the organization of a large market, in fact the whole industrialization process, is impossible without a broad transportation programme. Without means of transportation, the unlocking of the interior is unthinkable. South America's material suffering largely arises from the transportation problem. When we realize how important the horse was for the *gaucho*, we can then understand the economic revolution that is brought about by a new railroad, steamship line, automobile highway, or airplane route. For the interior the construction of any such line of communication is equivalent to shortening by a decade the natural course of development.

The transportation problem is closely allied with another kindred problem: the lack of capital. The national capital market is uniformly unorganized. Calderon is in error when he declares that "there is no national capital."[60] In several countries the formation of capital has already achieved considerable proportions. But the lack of any organized capital market whatsoever, the ineffective organization of the national banking systems, the embryonic state of the present securities markets[61]—all serve to impede the co-operation of national capital with industrialization.[62]

An investigation in Chile revealed that out of an aggregate of 32,000,000 pesos of capital, about 18,000,000 are of national origin.[63] But a part of the so-called foreign capital is in reality native. A large portion of these deposits in the foreign banks of South America is of local origin, while the investments and loans of these banks are considered foreign. Thus part of the financing of South America through her foreign banks is accomplished with native capital. German banks especially have applied this method (Germany has usually replaced her lack of capital by an exemplary organization).[64] This method is now used on a large scale by branches of the United States banks.

At the same time, several South American countries are beginning to export capital. Argentina and Chile undoubtedly show tendencies in this direction. Argentina capital dominates in Paraguay, is represented in the neighbouring parts of Bolivia, is penetrating into Uruguay, and until after the War was conspicuous in Rio Grande do Sul (at present, however, it is largely replaced by capital from the United States). Chile is participating in many enterprises in Bolivia and Peru. And in this manner there is developing in South America a situation which could have been witnessed in the United States at the beginning of the twentieth century; they are simultaneously borrowers and lenders.

"The United States was still, on the eve of the War, among the debtor nations; the amount of European capital invested there, principally in railroad bonds, was valued at between $4,000,000,000 and $5,000,000,000. On the other hand, the Americans had made investments, although for a much smaller amount, hardly equalling one-quarter or one-fifth of the former sum, in some countries of the New World, particularly Canada, Mexico, and Peru."[65]

The whole of South America depends upon foreign capital. It is evident that Paul M. Warburg's advice must and will be followed. His advice to South America is that the borrowed sums should be obtained not from one but from several states. It would be very helpful, if it were possible, to attract neutral capital, from countries such as Sweden, which is now witnessing a period of great exhilaration, Switzerland, Holland, or Belgium. But the fact is that without foreign capital the economic progress of the continent is impossible. South America can, of course, count also upon an influx of capital as a consequence of the probable increase of immigration from Southern Europe.

Another important source of capital is and will be industry of the United States which, as shown above, is constantly penetrating the several countries through the expansion of the "Big Thirty." It is also probable that convalescent Europe (and France chiefly) will open its capital markets to South America, and in doing so will undoubtedly neutralize to a greater degree the United States' financial influence in this sphere.

That capital will flow into the South American continent no one doubts. The high yield attracts the investor, and the possibility of great gains and the internal pressure toward expansion are sufficient incentives for industrial outlays.

The problem arises whether, foreign initiative excluded, the capitalistic spirit in South America is mature enough to play its designated part in this process of industrialization. This constitutes one of the most interesting and actual problems which confronts South America at the present time. Argentina's imperialistic policy constantly denies that the countries whose population is partly coloured (meaning Brazil, and thus emphasizing Argentina's "Europeanism"), or which lie in the tropics, are able to provide the much-needed leadership. The already well-known pessimistic taint goes farther than that. It declares that the *pereza*, the *arroganza*, and all those other imponderables are the inborn attributes of the South American soul and of the race.

We shall not bother about the embittered struggle between the experts on racial problems, on the one hand, and those who exalt popular desire for a homogeneous race, on the other. We shall set aside the consistent tendency of Argentina to become isolated from all that is native to South America; we shall omit from consideration the struggle between Lusitanians and Spaniards over racial problems, and the absence of pure races either in Spain or in other Latin countries. This absolute relativity of the racial principle, especially with regard to countries with great immigration, has been already emphasized by Bolivar.

"We are not Europeans," wrote Bolivar, "nor Indians either; but a kind of half-way species between the aborigines and the Spaniards; American by birth, European by right, we find ourselves forced to dispute our titles of possession with the natives, and to maintain ourselves in the country which saw our birth in spite of the opposition of invaders; so that our case is all the more extraordinary and complicated. . . . Let us be careful not to forget that our race is neither European nor North American; but rather a composite of America and Africa, than an emanation from Europe, since Spain herself ceased to be European by virtue of her African Arab blood, her institutions, and her character."[66]

The race is at present as it was in Bolivar's times; it is in the making. Even José Vasconselos is compelled to speak of "a conglomerate of types and races."[67] And Calderon is forced to join Vasconcelos and admit that in the problem of race we deal with "a caravan of races."[68]

But all this discussion about the purity of races does not throw any light on the problem of capitalistic spirit—the economic motivation of entrepreneurial activity, the *auri sacra fames*, the striving for gain—all these psychological qualities which have accelerated modern capitalism in Europe and in the United States. The problem is more interesting because the two prevailing economic theories cannot be applied to South America. Max Weber could not possibly find any Puritanism, and Werner Sombart any Judaism, on this continent.

In fact, by combining both theories, one could explain the economic success of the United States through the presence of the two elements. Followed to a logical conclusion, these theories deny the existence of capitalistic spirit in South

America. This opinion is corroborated by the fact that no large fortunes have been made in recent times in South America. This is, however, a pronounced vulgarization of these theories: they are not to be understood as universal theories; they are merely explanations of the historical European capitalism. Broadly considered, Puritan and Jew are simply historical illustrations of a more general type, which so often acts as the pioneer of capitalism: the foreigner, the immigrant uprooted from his customary way of life, who is fighting for his future and success under entirely new economic conditions, the innovator who in his new fatherland voluntarily forgets his former history and traditions. Oswald Spengler discovered "Puritanism" even in the Hindu, ancient and Arabic cultures. This is another proof that the capitalistic spirit is an historical and not a logical category.[69] Is it not more accurate to explain this interdependence not by racial and religious phenomena, but by the social peculiarities of the emigrant, who through social selection seems to be best fitted to unravel the destiny of his new country? Who were the Puritans in the United States? Pioneers, emigrants, and foreigners. Who are the Jews in the world?

This broader interpretation of the origin of the capitalistic spirit leaves no doubt as to its existence and activity in South America. It is continuously receiving new vigour with the influx of new blood from other continents. The opening of the interior and its subjugation by money economy automatically induces a capitalistic spirit together with the abandonment of the narrowness of natural economy. The change in the modes of economic activity brought with it a corresponding change in the outlook of that activity, while the opposite process is taking place simultaneously. There developed a permanently mutual interdependence, a levelling up, an adjustment.

One can notice that in South America (it already having taken place in Cuba) interest in politics is waning in the intellectual circles. This indicates the end of the previously existing belief (to-day still current in some countries, such as Bolivia) that politics and nothing else is the mission of the white man in South America. Interest is clearly becoming focussed on economic endeavour.

A sort of renaissance of the conquistadores and bandeirantes of colonial times is in sight. They will appear in new garb, and as knights of the new economic order, they will once again pass across the continent. Especially in Brazil the restless *Nortista*, the energetic *Paulista*, the freedom-loving *Gaucho*, the cosmopolitan *Carioca*—all of them promise to contribute to the rousing of the capitalistic spirit.[70] In São Paulo the day of *paciencia* and *ámanhã* has passed.

. . . . .

Industrialization must break through the monism of South American economy, the monism which consists of the predominantly mono-productive character of the countries. The economic life of each of the countries depends primarily upon one product only, so that no distribution of risk is possible. What coffee is to Brazil and Colombia, cattle is to Uruguay, nitrates to Chile, zinc and tin to Bolivia, cocoa and coffee to Ecuador, and wheat and refrigerated meats to Argentina. All of the South American states are in a greater or lesser degree subject to this tendency, and in this respect they resemble the *ante bellum* south of the United States. In their economic development they have followed the line of least resistance. They have constructed only one branch of economic production and allowed their other potentialities to remain untouched. And the result is that South America suffers more intensely from the world's cyclical fluctuations in production and prices of these chief and few products. The continent has become highly susceptible to temporary successes as well as to recurring crises. Thus Brazil lost its dominating position in the production of sugar, cotton, and rubber, and had also endangered, at present, its coffee supremacy. All this is a consequence of an attempt to carry all the eggs in one basket.

The growth of industrialization mitigates the risks involved in mono-production. At the same time, however, it extends the market, while commercializing and cheapening the cost of production. The force of the Brazilian slogan *O café dá para tudo*, will be weakened by this industrialization.

It is industrialization and not the newly fashionable "policy of defence" that will be able to free these countries from the dangers attending mono-production. The chief feature of this "policy of defence" is the attempt to regulate the market, and not to decrease the cost of production. Such a policy is a remnant of mediæval economy with its notion of "just price." The typical and best-known *defesa* is the regulation of coffee in Brazil. What has this regulation accomplished? Better prices? Stabilized prices? Eliminated crises? Lowered costs of production? History has shown that there were occasional successes, but continual defeats. Artificial regulation of prices through control of supply has called forth new competition from other countries. Prices fluctuated and broke down, and the situation became grave for the entire economy and finances of the country. It is sufficient to recall the situation which developed in the second half of 1929.

The defesa policy in South America seems to be developing into a popular game. In Brazil every state and every branch of production is crying and striving for a defesa similar to that of the coffee system. (Because the several states of Brazil are also suffering from mono-production.) Chile carries on its defesa policy in nitrates. In the districts of La Plata the sentiment for a defesa is growing.[71]

The economic aim of the defesa policy conforms with the interests of the "Big Thirty" of the United States; both are vitally interested in the regulation of world markets and world prices for specific commodities. The ways and methods of attaining this goal are different, however: the United States' industry strives to expand their mass-production internationally in order to lower the costs of production, while the South American defesa seeks to regulate the supply of commodities and is sealed up within the national boundaries.

But even if a trade alliance among the several countries could be realized for a single branch of production, the defesa nevertheless would not be efficient, just as the sugar convention of Brussels prior to the War had on the whole failed to achieve its aims.[72] The fundamental fallacy of the defesa system lies in the fact that the cost of production is being entirely neglected. The system's aim is to keep alive economic forms that are destined to die. It belongs to the realm of economic romanticism.[73]

Industrialization will undoubtedly affect the agrarian structure of the countries. The landlord is bound to relinquish a part of his political and social significance. The formation of the landlords and latifundios might well be compared to the plantation system in the south of the United States prior to the Civil War. In general, it may be said that the South American countries suggest comparison with the Southern States while they were hampered by the lack of adequate transportation. It will be interesting to watch the development of the relations between the latifundio—the present basis of mono-production—and industrialization. In Cuba they are complementary, driving out the small landowner. In Argentina and Uruguay the concentration of land in fewer hands seems to be growing stronger through the industrialization of cattle-raising and the meat industry. In Brazil, parallel to the existence of a plantation system, the class of rich farmers seems to be on the increase, thus recalling in several districts Canadian and Danish conditions.

Alejandro E. Bunge is entirely correct in stating: "We must agree, gentlemen, that this is *the last generation of importers and landlords*. In the next generation, that of our sons, the industrialists will have supremacy."[74]

Industrialization also means the defence against the "Peligro Yanqui." This danger is, in the first place, a part of the more general problem of the economic independence of the continent. During colonial times the continent depended largely upon the Iberian peninsula; in the nineteenth century upon

Great Britain,[75] which has aided the new-born states financially; in the last quarter of the nineteenth century upon Europe, for at the time the new industrial states, like Germany and France, and the small rentier states, like Belgium and Holland, joined England. "The new continent politically free is economically a vassal."[76]

The World War has shaken this European monopoly, but a new menace has arisen from the United States.

The European danger evoked neither fears nor cries. There was no hatred against Englishmen, no propaganda against British imperialism. Xenophobia, generally, is not a natural phenomenon in a country which is in its first period of development, where the largest part of the population consists of immigrants. "Citizens of Argentina, but of foreign blood,"[77] is a description which is analogous for all the national populations of the continent.

The "American Danger," as proclaimed in Europe, the conduct of the United States toward the Latin Americans in North America, the part played by the United States in the War and its liquidation, the growth of the United States' trade and investments in South America, and last, but not least, the economic nationalism of the freshmen of world history—all these factors brought to the surface the feeling of an "American Danger."

The problem, however, is broader, much broader. It reads: how can the disadvantages arising from this dependence upon foreign countries be ended? how is it possible, in the long run, to be emancipated from foreign influence? The answer to these questions is simultaneously a solution of the partial problem—the "Peligro Yanqui." From the economic point of view, it is a modern form of an old problem—the economic vassalage of the continent.

Clearly, this is not a question of complete emancipation from abroad. What Professor John H. Williams says of Argentina is valid for the entire continent:

"There are few countries whose economic life depends so

entirely on contact with the outside world. Without foreign trade and foreign capital Argentina would be a frontier community. . . . In Argentina foreign trade is the breath of life. If there is a bad harvest, there is immediately a 'slump' in exports; as a direct consequence, the spending power of the country is cut down; there is a decline of imports. The national budget of the following year shows traces of these effects of the bad harvest."[78]

"The whole economic structure, in a word, is erected on a single basis and with a single aim, that of buying and selling, borrowing and repaying, with the outside world."[79] The isolated state of von Thünen would be unthinkable here.

The peculiarity of the economy of this continent is that it exports the greatest part of its products and is obliged to import almost all of the needed manufactured commodities. A continental application of dictator Françia's methods in Paraguay, which transforms the whole continent into a walled China, is no longer possible. This would be a return to the Middle Ages. So it is not accidental that the political dictators and tyrants of the nineteenth century in South America were always idealizing the hermit state.[80]

This tendency towards isolation was a result of the Spanish colonial policy, a continuation of that period when the countries, intoxicated with their newly acquired independence, were still in a state of permanent perturbation. This mediæval ideal corresponds neither to the spirit nor the material needs of modern times. They fought against such isolation because it would be suicidal for South America, which thrives on foreign trade.

It is impossible to attempt to set an autarchial economy. On the contrary, it is impossible to avoid the geographical division of labour. One is necessarily tied up with world economy, which implies a rationalization of economic life. That an economic *αὐταρχία* is unthinkable is clearly demonstrated by the wartime blockade of Germany and embargo on communistic Russia. The distress and misery of the two countries was a result of isolation, an effect of a forced economic seclusion from countries abroad.

On the other hand, the development of a domestic industry in order to supply the needs of the population would certainly diminish the dependence upon foreign goods, upon foreign capital, and would foster capital accumulations. Was not the industrialization of Japan a defence against foreign capital? Was it not a protection programme of the United States, a programme distinctly formulated by Frederick List? "English national economy is *predominant*; American national economy aspires only to become *independent*." Hume tells of the influence of foreign capital in England during his time. Was England delivered into the hands of the money-lenders?

Most South Americans agree that without foreign capital the continent's future is uncertain. "This dependence is inevitable; without European capital there would have been no railways, no ports, and no stable government in America."[81] "Buenos Aires, Santiago, Montevideo, and Rio de Janeiro would have remained as backward towns if they were without English and French money. There would have been no railways in America had not the Englishmen and Frenchmen constructed them."[82] It suffices to glance at travel notes written at the beginning of the nineteenth century in order to understand what the continent would be without the foreign capital which organized transportation."[83]

It is a universal course of development that the nations of the world, in order to insure their political independence, were bent upon acquiring economic independence as extensively as possible. Accepting this formula involves fighting the "Peligro Yanqui" and all other similar dangers as well. Alberdi has already most clearly proclaimed the means of defence in a far-reaching programme. The danger "does not lie in foreign oppression, but in poverty, depopulation, backwardness, and misery. These are real enemies of America."[84]

The negative influence of the debtor position upon the United States was never of great importance. Why is it so? It is because foreign capital was employed to industrialize the country. Clearly, such a programme, like that once drafted in Washington for Brazil, would not be a defence against the "Peligro Yanqui." "The sub-committee recognizes that the resources of Brazil are so large that properly to develop them, not only can all the available domestic capital be used, but also as much foreign capital as might be secured. At the present stage of development, it is our opinion that the best interests of the country require the use of as much domestic capital as possible in commercial and agricultural pursuits, and that railroad, public utility, and industrial development can best be financed by foreign capital."[85]

Domestic capital must co-operate in industrialization, so that foreign capital may act as an ally only. It must not, however, be permitted to monopolize initiative and specific fields of economic activity.

"*Undeveloped* nations, reading in the lessons of history the inevitable domination of weak borrowing countries by stronger creditor nations, have sometimes sought to guard their independence by *setting up* restrictions against foreign capital."[86]

But history teaches us that economy in the process of development produces its own antitoxins. Industrialization is the insulin to counteract the foreign virus, and its action is facilitated by foreign capital itself. And if South America "is more defenceless than in the time of Bolivar"[87]—(with regard to ABC States, however, it certainly is false)—it is only because she did not enter upon the road to industrialization at the right time.

A purposive, conscious, constant, and consistent economic policy will demonstrate that the "Peligro Yanqui" is only a phase of the greater and more important problem—the problem of life, of industrialization in South America. Otherwise it is impossible that "a tortoise should overtake an automobile going at full speed" according to the bitter expression of Francisco Bulnes.

The path to independence is not through political struggles, but through economic progress. For, as Hamilton said, "Power without revenue in political society is a name."

The tempo of the continent's industrialization, given the necessary conditions, can exceed all expectations. Again one must refer to Alberdi: "Instead of inheriting a backward industry, build up the most progressive of twentieth-century Europe,"[88] and, we might add, the most advanced of the United States. The sweeping technological revolution of our times permits us to anticipate a storm-like tempo.

The great Venezuelan *caudillo* Guzman Blanco, who opened the doors of the country to foreign capital, stated in the year 1883 that under his authority Venezuela "had undertaken an infinite voyage towards an infinite future." The present voyage of the entire continent has a definite destination. It is a start towards modern capitalism.

(*b*) POLITICS

On the South American continent politics as well as economy is in the making. New political tendencies are internally connected with the first steps of the new economic order.

The growing industrialization requires a broad market, prefers not to depend and actually cannot depend on domestic purchasing power alone. Infant industry strives toward methods of mass-production in order that by producing more cheaply it may be enabled to compete with foreign producers. But, in spite of common language and habits, industry is limited in its natural growth by state boundaries. Infant industry strives to overleap these limits. The proposals for union current in the nineteenth century are now bolstered by economic reasons, and whereas the main impediment to the accomplishment of such an achievement in the first half of the nineteenth century was inadequacy of transportation, this obstacle is now more or less obviated.[1]

The advanced industrialization of Argentina already forms its own spheres of interest. Economically Paraguay is an Argentine colony. The contiguous regions of Bolivia are under pronouncedly Argentine influence, and in Uruguay Argentina's investments are active; even in Rio Grande do Sul—in spite of recent penetration by capital from the United States—one can find Argentine investments. The fortunate position Argentina holds in her exports, her possession of a geographically favoured market for her agricultural produce[2] tend to strengthen this influence. Argentina is now attempting to utilize the Pan-American Union for her programme of economic expansion in the same manner in which the infant industry of the United States did in the 'eighties.[3]

The evolution of Chile in its relations with its neighbours is similar. The first uncertain steps of an embryonic domestic imperialism are stimulated by the desire for a broader market.

On the other hand, the movement toward union and its continued propaganda in Hispanic-American countries made a slogan of the necessity for mutual economic and cultural intercourse based on recent progress in communication.

Parallel with the economic expansion of the larger states another current exists: a consequent mutual co-ordination of the various union plans in South America, and Argentina's desire for hegemony. Indeed, after exclusion of Brazil from the Hispanic-American bloc, the problem of hegemony is clarified by the fact that even Chile, in spite of her genuine progress and ambitions, cannot be considered a serious rival against Argentina. And Argentina, which has developed into the main centre of propaganda of the unionist movement, thereby inheriting in this respect the former position of Mexico and Peru, steers consciously and consistently towards an Hispanic-American union in South America.

The belief in the definite menace of "Peligro Yanqui" forces the smaller countries to seek common defence, and to find in Buenos Aires a leader; in Briand's Pan-European union a stimulating example; in Latinism and Hispanism helpers and allies; and in the remaining Spanish-American countries high hopes and goodwill.

Latin-American observers note that the situation of the United States in world politics is similar in some aspects to the situation of the German Empire prior to the War. The "German Danger" has its counterpart in the "American Danger," German imperialism in Dollar-Imperialism, the "made in Germany" in the "made in the United States." The rapid success of the "Kaiserreich" corresponds to the great progress of the economic empire of the United States, and Pan-Germanism may well be compared with Pan-Americanism when considered as an attempt of the United States to control the continent.[4]

A united solid front against the American danger does not yet exist. But the situation has changed since the War. Europe is not entirely ruined, but is recovering with the financial help of the United States, and is trying to regain her leading world position, to liberate herself from her financial tutelage, and to organize her economic forces anew. The Pan-European Union is an attempt at such a defence. The post-War continental spirit in Europe requires that tariff barriers be erected in an effort to arrest the growth of imports from the United States. The tariff offensive against motor-cars of the United States, started by France and Italy in Europe and Argentina in South America, is an example to the point.

South America recalls the European alliance against Germany, in which England joined at the last moment, and is attempting to study and imitate the Pan-European movement as a defensive programme against the "American Danger."

In spite of numerous difficulties, this defensive programme finds many followers in South America, while Europeans and Asiatics, as well as South and North Americans, are all preaching a crusade against the "Peligro Yanqui." The motive of several of these nations is fear; of the others—envy.[5]

The programme of Europe is especially inciting because it

aims to create a great continental market as a basis for modern mass-production and to obliterate custom barriers, the most important obstacle to free economic intercourse. South America is tempted to apply the same measures to her own new economic needs.

In spite of the differences in their respective stages of economic development, a peculiar similarity exists between the actual tendencies of evolution in Europe and in South America. Politically, the two continents are divided into numerous independent states; South America has the advantage of community of language (in nine out of the ten countries), religion, and habits. Both continents are striving for the organization of a huge united continental market. While Europe wishes to avoid the decline of modern capitalism, South America is attempting to advance toward modern capitalism. The two continents are seeking to strike out new paths, new industrial methods. The striving for a continental market and, consequently, for mass-production through standardization of products is an attempt to imitate the success of the United States, to Americanize domestic economy. The two continents are forced into this economic system by the American danger; both are seeking defence by adopting the methods of the enemy.[6]

Problems of market expansion, the "Peligro Yanqui," and the examples of Europe, are actually propelling the Spanish peoples in South America toward union. It is difficult to predict whether the realization of this aim will ever come to pass, either through local alliances and federations, or through the unifying leadership of a new Cavour or Bismarck. But the tendency is now existing and progressing. Rubên Darío greets this movement:

Vened cuidado. Vive la América española!

In the Spanish countries of South America the European evolutionary trends are most evident (Chapter V, *a*); European cultural and economic influence is great throughout the continent; with the exception of the Northern Coast the

European capital is preponderant, in spite of the recent successes of the United States. The dependence of South America upon European immigration also enhances European influence; and if, as several indications predict, France regains her leading position as a capital-exporting country, the defensive programme against the "Peligro Yanqui" seems quite settled. A union of the Spanish-American countries in South America would gravitate *financially* toward Europe (first in rank, France and England), and toward all other possible neutral markets; *culturally*, toward Latin Europe (Spain, France, Italy); *through immigration* toward Spain and Italy. These are substantial considerations in the defensive alliance. Of course, the programme would vary in different countries. Conflicts exist between Hispanism and Latinism, between France and Italy, and among those South American countries whose relations with each other are not always too friendly.[7] But the great line *à la longue* seems to be already crystallizing; the seducers and the courted have found each other, the "Peligro Yanqui" acted as the intermediary. The Spanish-American countries of the Southern continent are veering toward Europe.

The importance even of a partial success of this policy for the remaining countries of Latin America is not to be underestimated. Even a small federation will attract the other countries, and will advance the unionist movement in Central and North America, where conditions are quite favourable: "everyone who has examined the subject has come to the belief that Central America is destined to federate."[8]

The case of Brazil is different. "All is peculiar in the history of Brazil."[9] This country does not belong to the Spanish-speaking peoples, and the historical differences of Brazilian development are of the greatest importance. Brazil always was and still is the *United* States of Brazil, not only in name, but as a contrast to the *disunited* States of Spanish America. Brazil was never dismembered and does not need to seek the re-establishment of her lost union as does Spanish America, which was, of course, politically united in colonial time.[10]

The relation toward the former mother country was also entirely different. The colony itself assumed the rôle of the mother country during certain years. The monarchical form of government avoided dictatorships and tyrants and prepared for the transition to a republic; it was not a single leap from colony to republic.[11] "The Portuguese colonization of Brazil was less rigid, and the commercial isolation less rigorous; and religion was neither fanatical nor so powerful as in the Spanish colonies."[12] The Lusophobia was consequently not so virulent in Brazil, but the attraction of Portugal was never of such importance as that of Spain.

The chief peculiarity of Brazil is its extension. The area of Brazil is about 3,000,000 square miles, or a little greater than that of the United States. That Brazil, if as densely populated as Belgium, could furnish enough land for the entire population of the world is a popular overstatement. But, in fact, the population of Brazil, which was 30,600,000 in 1920, reached 39,100,000 in 1928, according to official calculations,[13] and now, in 1930, is over 40,000,000. Brazil has the largest population of any country in Latin America, and in all America is second only to the United States.

Brazil is a country of large dimensions in every aspect. For example, the delta of the Amazon reaches 250–320 kilometres in several places. The steamer requires thirty days in order to accomplish the famous Amazon journey. The superlative in South America in Brazilian.

Each epoch has its own country of "boundless possibilities." This banal expression was applied to Russia for a long period, later it was transferred to the United States, and virtually these two countries have confirmed this description, although in different directions.

To-day the country of "boundless possibilities" is Brazil. "Not even the great North American republic has a territory at once so large and productive. What will be its future?"[14]

This country of the future is still an enigma! The contrasts are too great to permit a solution of its mystery. Even to-day

75 per cent. of the population is illiterate; and in the year 1780, in a theatre 1,400 kilometres from the seacoast, tragedies of Voltaire were performed.[15]

"No one who has visited Brazil will have doubts as to the future of this State."[16] And similar verdicts have been numerous ever since Amerigo Vespucci said of Brazil: "Paradise must be here, or not very far from this place."

But it is clear that the industrialism of Brazil—a continent in itself—does not need to seek foreign markets in order to adopt the modern methods of production. Only the inadequacy of transportation is hindering the formation of what is potentially one of the greatest and most important markets in the world. This market will increase automatically as a consequence of industrialization. Each new railroad opens new territories, forcing them into a money economy, creates new markets, and at the same time new industries. Brazil will not be pressed to look for foreign markets even within the next century. Tendencies of Brazilian imperialism cannot be stated, as in Argentina and Chile. Brazil possesses colonies within itself. What is Amazonas, if not a colony? (Eduardo Prado has already mentioned Amazonas as a "tropical colony of Brazil"); and is Matto Grosso not a field for colonization?

Brazilian imperialism, which can be discerned in the pressure of expansion toward the Pacific coast, has actually no economic stimulus. The penetration of money economy into the immense interior and the dissemination of culture and cultivated habits among the population are the most important factors which are aiding the creation of a Brazilian market. A modern organization of transportation will alleviate the rigid isolation of many local markets existing now. To-day many states live relatively in economic isolation. A greater proximity of economic life among the Brazilian states is one of the most important factors in the creation of a wide uniform market in Brazil.[17]

The formation of this vast domestic market in Brazil is one of the conditions of mass-production, such as one finds it in the United States. The heterogeneous population of Brazil, which constitutes another point of resemblance with the United States, presents the problem of the creation of a *new* race. As formerly in the United States, there exists to-day in Brazil an ethnic anarchy, a variety of types which are already tending toward fusion. There are two racial strains: the Latin and the American. The American is a result of mutual psychical and physical assimilation between the immigrant and native elements. As the great Brazilian writer Graca Aranha said: "From this fusion of these two spirits, Latin and American, there may be several results, the secret of which Brazil possesses."[18]

The American line of evolution, previously considered (Chapter V, *a*), is now becoming a new force in view of certain similarities to the United States; but the Brazilian evolution, in spite of these, is not a mere copy, not a mechanical imitation of the Northern Colossus. It is an analogy, a parallelism on the Southern continent.[19]

Brazilian literature already gives evidence that this country is not only receptive, but it is also capable of original productions while keeping permanent contact with the native soil.[20] Professor Shepherd characterizes it as "The most pronouncedly American in Latin America, generally considered."[21]

The policy and ideology of Brazil are different from those of the Spanish-American countries. Here we can readily discern the preponderance of continental sentiment combined with a favourable attitude towards the United States.

This "American tendency," characteristic of Brazil, has become firmly entrenched in Brazilian diplomacy. "The diplomatic policy of Brazil, owing to her relative isolation from the other Latin-American countries, has been traditionally one of friendship with the United States," confirms Professor Haring.[22] In this direction lies the policy of the great Brazilian statesman, Baron Rio Branco.[23] This friendliness toward the United States, however, did not keep Brazil from demanding a clear and open interpretation of the Monroe Doctrine and its application, and from calling for the continentalization of the Doctrine.[24]

Brazil has no fear of the "Peligro Yanqui." Eruptions like the brilliant book of Eduardo Prado are infrequent; and this particular instance was a result of domestic politics.[25] The Brazilian point of view is revealed in the following: "We cannot fear imperialism while we are a country continually more powerful and more thickly populated."[26] Of all the countries of South America Brazil perhaps is most dependent on the market in the United States, for in Brazil coffee is king. The situation may be said to resemble the Cuban dependence on sugar production. Nevertheless, the Brazilian programme is clear, since the extension of communication and the application of foreign capital are necessary in order to develop the latent natural riches of the land.[27] In Brazil, therefore, we can find no resistance to penetration by the United States' capital. The United States is permanently invited on Brazilian soil. Prior to the War a Brazilian official publication was issued which clearly explained this programme and repeated this invitation: "We want, above all, two principal factors for our progress—the increase of population and the increase of capital. The former may be furnished a great deal by immigration; the latter is to be borrowed from the country or countries which are willing to lend or invest it in bettering conditions.

"Being so, it is apparent that the economic conditions of Brazil and North America are somewhat complementary to each other; the former possesses enormous natural resources and riches, and lacks capital for their profitable exploitation; the latter possesses an enormous surplus capital, and is trying to find out where to invest it in the exploitation of better returns."[28]

And after the War Brazil repeated this invitation: "What we wish to see now is a greater number of citizens of the United States at work in Brazil with their own money, just as the Chicago packers are developing our meat industries and the smelting interests are trying to bring about the same result with iron and manganese."[29]

One wonders why "North America has done remarkably little for Brazil."[30] If the invitation will be accepted, the liaison is complete, and for a long time: "Quitter Rio de Janeiro c'est toujours un acte heroique."[31] The United States is beginning to understand the importance of such co-operation.[32]

Just as in Spanish America the predilection for European suitors seems to dominate, so in Brazil sympathy for the United States prevails. This tendency in Brazil will be strengthened in case of the eventual success of a Spanish-American bloc, which at the same time will force the United States to give greater attention to her Brazilian friendship. The United States of America and the United States of Brazil are surrounded by Spanish peoples, and will be confronted with isolation through the formation of a Spanish bloc.[33]

If we compare the maps of the two American continents, we can note a certain parallelism: numerous disunited Spanish peoples in each, and two federations of states: the great North American Republic and the United States of Brazil in the south, two continents in themselves, two empires, which, in view of Russia's self-exclusion from international life and permanent disorders in China, territorially occupy first rank together with Great Britain. Both United States possess the natural hegemony of their respective continents. They are both remote from the unionist movement in the Spanish-American countries, which regard the United States not as a partner, but rather as an enemy. Brazil, which was always indifferent to these movements, has been and still is almost entirely excluded from Spanish-American political combinations.

The results of such co-operation between the northern and southern federations may become very important. The consequence for Brazil will be an acceleration of her industrialization, an increase in the importance of her political rôle on the continent and in world politics which may be the first step toward attaining a position of world power. The United States will secure through this partnership a field of operation: the potentially largest market in South America, the country with the largest population. Brazil may be in the future not only a field for investments and trade for the United States, but also the country for the emigration of her sons. The time seems not distant when the United States will be looking for an outlet for her overpopulation. Politically this *rapprochement* signifies an equilibrium on the American continent.[34]

Of course, all these currents are only vague manifestations and tendencies; it is impossible to prognosticate the forms and methods of the development. One thing is clear: a new period in the history of South America is dawning, a new chapter in its romantic biography.

NOTES

PREFACE

1. *The Decadence of Europe*, New York, 1923, p. 30.

2. Rafael Reyes, *The Two Americas*; translated from the Spanish, London, 1914, p. 14. "In this hemisphere the twentieth century will sooner or later come to be known as that of the Southerner." Charles H. Sherrill, *Modernizing the Monroe Doctrine*, Boston and New York, 1916, p. 52.

3. R. E. Enock, *Republics of South and Central America*, London, 1922, p. 519.

4. *Ibid.*, p. 520.

5. *Ibid.*

6. *Conflicto y armonias de las razas en América*, Buenos Aires, 1915, p. 63.

7. *Liberty and Despotism in Spanish America*, Oxford, 1929.

8. It is perhaps significant that Victor Orban, the French specialist in Brazilian literature, is at the same time the author of the book *Sur l'Œuvre de Pierre Loti*, Paris, 1907.

CHAPTER I

Economy

(*a*) *Trade*

1. It must be emphasized that the aim of this chapter is not statistical. Figures will be called in only to demonstrate trends, and no attempt is to be made at an exhaustive statistical description. Accordingly, I do not propose to correct data by reference to movements of the price-level or by comparison with figures representing volume of commodities. For the purposes of the present study, primarily concerned with determining the relative ranks of the competitors in South America, these otherwise important adjustments are superfluous. Their omission is further justified by the fact that the decade in which the great price-changes occurred—1914–24—is a period of quite subordinate importance so far as the purposes of this investigation are concerned.

2. *Intensificacão economica no Brasil*, São Paulo, 1918, p. 7.

3. This was realized, even at the time, in the United States. We read in one of the best contemporary works of political economy (now unfortunately forgotten):

"And this deed certainly did not originate in disinterested love of freedom and humanity, but a desire, as he confessed it himself, to open for England immense markets." *Appendix to "Outlines of Political Economy," in three additional letters addressed by Professor Frederick List to Charles J. Ingersoll*, Philadelphia, 1827, p. 3.

Hobbes was among the fathers of the great scheme to acquire South America for England.

4. "When one brings these figures together it appears that with regard to the whole South American foreign trade situation Great Britain is numerically in the lead; but that Germany—coming from the south—is more and more nearly equalling her share in Argentine, Chile, Brazil, Uruguay, Paraguay, and Bolivia; while the United States—coming from the north—is making notable gains and capturing an ever-increasing share of the business of the northern states of South America." Otto Kasdorf, *Der Wirtschaftskampf um Südamerika*, Berlin, 1916, p. 42.

5. *Foreign Commerce and Navigation of the United States.*

6. *United States Trade with Latin America in 1928*, United states Department of Commerce, Trade Promotion Series No. 88, Washington, 1929, p. 11.

7. Compare *Commerce Year Book*, 1929, Vol. I, p. 109. Table 14. "During the past year there were large increases in exports of finished manufactures and crude materials from the United States, as compared with a sharp decline in exports of crude foodstuffs. Finished manufactures amounted to about 45 per cent. of the total exports, a larger proportion than in any earlier year except 1916. About two-fifths of the increase in this group resulted from larger shipments of automobiles. Exports of office equipment and other kinds of machinery also showed substantial gains." *Ibid.*, p. 87.

8. In this sense, perhaps, Count Keyserling is symbolically right in declaring that "the human type of the future civilization is to be the taxi-driver."

9. *Department of Commerce Trade Information Bulletin*, No. 379, p. 2.

10. *Commerce Year Book*, 1929, Vol. I, p. 107.

11. *United States Trade with Latin America in 1928*, United States Department of Commerce, Trade Promotion Series, No. 88, Washington, 1929, p. 7.

12. *Ibid.*, p. 10, and also:

"Argentine Typewriter Market Expanding. . . . Seventy per cent. of all the typewriter imports during 1924 were from the United States. German and Italian prices have been considerably below those of the American companies, but the sales of the latter are made chiefly on quality and reputation. The most successful importers have been those with comprehensive organizations and who have advertised extensively. Three American machines have about half of the market."

Phoebus, M. A., *Argentine Markets for United States Goods*, United

States Department of Commerce, Bureau of Foreign and Domestic Commerce, Trade Information Bulletin, No. 384, 1926.

13. *Commerce Year Book*, 1929, Vol. I, p. 98.

14. *Ibid.*, p. 134.

15. *Ibid.*

16. Federal Trade Commission, *Report on Trade and Tariffs in Brazil, Uruguay, Argentina, Chile, Bolivia, and Peru*, Washington, 1916, p. 20.

17–19. See pp. 249–250.

20. *1928 Retrospecto Commercial do "Jornal do Commercio,"* Rio de Janeiro, 1929, p. 393.

21. "For the most part in relation to Latin America, our economic activities are complementary and not competitive. The products of Latin-American countries are typically those which either are not produced in the northern part of North America or are produced there only to a degree insufficient to fill the national needs. . . . There has been also a rising purchasing power in many Latin-American countries." Charles E. Hughes, *Our Relations to the Nations of the Western Hemisphere*, Princeton, 1928, pp. 4–5.

Compare what Mr. J. J. Arnold of Chicago says:

"Trade between two countries must be based upon an exchange of commodities in as far as it is possible. The United States of America is rapidly becoming an urban instead of a rural country. This is why we are now seeking, perhaps as never before, a market for our manufactured articles. In your countries the reverse is still true, and on this account your natural products will necessarily be wanted in our land in increasing quantities." *Proceedings of the First Pan-American Financial Conference*, issued by direction of the Secretary of the Treasury, 1915, pp. 226–227.

22. See especially Hiram Bingham, *Across South America*, Boston, 1911.

23. Compare Clayton Sedgwick Cooper, *Understanding South America*, New York, 1918. His impressions were, in practically all the countries, that European competition would win back its old position after the War. See pp. x, 175, 198–199, 209, 275.

(*b*) *Investments*

1. It is often remarked that in the War, especially in Latin America, a great number of foreign enterprises changed their nationality. "To the case of North America especially can it be applied that its capital investments were very high in Latin America before the War, but after it they were even higher than one is able to conclude from estimates." Dr. Jens Jessen, *Die ökonomische Grundlage der panamericanischen Idee*. Schmoller's *Jahrbuch für Gesetzgebung, Verwaltung und Volkswirtschaft*, 52 Jahr, Heft 5, pp. 103/873.

2. An interesting but not detailed attempt can be found in the

17. The main lines of the shift in United States export trade will be evident from the following table:

PERCENTAGE INCREASE OR DECREASE IN FOREIGN TRADE BY ECONOMIC CLASSES

Class	Per Cent. Change in Value from 1928 Exports from:			Per Cent. Change in Value of 1928 Imports from:		
	1910–14	1921–25	1927	1910–14	1921–25	1927
Total	+ 136·1	+ 16·7	+ 5·7	+ 142·3	+ 18·6	− 2·2
Crude materials	+ 81·3	+ 9·0	+ 8·4	+ 146·5	+ 13·7	− 8·4
Crude foodstuffs	+ 132·0	− 30·1	− 30·3	+ 170·4	+ 43·7	+ 8·9
Manufactured foodstuffs ..	+ 58·4	− 22·3	+ 1·0	+ 108·7	− 9·5	− 10·1
Semi-manufactures	+ 109·7	+ 33·5	+ 2·4	+ 148·4	+ 25·2	+ 1·7
Finished manufactures ..	+ 345·4	+ 44·3	+ 14·0	+ 132·9	+ 26·0	+ 3·2

Commerce Year Book, 1929, Vol. I, p. 110, Table 15.

18. This object is quite unmistakably set forth by Mr. Robert Porter, Special Commissioner for the United States to Cuba and Porto Rico:

"If Cuba then belongs to the United States, we shall control the sugar market of the world just as we now control the world's market in so many other staple products." *Industrial Cuba*, New York, 1899, p. 301.

Compare also: "It can be said that the United States controls the production of cotton, copper, petroleum, and, in a certain degree, sugar." Jacques Auboyneau, *Le marché des capitaux de France de 1924 à 1926*, Paris, 1927, pp. 169–170.

19. *Foreign Commerce and Navigation of the United States*, 1928, p. xiii, Table V.

The following table shows the relative treatment accorded typical South American products under the tariff laws now in force in the principal countries to which they are exported:

Articles	United States	Canada*	United Kingdom	Germany†	France†	Italy†	Spain	Portugal
Cacao	Free	Dutiable	Dutiable	Dutiable	Dutiable	Dutiable	Dutiable	Dutiable
Coffee	Free	Dutiable	Dutiable	Dutiable	Dutiable	Dutiable	Dutiable	Dutiable
Cotton	Free	Free	Free	Free	Free	Dutiable	Dutiable	Dutiable
Rubber	Free	Free	Free	Free	Free	Free	Dutiable	Dutiable
Hides	Free	Free	Free	Free	Free	Free	Dutiable	Dutiable
Meat, frozen and chilled	Free	Dutiable	Free	Dutiable	Dutiable	Dutiable	Dutiable	Dutiable
Wool	Free	Free	Free	Free	Free	Free	Dutiable	Dutiable
Copper	Free	Free	Free	Free	Free	Ingots Dutiable	Dutiable	Dutiable
Tin	Free	Free	Free	Free	Free	Free	Dutiable	Dutiable
Nitrate of soda ..	Free	Free	Free	Free	Free	Crude free; Refined dutiable	Dutiable	Free

* No account taken of the War surtax of 7·5 per cent. *ad valorem* on certain products of other than British origin.

latest compilations of the League of Nations (*Memorandum on International Trade and Balances of Payments*).

3. *La Economia Argentina*, Vol. II.

4. *Investments in Latin America* (mostly in co-operation with others), Department of Commerce, Special Agents Series, No. 169; Trade Information Bulletins, No. 362, 382, 466.

5. *American Foreign Investments*, New York, 1926.

6. *Investments of United States Capital in Latin America*, World Peace Foundation pamphlets, Vol. XI, No. 6, Boston, 1928.

7. *Nuestros Banqueiros en Bolivia*. Spanish translation, Madrid.

8. *1928 Retrospecto Commercial do "Jornal do Commercio,"* Rio de Janeiro, 1929, p. 68.

9. *L'Avenir de l'Expansion Économique de la France*, Conférences faites au Collège Libre des Sciences Sociales, pp. 330–331, Paris, 1918, article by Monterroyos.

10. *Eulogy of President McKinley*, February 27, 1902. Congressional Record, 57th Congress, First Session, 2201. See also Professor Achille Viallate, *Economic Imperialism and International Relations during the Last Fifty Years*, New York, 1923, p. 37.

11. Enock, *op. cit.*, p. 490.

12. "The New Machinery for American Financing Abroad," *The Two Americas*," Vol. II, No. 2.

13. The United States during the War attempted to buy up European capital in South America and wished to receive Latin-American bonds and financial obligations in payments for Allies' debts (see *Proceedings of the First Financial Conference in Washington*, 1915). That is to say, to apply the famous Knox Central-American policy to the South American continent.

14. "The twelve Federal reserve banks could, with the consent of the Federal Reserve Board, establish *joint* agencies in each of the countries of Latin America, their interest in such agencies to be in proportion to the capital stock and surplus of each participating Federal bank. The combined capital stock and resources of our Federal Reserve banks, utilized in this way for the extension and promotion of our foreign commerce, would give them unrivalled financial power. They could maintain themselves in foreign fields in competition with the world and perform a service of incalculable value to the American people." *Proceedings of the First Pan-American Financial Conference*, 1915, pp. 10–11.

15. "Resolved, That it is recommended that the banking interests of the United States study the possibility of financial relief to Europe by means of new loans granted in the United States to the respective Latin-American countries." *Ibid.*, p. 15.

16. *Ibid.*, pp. 207–208.

17. In this comparison it should not be forgotten that the importance of the foreign investments of England diminished even before the War. So the North American securities returned to the Western

World, Russian securities to France and Germany. Foremost among English investments are their own colonial loans, in connection with the political aim to support financially and to unite the British Empire.

18. *L'Avenir de l'Expansion Économique de la France*, *op. cit.*, p. 333.

19. Compare Le Baron L'Authouard, *Le Progrès Brésilien*, Paris, 1911, p. 360.

20. Enock, *op. cit.*, p. 488. In 1930 a Chilean investigation was published (*Informe del departamento de Comercio*) which estimated the English capital in Chilean railroads to be 42 per cent., United States as 3 per cent., Chilean Government as 46 per cent., and other countries as 9 per cent Quoted in *La Prensa*, New York, June 6, 1930.

21. Enock, *ibid.*

22. Hiram Bingham, *Across South America*, Boston, 1911, p. 33.

23. In the process of investigation, after finishing this chapter, similar ideas were found in an analogous passage in the book by the German-American economist, Dr. Hermann A. L. Lufft, *Die Nordamerikanische Interessen in Südamerika vor dem Krieg*, Jena, 1916.

24. This is typical also of a country like Paraguay: "As an important investment fact, it is reported that three large packing plants, affiliated with three of the largest Chicago packing companies, have been established in Paraguay since the first Pan-American Conference met in 1915." *Report of the Secretary of the Treasury to the President on the Second Pan-Amercian Financial Conference at Washington*, Washington, 1921, p. 150.

25. The same is stated by C. H. Hobson in regard to United States' investments in Canada. *The Export of Capital*, London, 1914, pp. 28–29.

26. What is the aim of this concern? The building of a world monopoly "in order to receive through the world organization the special great savings on the production of this small commodity of daily use." Sven Helander, *Die Kapitalausfuhr Schwedens* in "*Die Auslandskredite*" (*Schriften des Vereins für Socialpolitik*, Vol. 174, Heft III), edited by Professor Walter Lotz, München and Leipzig, 1928.

27. Characteristic of this capital export: "During 1928 there were sold abroad 230,000 automobiles assembled in branch plants of American automobile companies from parts, most of which were imported from the United States; this was 16 per cent. more than in 1927. Active assembly of American cars abroad began in 1923, and the practice was found so economical and efficient that the number of assembling plants has increased steadily.

Assembly parts exported from Canada are invariably declared as a given number of complete car units. Not all exporters in the United States ship parts on a car-unit basis; thus cars assembled abroad in plants under control of United States' companies are declared on export either as "parts for assembly" and "engines," or as a given number of car units. Exports during 1928 as "Parts for Assembly" resulted in 67,000 automobiles, a decrease of 8·6 per cent. from the total of 1927." *Commerce Year Book*, 1929, Vol. I, p. 463.

28. *The New York Times*, June 2, 1930.

29. Dr. G. von Schulze-Gaevernitz, *Britischer Imperialismus und englischer Freihandel zu Beginn des zwanzigsten Jahrhunderts*, Leipzig, 1906, p. 310.

30. Benjamin H. Williams, *Economic Foreign Policy of the United States*, New York, 1929, p. 23.

31. "Rhodes appears as a precursor of that type of Cæsar for whom the time is not yet ripe." Oswald Spengler, *Der Untergang des Abendlandes*, Vol. I, München, 1920, p. 52.

32. M. and Charles A. Beard, *Rise of American Civilization.*

33. Viallate, M. A., *La Concurrence Américaine*, Société d'Encouragement pour l'Industrie Nationale, Paris, 1907, p. 87. But, on the other hand, the automatical and mechanized extension of the corporation does not depend more from the person.

34. South America is already beginning to understand the true character of this organization. *L'Avenir de l'Expansion Économique de la France*, *op. cit.*, p. 335.

35. "As for Great Britain, its surplus of capital disposable at present for capital exports is smaller than it was prior to the War, in spite of recent increases." Francis W. Hirst, *Kapital und Kapitalanlagen Grossbritanniens seit dem Krieg* (in *Die Ausländskredite*, *op. cit.*, p. 37).

36. "My own belief is that capital in the old world will find so vast a field in work of reconstruction and colonization in 'darkest Europe' that it will not be able to devote itself as liberally to the development of the countries of this hemisphere as it did in the past. The three Americas will, therefore, be drawn together in a commercial and financial union of growing strength and intimacy," declared Paul M. Warburg in the year 1921 under the influence of the War events. *Report of the Secretary of the Treasury to the President on the Second Pan-American Financial Conference at Washington*, January 19–24, 1920, Washington, 1921, p. 49.

More cautious is the excellent recent publication of the National Industrial Conference Board (*The International Financial Position of the United States*, New York, 1929). "The United States is not a mature creditor nation, as Great Britain is, for example, and continues to experience an almost constant rate of internal economic growth. Capital requirements may steadily expand. On the other hand, there is no denying the fact of a wider interest in international trade, industry, and finance. The United States may be expected to be both an importer and exporter of capital, according to the judgments of individual investors and corporations both here and abroad. The assuming of a permanent rôle as a nation predominantly in a creditor position, however, may be predicted. No volume of foreign indebtedness such as has become owed to the United States could be rapidly liquidated. Nor could it be rapidly exceeded by the growth of indebtedness to foreigners. The present net creditor position could easily be maintained or even gradually increased" (p. 270).

Gustav Cassel is more reserved in his opinions: "Since the War, the United States have presented themselves as lenders on a large scale. The situation has, of course, been considerably improved thereby as compared with what it would otherwise have been. One should be careful, however, not to form exaggerated ideas of the importance of the American capital export. America has at the same time imported a considerable amount of capital, particularly in the form of sales of securities to foreign countries. The net capital export is therefore much lower than would appear from the figures for new loans, to which public attention is usually drawn. It is true that, in the years immediately following the War, the net export of capital from the United States was also very important. Since that time, however, a change has taken place. For the year 1923 reverse capital payments actually exceeded new loans, so that capital movements showed a net import of 109 million dollars. For the years 1924 and 1925, the American net export of capital is stated to have been respectively 522 and 432 million dollars. If British gross and American net figures for investments abroad in 1925 are taken together, we arrive at a sum of 857 million dollars. This seems to show that the capital export of the United States and England together does not nearly amount to the sum attained in 1913 by England alone. The comparison will, of course, give a still more unfavourable result if the fall in the value of money is taken into consideration." *Recent Monopolistic Tendencies in Industry and Trade*, League of Nations, 1927, Geneva, pp. 38–39. *The Balance of International Payments of the United States*, 1929, recently published by the Department of Commerce, confirms this opinion.

(*c*) *Foreign Trade and Investments of the United States as an Appendage to Domestic Mass-Production*

1. A recent investigation relates the Belgian capital exports prior to the War with the wish of industry to gain new outlets (railroads, trainways). On the other hand, after the War Belgian capital exports an extension of domestic business abroad dominated mainly by their quest for raw materials. Dr. Leon Dupriez, *Belgien und die Internationale Kapitalbewegungen 1919–27*, in *Die Auslandskredite*, *op. cit.*

2. Henri Hauser, *Les Méthodes Allemandes de l'Expansion Économique*, Paris, 1916, p. 40.

3. An opposite opinion represents Andre Siegfried: "The com-

position of the foreign dollar investments emphasizes their financial character in contrast to the commercial character of similar British investments." *America Comes of Age*, translated from French, New York, 1927, p. 224.

Gustave Cassel, in the cited publication, is not far from the conclusion that the motivating force of foreign trade and investments is industry, but he does not state it explicitly.

The United States Federal Trade Commission suggests investments in South America, which "Indirectly they will increase our commercial intercourse. They will, on the one hand, create a preference for American goods, and, on the other, acquaint our people with South American products and resources." *Report on Trade and Tariff in Brazil, Uruguay*, Washington, 1916, p. 22. That is the traditional thought.

In German literature one finds only a one-sided view. Jessen in the above-mentioned article believes that the United States seek only raw materials in South America, and have no special interest in the marketing of manufactured goods. This point of view is certainly in error. But also one-sided is the view of von Reibnitz (*America's Internationale Kapitalwanderungen*, Berlin, 1926), against whom Jessen argues. von Reibnitz believes that South America is important mainly as a market, and that the aim of the investments is to expand the market.

(*d*) *Competition*

1. Sometimes the very peculiar conduct of the official representatives of a country invigorates this Caribbeanization. In a publication of the League of Nations we may read: "The Colombian Members of the International Economic Conference are of the opinion that the best way of making known the economic position of their country to the other members of the conference is by placing before them a statement regarding Colombia's credit and present position drawn by Mr. James C. Luitweiler, of the banking firm of Baker Kellog, and one of the most important financiers who has visited Colombia in recent years." League of Nations, Economic and Financial Section, International Economic Conference, Documentation, *Principal Features and Problems of the War Economic Positions from the Point of View of Different Countries—Colombia*, Geneva, 1927, p. 22. It is very strange and unusual for officials of a sovereign state to refer in their relations to the League of Nations to the judgment of a private foreign business man.

2. Prior to the War Viallate already emphasized that the United States industry cannot be of great competition to France, and the economic development of the twentieth century has made more distinct the high degree of specialization in the United States. *La Concurrence Américaine*, *op. cit.*, p. 88.

3. *Directorio Comercial de depositadores interestados en el negocio extranjero con la América Latina*. This directory was published during the War, 1915, when everybody dashed at foreign trade. The new specialization in foreign trade through the great United States' firms and their affiliates cannot be without influence in the structure of the national trade organization in South America, where the *almacen* system still prevails. This system is typical not only of the rural *tienda* which must naturally be of this character, and not only for the department store which is at the beginning of its development on this continent, but also for all trade. Of course, there are exceptions among large trading firms of many branches. Most characteristic, however, is the lack of specialization in trade and in the branches.

4. "It is true that the Americans cannot offer their manufactured products cheaply enough on foreign markets except for several special articles." *La Cultura Latino-Américana*, Cöthen, 1916, Vol. I, No. 2, p. 144.

5. "According to the American Consulate-General in Buenos Aires, two entirely different systems are used by American firms in that market. The first and most successful is that employed by the large American houses which have established their own branches in Argentina, operated by personnel under the direct control of the Home Office. These firms are well acquainted with the market, and need have little fear of foreign competition. They are firmly established units of the Home Office, and can depend on the parent organization for the support and financial backing that are necessary.

"It is the other type of representation in this market which, it is feared, may find difficulty in meeting competition, after the complete recovery of Central Europe. . . .

"A small firm cannot, of course, establish its own branch in Argentina. The volume of business would not justify the expense." Phoebus, M. A., *Argentine Markets for United States Goods*, United States, Department of Commerce, Bureau of Foreign and Domestic Commerce, Trade Information Bulletin, No. 384, Washington, 1926, p. 12.

6. Clarence H. Haring, *South America looks at the United States*, New York, 1929, p. 188.

7. Federal Trade Commission, *Report on Trade and Tariffs in Brazil, Uruguay, Argentina, Chile, Bolivia, and Peru*, Washington, 1916, p. 146.

8. *Ibid*., p. 20.

9. *Ibid*., p. 18.

10. *Ibid*., p. 19.

11. Compare Helio Lobo, *A Democracia Uruguaya*, Rio de Janeiro, 1928.

CHAPTER II

The Ideology

(a) *The Seducers*

1. The Non-American

1. "Study Pan-Americanism, Pan-Slavism, the Doctrine of Greater Britain, Italian Nationalism, for the greater part of the great powers, you will see, in the making or in full evolution, a myth similar to that of the Pangermanism"—says Maurice Milloud in his Preface to the French translation of the book by Otto Richard Tannenberg, *Gross-deutschland* (*La plus grande Allemagne*), *l'Œuvre du XX siècle*, Paris, 1916.

2. *Latin America, Its Rise and Progress*, English translation, London, 1913, p. 281.

3. Compare Dr. Pietro Ualdi, *L'Espansione coloniale e Commerciale dell' Italia nel Brazil Roma*, 1911, pp. 230–231.

4. Haring, *op. cit.*, p. 187.

5. Emile Boix, *El libro en la Argentina*, p. 118.

6. Percy A. Martin, *Latin America and the War*, Boston, 1919, p. 229 (World Peace Foundation Publication).

7. A sample of a common commercial propaganda, legitimate withal, now carried on by France, is shown in an article in the *Paris Review* by D. Lafond. And another one by Georges Lefor, in a recent issue of *Revue Minerva*, entitled "Captured Latin-American Markets." Quoted by Samuel Guy Inman, *Problems in Pan-Americanism*, New York, 1921, pp. 345–346.

8. These methods have often been described. A good résumé is to be found in Haring's book, *op. cit.* With special reference to France, see Garcia Caminero, *op. cit.*, Chapter IX.

9. T. H. Lathané, *The Diplomatic Relations*, *op. cit.*, p. 221.

10. Clemenceau, on the contrary, says: "Latin idealism has kept the South American populations oriented toward the great modern nations which had their origin in the Roman conquest." *Notes de voyage dans l'Amérique du Sud*, Paris, 1911, p. 48.

11. Emile Boix writes: "The cultured classes of Argentina, owing to a number of causes, are *essentially French* in formation. French culture and books dominate in the universities and exercise an irresistible tutelage on the classes of people mentioned, and therefore on all the great mass of the population of the country; and French is the daily bread in all the intellectual work of Argentina." *Ibid.*

A pertinent picture of the part which the older nations play in the intellectual provision of the aspiring peoples of South America is given by the following statistics of the medical books used in Buenos Aires and Montevideo. In a recent year there were used in the Library of the Faculty of Medicine in Buenos Aires—a majority of whose books are of French origin—an aggregate of 27,980 volumes, of which

13,716 were French	1,449 Italian
7,716 Argentinian	211 German
4,821 Spanish	53 English
	14 Portuguese

In the Library of the Faculty of Medicine in Montevideo there were used an aggregate of 10,476 volumes, of which

5,816 were French	239 English
2,793 Spanish	231 Portuguese
1,243 Italian	154 German

La Cultura Latino Américana, *op. cit.*, Vol. I, No. 2, p. 340.

If we read Francisco G. Calderon's book, of which Poincaré said that "from beginning to end of this book we hear the rallying cry of the Latin republics" (p. 13), we immediately agree, but only so far as the educated classes are concerned—a fact which Calderon overlooks—that "America, Spanish, and Portuguese by origin, is becoming *French* by culture" (p. 17).

Without distinction of country or person, the influence governing South American heroes and their associates is always French. Guzman Blanco in Venezuela was an admirer of French art. "From the enchanted banks of the Seine he directed the febrile development of Venezuela," writes Calderon. And this was approximately the case with the other South American dictators.

Is not Calderon's fine book typical of Latin-Americanism in form and content? He begins as a researcher, writes like a poet, and ends as a prophet. The ever enthusiastic character of the narrative makes his history—an outspoken history of persons—a typical South American product of high quality in French dress. His "history" has much in common with the now fashionable biographical novel which may also be called romantic biography.

12. S. Dutot, *France et Brézil*, Second Edition, Paris, 1859 (Introduction).

13. Le Comité *France Amérique*. Son activité de 1909 à 1920, Paris, 1920, p. 2.

14. *La Nación* (Buenos Aires), 1929, quoted in *Living Age*, December 1, 1929.

15. Haring, *op. cit.*, p. 185.

16. Constantino Suarez (Españolito), *La Verdad desnuda*, Madrid, 1924, p. 38.

17. *Ibid.*, p. 40.

18. Fourth Centenary of the Discovery of the Pacific Ocean. Congreso de Historia y Geografia Hispano-Americano celebrated in Seville, April 1914, *Notas y Memorias*, Madrid, 1914, p. 313.

19. *Ibid.*, p. 316.

20. II Congreso de Historia y Geografia Hispano-Americanas, Seville, 1921. *Notas y Memorias*, Madrid, 1921, p. 355.

21. *El problema Ibéro-Américano*, Madrid, 1926, p. 83.

22. *Op. cit.*, p. 43.

23. Calderon, *Latin America, op. cit.*, p. 233.

24. See the article by Gabriel Franko in *Wirtschaftstheorie der Gegenwart*, Vol. I, Vienna, 1927, section on Spain.

25. Compare J. Goldberg, *Studies in Spanish-American Literature*, New York, 1920.

26. Compare with the line of thought of the Argentine Francisco Silva, who speaks of the "reconstitution of the Catholic Hispanic Empire."

27. "But when the prolongation of the War was considered as an inevitable ill for an indefinite period, and in Spain one had to take into account the imposed necessity of the nation to help herself . . . our country made such progress to invert itself into an industrial nation that one may affirm that at present industry plays the leading rôle in Spain." Jean Baelen, *Principaux traits du développement économique de l'Espagne*, Paris, 1924, p. 8.

28. Compare Gabriel Franco, *op. cit.*, pp. 232–233.

29. "To produce what one can no longer receive, to produce in order to sell to others what they cannot produce themselves, that is the task which the War imposes on Spain, revolutionizing the customs of her population which hitherto had been chiefly agricultural and imported manufactured objects." Jean Baelen, *op. cit.*, p. 7.

"This state of mind, this desire for independence, was translated during the War into a formula which frequently recurs to the pen of publicists: 'to attain sufficiency,' 'to be sufficient unto ourselves,' which is the aim of Spanish political economy." *Ibid.*, p. 46.

30. *The Catholic Association for International Peace, Latin America and the United States*, Pamphlet No. 2, 1929, p. 20.

31. *Para América desde España*, Paris, 1910, p. 70.

32. Badia Malagrida is mistaken when, in his eminently industrious book prepared on the lines laid down by German examples (*El factor geografico en la politica Sudamericana*, Madrid, 1919, p. 3), he says: "Everything is propitious for us, and there is no longer any serious obstacle except our own indifference." José Franco Rodríguez, the traditional writer of introductions for Hispano-American authors in this field, is much more modest. He recommends investigating "the causes of this lack of union, to obtain efficacious remedies for them, instead of proclaiming what does not exist." (Prologue to Constantino Suarez's book quoted above, p. 30.) Compare with his introduction to the book of Garcia Caminero (*supra*).

33. Thus Luis Araquistain says: "With the co-ordination of the capital of the Spaniards in America only, for the foundation of banks and other continental organizations, the economic emancipation of

the Hispanic states and people would soon be a fact. The only thing lacking is vision of the future. Napoleons are lacking for the new international struggles." *El Peligro Yanqui*, Madrid, 1921, p. 105.

Emilio Zurano Muñoz advocates a bank organization of Hispano-Americanism (*Apuntes para la organización economica entre los pueblos Hispanos*, Madrid (?), second edition—a remarkable mixture of philosophy and retail trade); Rodrigo Zárate proposes a Spanish Export Bank (*España y America. Proyecciones y problemas delirados de la Guerra*, Madrid, 1917).

As early as the year 1900 the "Congreso Social y Economico Hispano-Americano" in Madrid proclaimed: "It would be appropriate to create a bank with its head office in Madrid and with branches in all the capitals of Latin America. (*Memorias*, Madrid, 1902, p. 767.) The history of the "Idea Banks" has shown that they all go the same way—to collapse. It is all the same whether they are great socialistic experiments, like the Crédit Mobilier of the 'fifties in France, a favourite child of the Saint-Simonians; or small quasi-socialistic experiments like that of Robert Owen; or the desire of the Church to exercise money power, like the Bontoux Group in France. Their end was always the same. In banking it appears to be impossible to serve two gods at the same time.

34. Conde de Romanones said of intellectual Pan-Hispanism: "There are three Spains: one, that which lives in the territory under our jurisdiction; another, that composed by those compatriots who have carried our name and our race to distant latitudes; another, and greater, that formed by those ramifications of the old Iberian stock, which have flowered in the republics which people the centre and south of America. The three are Spain; the three are our country. The second is such because the motherland is not a geographical expanse but a spiritual expanse, a dominion of the soul, composed of the community of memories, the solidarity of affections, by the identity of experiences." Conde de Romanones in *The Revista de la Union Ibéro-Américana*, as quoted by Luis Felippe Contardo, *Medics prácticos de un acercamiento más estrecho entre España y la América Espanola. Fiesta de la Raza*, 1492–1916, Juegos Florales Concepción, Chile, 1917, p. 106.

35. "A Hispano-Americanism made up of good wishes is not sufficient." *La Agonia Antillana*, Madrid, 1928, p. 28. "Hispano-Americanism will not go beyond empty rhetoric or chimerical dream." *Ibid.*, p. 102.

36. Posada says: "It can only treat of reciprocal influences and realization of coinciding efforts to save, in the confused process of history, a common spiritual patrimony, an individual tone of culture, an intense and vibrant note of a civilization and an ideal. What else is a language with which so many sublime things have been expressed, a language spoken by so many millions of men?" (*op. cit.*, p. 72). This is a purely cultural movement: spiritual interpenetration; he declines

to "elaborate a program of . . . Hispano-American intimacies. Only words . . . there is no occasion for anything else" (*ibid.*, p. viii). Posada's programme would correspond to the cultural community of the "English-speaking people"—"Naciones de habla español."

"Our old and beloved Spain does not desire, nor is she able, nor ought she, to think of exercising any hegemony over the Ibero-American peoples. We desire, and we aspire to, only a fraternal communion," said Juan Ortega Rubio, *History of America*, p. 212.

37. Bahia de Malagrida says of "supernational solidarity": "When we talk of 'Hispano-American political unity' we do not allude to the unitary concept of the national state, within whose orbit the geographical dictates have a decisive value, but rather to the idea of solidarity among different states, consented to and stimulated by the action of an identical sentiment, a single idiom, and a common tradition" (*op. cit.*, p. 113; cf. p. 559).

38. Luis Jiménez de Asua underestimates the Spanish influence, when he says: "Let our (Spanish) actuation be rather that of friends than of kinsmen, separated both by time and distance." (*Politica, Figuras, Paisajes*, Madrid, 1927, p. 78.) On the other hand, Haring is perhaps not too optimistic when he says of Hispano-Americanism: "It is a dream, like primitive Christianity, but possessing the possibilities of an immense future" (*op. cit.*, p. 182).

Rippy remarks in one passage: "And there was some attempt to put this idea of solidarity into practice. Early in 1856 the Spanish Minister at Washington held conferences with the diplomatic agents of the Hispanic countries resident in the United States for the purpose of discussing plans of union. A project was drawn up which proposed to bind the nations to the south of the Rio Grande not to consent to the abridgment of the independence or the infringement of the territorial integrity of any of the signatory Powers, but to treat the invader or offender of any member of the prospective alliance as a common enemy. No provision was inserted, at the time, that would include Spain in the union, but the action of the Spanish Minister was approved and the Spanish Secretary of State considered the matter of sufficient importance to communicate it to the Captain-General of Cuba." J. Fred Rippy, *Latin America in World Politics*, New York, 1928, p. 20.

39. See his works, *La politica exterior norteamericana de la post-guerra*, Valladolid, 1924, and *El imperialismo del petroleo y la paz mondial*, Valladolid, 1925.

Camillo Barcia urges the American republics of Iberian origin to unite in a conference where they may consider their attitude with regard to the problem of the Pacific and the question of immigration. The unjust exclusion from the Washington assembly gives the right to the Iberian peoples to unite for the study of problems which affect them in a vital manner. "If cordiality is imposed," says the author in conclusion, "the sister nations will be able to work within a productive fraternity, in intimate collaboration, which, while safeguarding their interests, will enable them to show the world nobly constructive pathways." Luis Jiménez de Asua, *op. cit.*, pp. 156–157.

40. *La Unión Ibérica, Estudio crítico-histórico de esta problema*, Madrid, 1914.

41. *Op. cit.*, p. 53.

42. *Ibid.*, p. 57.

43. *Ibid.*, p. 37.

44. *Ibid.*, p. 52.

45. "Everything is common between it (Brazil) and the remaining countries, except the accident of language—modal and of no effect whatever. Portugal, which colonized it, was a simple sociological remnant of Spain, which colonized all the others (and in truth at that time it had not long ceased to be a geographical part of the same). Consequently the types, customs, and clothing, the aims, practices, and methods of colonization were identical and left analogous traditions. They have even risen to autonomy together, if we ignore, as is fitting, a small number of years which cannot count for anything." *Los paises de la América Latina*, Madrid, 1915, p. 8.

46. José Pequito Rebello, "*Aspectos economicos*," in *A questão ibérica*, Lisbon, 1916.

47. *Ibid.*

48. *Ibid.*, p. 349.

49. Only in an unimportant and typical congressional speech can we find a Portuguese statement of a different purport: Adriano Anthero, *Hespanha e Portugal e suas affinidades*, Oporto, 1921.

50. See Francisco Ribeiro Salgado, *Interesses economicos luso-brasileiros*, Oporto, 1927. He gives an historical sketch of these ideas in Portugal (pp. 48–51).

51. João de Barros, *Sentido de Atlantico*, Paris-Lisbon, 1921, p. 14.

52. Salgado, *op. cit.*, p. viii.

53. *Ibid.*, p. 45.

54. Compare with Barros, *op. cit.*

55. Rafael Reyes, *op. cit.*, p. 11.

56. *The Living Age*, December 1, 1929.

57. Compare with Leon Foucher, who suggested in 1837 the foundation of a "Union du Midi," Leroy-Beaulieu (1879), a "Union Latin," and so forth.

58. Haring, *op. cit.*, p. 131.

59. "The German has obtained greater and more permanent results as colonizer than in the commercial field. German colonies extend from the island of Chiloe, with its cold damp climate, to the Brazilian tropical town of Espirito Santo, and even as far as Venezuela. The number of German colonists in South America is thought to be in the neighbourhood of half a million." *La Cultura Latino-Américana*, *op. cit.*, p. 146.

60. *Op. cit.*, pp. 497–498. "The word of the Englishman is the gold

standard of commercial honour throughout Latin America." See Warshow, *The New Latin America*, New York, 1922, p. ix.

61. Enock, *op. cit.*, p. 10.

62. "Without doubt the number of Chileans who have been affected by English influence is less, because of the difficulty of the language, and the very originality of the British institutions and mentality, which make them assimilable with difficulty by peoples of our origin; but its liberalism, its schools of economy, its literature and art have awakened great sympathy and have been the object of study and admiration." *South American Opinions on the War*; Carlos Silva Vildósola, *Chile and the War* (Carnegie Endowment for International Peace), Washington, 1917, p. 4.

63. *América*, Gante, 1867.

64. "The Latin countries of Europe are to-day seeking a place of dominant influence in the political, economic, and intellectual life of the South American republics, generally in frank opposition to the influence claimed by the United States." Haring, *op. cit.*, p. 168. This relates also to England and Germany.

2. The United States

1. ter Meulen, *Der Gedanke der internationalen Organization*, Vol. II, The Hague, 1929, p. 174.

2. "We are of different races and tongues and creeds, but we have this heritage in common: Our ancestors all had the virtue and vigour of the pioneer. They sought betterment for themselves and their children. They came to a new country; they dreamed dreams, and endured hardships for the sake of their dreams. They dedicated the best years of their manhood and all of their interests to create, serve, and perpetuate a Government that should be dedicated to the common good of all men. This service they have rendered to their country and to us, their children. We therefore have in common the hopes and aspirations of our fathers. We have in common bequeathed to us those ideals which Bolivar, Rosas, and San Martin, and the founders of this Government fought for, and on which our Governments were founded." *Proceedings of the First Pan-American Financial Conference*, 1915, *op. cit.*, pp. 199–200. Address of Hon. Joseph E. Davies, Chairman of the Federal Trade Commission. These reminiscences strike the spirit of those times.

3. James Bryce, *South America. Observations and Impressions*, New York, 1913, p. 484.

4. Frederick Scott Oliver, *Alexander Hamilton*, London, 1907, p. 450.

5. *The Federalist*, No. 11. Hamilton was in personal contact with representatives of South America, especially with Francesco de Miranda, one of the first propagators of the unionist movement on the Southern continent.

6. Oliver, *op. cit.*, p. 356.

7. *Op. cit.*, Introduction, p. xix.

8. Chapter VII of the excellent study by Joseph Burne Lockey (*Pan-Américanism: Its Beginning*, New York, 1920), dedicated to the history of continentalism, does not mention this term. It seems strange that Hamilton's views are disregarded by Lockey.

9. The term "continentalism" denotes something different from "official Pan-Americanism." Ernesto Quesada, however, is of another opinion. To him Pan-Americanism is a continentalist movement in contradistinction to all other "isms" (see *La Evolución del Pan-Americanismo*, Buenos Aires, 1919). His efforts to present Pan-Americanism as a natural expansion of old theories is chronologically false. Samuel Guy Inman, on the other hand, goes too far in his attempts to show the existence now of a continental solidarity. It is true that "in the early development of American life both Anglo-Saxon and Hispanic-America were strongly in favour of continental solidarity" (*op. cit.*, p. 99). But Inman finds continental tendencies in the attitude of Rivadavia and Rosas, and considers alliances among several states of South America as a kind of continental solidarity; and even the supporters of Spanish American union who exclude the United States are, according to Inman, continentalists. The question then arises as to what all this has to do with "continentalism."

10. *The Life and Speeches of the Hon. Henry Clay*. Compiled and edited by Daniel Mallory, fourth edition, New York, 1844 (*Mission to South America*, House of Representatives, May 13, 1820), p. 429. South Americans often understood quite clearly the intentions of the United States. Thus the first Brazilian diplomatic envoy declared to his Government in 1885: "This Government desires the same relationship with American Governments which already exists between it and Colombia: commerce, but not alliances which carry obligations, is the only and desirable aim." Helio Lobo, *Brazilianos e Yanquis*, Rio de Janeiro, 1926, p. 180.

11. "The first intimation that the presence of the United States was desired was made by the representatives of Colombia and Mexico in conversation with Clay, who had become Secretary of State" (John Bassett Moore, *op. cit.*, p. 353). Bolivar's invitation did not include the United States. Then Clay planned to promulgate at the Congress "a joint declaration of the principle of the Monroe Doctrine," "a joint support for an isthmian canal" (see Pitmann B. Potter, *The Myth of American Isolation. Our Policy of International Co-operation*, World Peace Foundation, Boston, 1921, p. 445). The United States at this time "was engrossed in the problem of slavery, and was led by the slave-owners, who had raised the chief opposition in Congress to the Conference at Panama, into a career of conquest in the south-west, which resulted in neglect and tacit repudiation of the Pan-American Policy" (*ibid.*, p. 446).

12. John Bassett Moore, *op. cit.*, p. 357.

13. The title of this booklet is *A Plan to Stop the Present and Prevent Future Wars.*

14. "We were all in the same boat afloat between the Atlantic and the Pacific." *Proceedings of the First Pan-American Financial Conference, op. cit.*, p. 196 (address of Hon. Joseph E Davies, Chairman of Federal Trade Commission).

15. *Ibid.*, p. 204 (address of Hon. John Barrett, Director-General of the Pan-American Union).

16. *Una Evolución Trascendental de la Vida internacional en América*, Buenos Aires, 1918, p. 147.

17. *Proceedings of the First Pan-American Financial Conference, op. cit.*, p. 114.

18. While the Secretary of the Treasury tried to revive old continental thought, his colleague, the Secretary of Commerce, was in his address closer to the facts of history. "Gentlemen, we are gathered here representing two great continents with many common ideals but too little in touch with one another in the past." *Proceedings of the First Pan-American Financial Conference, op. cit.*, p. 122 (address of Hon. William C. Redfield, Secretary of Commerce).

19. Guillermo A. Sherwell, *The Inter-American High Commission. Its Rôle in the Economic Studies of the Continent*, Washington, 1925, p. 2.

20. *Latin America and the War, op. cit.*, p. 265.

21. *Proceedings of the First Pan-American Financial Conference, op. cit.*, pp. 32–33; report of the Secretary-General.

22. However, few considered the moment of these changes. For example, the Secretary of State, Richard Olney, used the old arguments: "The States of America, South as well as North, by geographical proximity, by natural sympathy, by similarity of Government constitutions, are friends and allies, commercially and politically, of the United States." With regard to the first motive, Hiram Bingham remarks appropriately: "Most of our statesmen studied geography when they were in the grammar school, and have rarely looked at a world atlas since" (*The Monroe Doctrine an Obsolete Shibboleth*, 1913, p. 18). The history of peace negotiations in Versailles has confirmed this statement.

23. J. Fred Rippy denies the term Pan-Americanism. He makes no distinction between continentalism, Pan-Americanism, and between movements organized in Europe or America; he regards these ideas as "the International movement in America." What misconceptions such a generalization may leave is illustrated by the following: "By the international movement in America, I mean the attempt to solve some of the problems of the United States and Latin America by the employment of multilateral diplomacy, the diplomacy of congresses and conferences. Some people would call the movement Pan-Americanism, but this is not quite correct. Canada has not been included in the movement. On one occasion England was present. On the

same occasion Holland was present. On many occasions the United States has not been present. Sometimes by no means all of the Latin-American countries have been present. So I have decided to call this, 'The International Movement in America.'" . . . "Leadership in this multilateral diplomacy was assumed by Latin America for the first sixty-five years of its employment, but since 1889 the United States has played the leading rôle. Under Latin-American leadership little was accomplished. Although more than twenty conferences were assembled under this leadership, never were there more than nine States represented, and sometimes not more than three had delegates present. Indeed, some seven or eight calls were issued without assemblies actually convening, and, what is more important, few of these early agreements and recommendations were ever ratified by the Governments back home.

"After the United States became interested, however, attendance improved, and no calls were issued without resulting in assemblies. This result has been due not alone to the United States, but to the growing interest in multilateral diplomacy in the modern world." *The Seminar in Mexico* (Committee on Cultural Relations with Latin America). Fourth Annual Session, 1929; Rippy, *The International Movement in America*, p. 90. In Spanish literature on the subject one is confronted with the same confusion. "Pan-Americanism, as a noble aspiration to fraternity, has its roots in Spanish America." Nestor Carbonell, *Las Conferencias Internationales Américanas*, Habana, 1928, p. 8; also see p. 54.

24. Archibald C. Coolidge, *United States as a World Power*, New York, 1909, p. 299. In general this situation was similarly understood in South America. "During the first two-thirds of the nineteenth century it was in the interests of the United States to avoid entirely being mixed up in anything that happened outside of the country or the surrounding zone. Such an attitude lasted until the interests of the United States changed so that they drove the country to intervene in the policies and especially the commercial relations of the other America." Ernesto Quesada, *La Evolución, op. cit.*, p. 39.

25. The original plan of the Pan-American Union, practically similar to that accepted in 1889, had been proposed by General Carlos Butterfield as early as 1868. (See his pamphlets, *Value of Spanish America to the United States*, New York, 1868, and *The National Debt and the Monroe Doctrine*, New York, 1866.)

26. An interesting description of Blaine is given by Eduardo Prado: "Peculiar and strange is the personality of this quasi-statesman. He was like a last and belated heroic breath of the period of independence and intellectual grandeur of American statesmen. He was a kind of Hamilton, Clay, Webster, or Seward, but incomplete, not sustained, and unbalanced." *A Illusão Américana*, São Paulo, third edition, 1912, pp. 124–125.

27. "Blaine was a tariff man, a follower of Henry Clay and a believer in the American system from boyhood." Edward Stanward, *James Gillespie Blaine*, Boston, New York, 1905, p. 356.

28. It would be highly interesting to study the origin of the ideas of both statesmen and their personal relations in Europe. Especially the activity of Blaine (railroads, his attitude to the Crédit Mobilier, and his interest in the Panama Canal) seems to indicate a certain influence by practical Saint-Simonism.

29. Dr. William Notz, *Friedrich List in America*, Jena, 1925, p. 282.

30. Swanton, *op. cit.*, p. 252.

31. "A personal note accompanied the formal offer of the State Department. General Harrison expresses himself as 'especially interested in the improvement of our relations with the Central South American States.' " Swanton, *op. cit.*, p. 311.

32. "In Europe the simple announcement that an American Congress will take place made the Governments feel anxious. Europe saw danger in the tendency of Panama to invite the Hispanic-American countries." Carbonell, *Las Conferencias*, *op. cit.*, p. 20.

But still stronger was the effect of the new scheme. "In Europe as well as in America this proposed meeting has produced an immense sensation, because it was believed that this was the beginning of a definitely aggressive policy with a tendency to establish political and economic hegemony of the United States in America, through absolute exclusion of any interference and intervention by Europe.' Ernesto Quesada, *op. cit.*, p. 42–43.

33. Achille Viallate, *Economic Imperialism and International Relations during the Last Fifty Years*, New York, 1923, p. 29.

34. Ernesto Quesada, *op. cit.*, p. 46.

35. Joaquim Nabuco, *The Approach of the Two Americas* (address before the University of Chicago, August 28, 1908).

36. *Op. cit.*, p. 496.

37. A German writer, however, states: "Thus we see North American propaganda in South America in all fields. These activities are being carried on in such a way that no other commercial power is able to accomplish anything of equal proportion. Through this propaganda the economic penetration of the United States in South America is made substantially easier." Dr. Walter Meissner, *Die Vereinigte Staaten und Süd Amerika*, Gluckstadt, 1918, p. 14. But where are the proofs?

38. An attempt towards the history of economic thinking in the United States would consist not in the history of the literature on that subject, but in the history of the principles of governmental policy. This country seems to have a pronounced aversion against theorizing. It is surprising how deeply Frederick List understood the peculiarities of the United States: "The best work on political economy in this country that one can read is life." *Das Nationale System der Politischen Oekonomie*, Jena, 1922, p. 11.

39. The Sixth International Conference of American States "Resolves: (1) To maintain in full force the resolutions of the previous conference, which provide that the Pan-American Railway shall be constructed along the Andes route which it follows at present, and which was outlined in 1890." *Report of the Delegates of the United States of America to the Sixth International Conference of American States*, held at Habana, Cuba, January 16 to February 20, 1928. Appendix 44, Resolution (Pan-American Railway), p. 278.

40. Pedro Martinez Fraga, *El Panamericanismo y su Evolución* (Sociedad Cubana de Derecho Internacional, Anuario, 1924, Habana, p. 427). It is erroneous to explain the origin of official Pan-Americanism by declaring it a continuation of Bolivar's idea.

41. "To some, Pan-Americanism is the Utopia of peace, a demonstration of the superior morality of the Western over the Eastern Hemisphere, of the New World and its Christianity over the Old. To some it is a dream of the monopolization of South American trade by the United States; to others, the Monroe Doctrine and our chivalrous protection of the weak against aggression; to others, a vision of empire in the Western Hemisphere." Roland G. Usher, *Pan-Americanism*, New York, 1915, p. 203.

42. W. S. Robertson, *Hispanic-American Relations with the United States*, New York, 1923, p. 378.

43. "Intercourse policy," as Alfred H. Fried calls it (*Pan-America*, Zürich, 1918). Fried exaggerates the importance of the Union.

44. Haring appraises the Pan-American Union in the following way: "The Union is coming to be a dynamic centre for all inter-American activities. Only in the political sphere has its influence proved incommensurable with the possibilities offered. *Op. cit.*, p. 55. Inman, however, does not realize that his description of the Pan-American Union (*op. cit.*, p. 206) emphasizes the decline of the movement.

45. *The Rediscovery of America*, New York, 1929, p. 270. How inconsistent and superficial is the following: "What could be more symbolic of our embryonism than the fact that we lack 'even names'? What is our America? Even the conglomerate phrase United States is not exclusively ours. And the other America? To call it Latin America, Indo America, Ibero America, or severally Mexico, Central America, South America, is equally inadequate. Only America is a good name, and prophetically it covers us all. I shall use the term America Latina as a reluctant convenience. Let it not be forgotten that America Latina is even less Latin than America Sajona (as they sometimes call us) is Saxon." *Ibid.*, p. 267.

46. *The Basis of Co-operation between the Two Americas* (The Seminar on Mexico, report 1929).

47. Warren H. Kelchner, *The Development of the Pan-American Union*, Bulletin of the Pan-American Union, April 1930, p. 333. The staff of five in 1890 enlarged to eighty-six. According to an in-

formation from the Pan-American Union from May 14, 1930, the incoming letter mail has been as follows:—

1922	40,700
1924	44,977
1926	51,052
1929	62,474

48. In spite of the fact that the Union as a whole is of minor importance to the United States at present, the information service in Washington is still of great value. The tendency of standardization of commercial and legal relations is but one more factor to facilitate the flow of the United States' mass exportation.

49. As Jessen maintains (*op. cit.*, p. 111/881), and as was believed in the United States at the time of the organization of the Pan-American Union.

50. *Op. cit.*, p. 203.

51. *Ibid.*, p. 215.

52. Address by Secretary of State, Lansing. Second Pan-American Scientific Congress, December 27, 1915. *New Pan-Americanism* (World Peace Foundation Pamphlets), Boston, 1916, Part II, p. 108.

53. Sometimes at the conferences one can discern the old strains of continentalism rising again—an echo of old melodies. As an example may be cited the utterances of the representative of Santo Domingo at the closing meeting of the Fourth Conference in Buenos Aires.

Very pungent indeed are the revived memories in the address by Antonio Sanchez de Bustamante, the famous Cuban scholar. (*Report of the Delegates of the United States of America to the Sixth International Conference of American States, op. cit.*, pp. 82–83.)

(*b*) *The Courted*

1. Quesada, *La Evolución, op. cit.*, p. 10.

2. Lathané, *op. cit.*, p. 21.

3. Helio Lobo, *Cousas Américanas, op. cit.*, p. 517.

4. Inman, *op. cit.*, pp. 101–102.

5. See in the various writings of Helio Lobo interesting data on the activity of this first Brazilian diplomatic representative in the United States, one of the first Pan-Americanists. Especially see the article: "Um creador da bóa amizade" (in *Brasilianos y Yankees, op. cit.*, p. 171), and his address in the Pan-American Society: "Uma velha amizade internacional" (in *Cousas Américanas, op. cit.*).

6. Helio Lobo, *De Monroe a Rio Branco*, Rio de Janeiro, 1912, p. 149.

7. *The Pan-American Conferences and Their Significances*. Supplements to the Annals of the American Academy of Political and Social Science, Philadelphia, 1906, p. 3.

8. Joaquim Nabuco, *The Approach of the Two Americas, op. cit.*

9. "The Pan-American movement, hitherto oftentimes regarded as

a platonic sentiment or a subject for debate before international congresses or in after-dinner speeches, suddenly took on a new and vital significance. As will be presently pointed out, this feeling of continental solidarity and community of ideals among the democracy of the New World was one of the causes which led Brazil actively to participate in the War." Martin, *op. cit.*, p. 230.

10. Quoted from Martin, *op. cit.*

11. Bingham declares that "Brazil . . . has always been more kindly in its criticism of us than many of the other countries" (*Monroe Doctrine*, *op. cit.*, p. 69). Clarence H. Haring explains this attitude: "These suspicions of American motives in the Caribbean region are of Spanish, not of Portuguese origin, and the Pan-Hispanic propaganda by which they are so sedulously nurtured finds no foothold in Brazil" (*op. cit.*, p. 208).

"On the whole, however, the Brazilian entertains little fear of the United States. Although he takes a keen interest in foreign affairs, he is not interested in American interventions in Central America and the West Indies, and although the news is reported in the papers of the day, there is little comment. Brazil, moreover, because of her climate and soil, is economically a supplement, not a competitor, of the United States. She is a producer of the commodities we need, tropical wares such as coffee, cacao, and rubber, the importation of which into this country is vastly increasing, and the output of which in Brazil is limited only by the present lack of capital and competent labour" (*op. cit.*, p. 212).

12. Martin, *op. cit.*, p. 238. When the United States and Great Britain agreed to submit the Alabama claims to arbitration, the Brazilian Emperor, Don Pedro II, was requested to name one of the arbitrators. After the recall of the United States Ambassador from Mexico, Brazil represented the interests of the United States there (*ibid.*).

13. Bunge, *La Economia Argentina*, *op. cit.*, p. 121.

14. Helio Lobo, *De Monroe*, *op. cit.*, p. 57.

15. *Ibid.*, p. 153. Lobo's explanation that Brazilian opinion was more or less the same is not precise. The causes were different.

16. Quesada, *op. cit.*, p. 20.

17. *Ibid.*, p. 31. In spite of this, Quesada declares that the initiative of an Hispano-American federation belongs to Argentina (p. 11). The facts are against his opinion.

18. Calderon, *Ideas e impresiones*, *op. cit.*, p. 117.

19. *Ibid.*

20. Sáenz Peña, *Escritos y discursos*, Buenos Aires, 1914, Vol. I, p. 81.

21. The consumption of the nations of Latin America represented in this conference amounts to $560,000,000, but the United States share in those importations to the amount only of $52,000,000, not being 10 per cent. of our purchases from Europe. The relation of these

figures to the trade of the United States reveals the poverty of the exchanges with greater clearness. Out of their total export trade, amounting to $740,000,000, Latin America buys only $52,000,000, that is to say, 7 per cent. of the total exports. *International American Conference*, Washington, 1890, Vol. I, p. 113.

In connection with this situation Señor Peña had the following apprehensions: ". . . it is easy to foresee the squirmings of Europe when she should feel the effects of a continental blockade, maintained, it is true, not by warships but by belligerent tariffs. It would not be countries bound together by political bonds that would enter into compacts inspired by a national sentiment. It would be the war of one continent against another, eighteen sovereignties allied to exclude from the life of commerce that same Europe which extends to us her hand, sends us her strong arms, and complements our economic existence, after having apportioned us her civilization and her culture, her sciences and her arts, industries and customs that have completed our sociological evolutions."

22. "Patriotism among the Argentines amounts to a mania." Bryce, *op. cit.*, p. 346.

23. *Nuestra América*, Madrid, 1926, p. 46.

24. This attitude did not change during the War. The former Secretary of Foreign Affairs appears worried about this fact, and claims (*La Razon*, April 10, 1917): "We should constitute the material and moral union of this continent for the defence of law and democratic principles in international relations." Martin, *op. cit.*, p. 252.

25. *El Ideal Latino-Américano.* Collección de documentos raros protocolos de diversos congresos, memorias de eminentes pensadores y otras materias de muy vivo interes que se refieren a la proyectada Union y Confederaciones de los paises Centro y Suramericanos. Mexico, 1919.

In 1926 the Mexican Government published in *Archivo Historico Diplomatico Mexicano* very interesting documents concerning the same subject (*El Congreso de Panama y otros proyectos de Union Hispano-Américana*. Prólogo de Antonio do la Pena y Reyes. Mexico, Publicaciones de la Secretaria de Relaciones exteriores, 1926.) The specific interest of Mexico in this problem is significant.

26. From the South American the Venezuelan, Chilean, and Peruvian were the most active.

27. Many projects not included in the Mexican collections are published by the Sociedad de la Union Americana de Santiago de Chile. The Mexican as well as the Chilean publication was used in the explanation of these projects.

28. "French intervention in Mexico provoked an interesting propaganda in Spanish America. Under the auspices of certain thinkers, patriotic societies were organized in various Spanish-American countries. The most influential of those societies was that founded by prominent Chilean Liberals on May 25, 1862, in Santiago, a society

which was designated the "American Union." In its statutes this society declared that its objects were to sustain the independence and to promote the union of various American States. Its statutes also provided that a junta of its members should correspond with similar societies in other parts of America, and should make known to the public the principles which might promote a union of the American nations. The junta of the "American Union" carried on an extensive correspondence with similar societies which sprang into existence in the towns and cities of Chile, Bolivia, Peru, and Mexico. An important measure of that junta provided for the collection and publication of essays and documents concerning a union of the South American nations. To this junta on May 14, 1864, there was submitted the design of a badge for the society, which was to be a five-pointed star composed of sixteen small silver stars upon a blue back-ground. Each silver star should represent one of the republics belonging to the "American Union." In the discussion concerning this proposed badge the significant question was raised as to whether or not a silver star representing the United States should be included in the cluster of stars." William Spence Robertson, *Hispanic-American Relations with the United States*, New York, 1923, p. 387.

29. *Allianza Sur Americana*, Guayaquil, 1868.

30. *La Union Americana*, Santiago de Chile, 1868.

31. *Ibid.*, p. 17.

32. An adequate account of the Panama Congress would require a separate volume. I have included a mere general sketch.

33. Marriano A. Pelliza, *Federación Social Americana*, Buenos Aires, 1895, p. 29.

34. Calderon, *La Creación de un Continente*, Paris, 1912, p. xi.

35. Oliveira Lima emphasizes that Bolivar strived for a military dictatorship. *Pan-Americanismo*, Rio de Janeiro, 1907, p. 95.

36. Samuel G. Inman, *op. cit.*, pp. 103–104. Calderon notes concerning this question: "The contemporary writers of the Revolution did not forget the instruction received in Spain, in the universities of the eighteenth century, where they studied in Latin and commented upon the classics of Greece and Rome. They read and imitated Horace and Virgil, and were inspired by the ancient democracies and the heroes of Plutarch; the Isthmus of Panama was compared to that of Corinth. At their birth the Republics appointed consuls and triumvirs. In speeches and proclamations of the time we find numerous classical reminiscences; politicians and poets borrowed their images from Pindar, Horace, Homer, and Virgil." *Latin America*, *op. cit.*, p. 251.

37. The opinion was popular that a danger also threatened from Brazil. Compare Monteagudo's pamphlet.

38. This idea seems to have found a propagandist in Central America—Cecilio Valle—independently of Bolivar.

39. *Archivo Historico Diplomatico Mexicano, op. cit.*, pp. vii–viii.
40. *Ibid.*, p. 12.
41. *Ibid.*, p. 9.
42. *Ibid.*, p. 33.
43. *Ibid.*, p. 18. "An eminent Brazilian historian and diplomatist, Oliveira Lima, has even demonstrated that when Bolivar, after convoking the Congress of Panama in 1826, had thereupon proposed, as the last stage of his vast epic, to give liberty to Cuba, it was the United States that prevented him. For they knew that independence would also mean the enfranchisement of subject races, and they needed slaves for the proud and wealthy feudal State of Virginia.' Calderon, *Latin America, op. cit.*, p. 316.
44. Bolivar counted on aid from Great Britain, and was pronouncedly opposed to invitation of the United States. Compare Robertson, *op. cit.*, p. 380.
45. Letter of September 6, 1815. It would be interesting to compare Bolivar's ideas with those of Napoleon. "L'Europe n'eut que même peuple, et chacun en voyageant, partout se fut trouvé toujours dans la patrie commune," said Napoleon (*Mémorial de Sainte-Hélène*, Vol. V, pp. 353–354). Especially the "acte additionale aux Constitutions de l'Empire," 1815, really written by Benjamin Constant (the "preambule" has a pronounced style of Napoleon himself), seems to be of importance in the investigation of this problem. Compare Thiers, *Histoire du Consulat*, Vol. 19, pp. 424, 438 (remark).

Even the cult of Bolivar in South America can be compared with that of Napoleon in France; and Rufino Blanco Fombona reminds one in this respect of Stendhal.

46. *Archivo Historico Diplomatico Mexicano, op. cit.*, p. xxi.
47. Pelliza, *op. cit.*
48. *Archivo Historico Diplomatico Mexicano, op. cit.*, p. xxvi.
49. Compare Constantino Suarez (Españolito), *La verdad desnuda*, Madrid, 1924, p. 53.
50. Fernando Ortíz, *La Reconquista de América*, Paris, 1911, p. 189.
51. Ortíz continues the traditional policy represented partly by the Argentine Domingo F Sarmiento.
52. *Op. cit.*, p. 105.
53. *Ibid.*, p. 184.
54. *Ibid.*, p. 105.
55. Calderon, *La creación, op. cit.*, p. 49. One can note an interesting analogy in the relations of the United States and England. Compare v. Schulze-Gaevernitz, *op. cit.*, pp. 97–98.
56. *Op. cit.*, pp. 197–198, 206.
57. *Op. cit.*, p. 124.
58. Fernando Ortíz, *Ni racismos ni xenofobia* (*Revista Bimestre Cubana*, Vol. XXIV, No. 1, Habana, 1929).
59. Rufino Blanco Fombona, *La evolución politica y social de Hispano-América*, Madrid, 1911, p. vi.

60. An analogy can be found in the well-known Epitalamio by Amado Nervo to Alfonso XIII.

61. *Ideas e Impresiones*, *op. cit.*, p. 83. Compare his *Latin America*, *op. cit.*, p. 337. He forgets that common tongue does not always signify common culture and friendly relations; for example, England and Ireland. Joaquim Nabuco urges the same objection against a union between Brazil and Portugal.

62. Introduction to the English translation of Manuel Ugarte's *The Destiny of the Continent*, New York, 1928, p. viii.

63. The famous "Isthmo de Panama" has a peculiar mixture of the old continental sentiment and radical socialistic notes.

64. *La Agonia Antillana*, *op. cit.*, p. 12.

65. Constantino Suarez, *op. cit.*, p. 49.

66. Luis Jiménez de Asua, *op. cit.*, p. 74.

67. *Op. cit.*, p. 139.

68. *Ibid.*, p. 218.

69. *La evolución*, *op. cit.*, p. 128.

70. *Latin America*, *op. cit.*, p. 288.

71. *Op. cit.*, p. xxiv.

72. *Politica Américana*, Buenos Aires, 1920, p. 21.

73. M. Romero Navarro, *El Hispanismo en Norte América*, Madrid, 1917, p. 7.

74. *A Illusão Américana*, *op. cit.*

75. Nido y Segalerva, *op. cit.*, p. 365.

76. Calderon pointedly says that Ugarte ends as a poet a book which he began as a sociologist. But who in Latin America is free from this weakness? "Románticos somos; Quien que es, no es romántico?" (Rubén Darío in his famous "Canción de los Pinos"). Even Sarmiento devoted himself to poetry.

77. Compare especially *El Porvenir de América Latina*, Valencia (?).

78. *La Patria Grande*, Madrid, 1924, pp. 13–14.

79. *Ibid.*, p. 10.

80. *Ibid.*, p. 16.

81. Rafael Altamira, in his *Psicología del pueblo español*, attempts to explain the Spanish pessimistic tendency by the fact that Spain's history in the nineteenth century shows more years of warfare than any other one. Latin America to a certain extent has perhaps taken infection from Spain.

82. *Latin America*, *op. cit.*, p. 76.

83. Compare Arguedas, *Pueblo enfermo*, *op. cit.*, p. 189.

84. *Op. cit.*

85. Calderon, *Latin America*, *op. cit.*, p. 32. "Yet it is strange to find that, both here and in other parts of South America, men of undoubted talent are often beguiled by phrases, and seem to prefer words to facts. . . . Exuberant imagination takes its hopes or predictions for realities, and finds in the gilded clouds of fancy a foundation on which to build practical policies." Bryce, *op cit.*, p. 417.

86. *Op. cit.*, p. 84.
87. Alberdi, *Estudios Economicos*, Buenos Aires, 1916, p. 43.
88. *Ibid.*, p. 128.
89. *Ibid.*, p. 43.
90. *Ibid.*, p. 191.
91. Manoel Bomfim, *A América Latina*, Rio de Janeiro, 1903, pp. 114, 391; Alberdi, *op. cit.*, p. 89.
92. Bomfim, *op. cit.*, pp. 184–185. Compare with expressions of Mariano da Fonseca.
93. *Op. cit.*, pp. 260–261.
94. Calderon, *Latin America, op. cit.*, p. 62.
95. *Ibid.*, p. 61.
96. Alberdi, *op. cit.*, p. 124.
97. *Latin America*, p. 201.
98. Ingenieros in his introduction to Carlos O. Bunge, *Nuestra América*, Madrid, 1926, p. 27.
99. Not so sharp and pessimistic, but calm and correct, Bryce gives a description of the same problem in Brazil. "The landowner loves his rural life, as did the Virginian planter in North America before the Civil War, and lives on the fazenda in a sort of semi-feudal patriarchal way, often with grown-up sons and daughters around him. Estates (except in the extreme South) are extensive; near neighbours are few; families are often large; the plantation is a sort of little principality, and its owner with his fellow-proprietors is allowed, despite all democratic theory, to direct the politics of the district just as in England eighty years ago the country families used to control local affairs and guide the choice of representatives in Parliament" (*op. cit.*, pp. 415–416). Bryce understood the historical character of the Caciquism.
100. Calderon, *Latin America, op. cit.*, p. 376.
101. *Op. cit.*, p. 131.
102. Bomfim, *op. cit.*, p. 187.
103. Alberdi, *op. cit.*, p. 134.
104. Calderon, *Latin America, op. cit.*, p. 29.
105. Shepherd, *La América Latina*, Traducción español, Madrid, p. 274.
106. Bingham, *Across South America, op. cit.*, p. 5.
107. Calderon, *Latin America, op. cit.*, p. 395.
108. Francisco Bulnes, *Los Grandes Problemas de México*, Mexico, 1927, p. 330.
109. Eduardo Prado, *op. cit.*, p. 6.
110. Bulnes, *op. cit.*, pp. 323–324.
111. Guillermo Padilla Castro, *Évolution politique du continent Ibéro-américain*, Paris, 1927, p. 51.
112. Vargas Vila, *Ante los bárbaros*, Barcelona, (?), p. 55.
113. *Op. cit.*, p. 331.
114. Arguedas, *op. cit.*, p. 221.

115. Parker Thomas Moon, *Imperialism and World Politics,* New York, 1928, p. 6.

116. Blanco Fombona, *La evolución, op. cit.*, p. 128.

117. Calderon, *Latin America, op. cit.*, pp. 349–350.

118. Alberto Ghiraldo, *Yanquilandia barbara*, Madrid, 1929, p. 154.

119. Malagrida, *op. cit.*, p. 543.

120. *La Creación, op. cit.*, p. x. Compare his *Latin America, op. cit.*, p. 298, and José S. Carranza, *Cuestiones Américanas*, Ligugé, 1912, p. 4.

121. Haring, *op. cit.*, p. 142. Haring considers Argentina as the inspirator of the Central American bloc in the Conference of 1923 in Santiago de Chile. *Ibid.*, p. 199.

122. Malagrida, *op. cit.*, p. 207.

123. "Buenos Aires, however, will always maintain her political and commercial supremacy. She is not only the capital of Argentina, but out of every five Argentinos she claims at least one as a denizen of her narrow streets. Already ranking as the second Latin city in the world, her population equals that of Madrid and Barcelona combined." Hiram Bingham, *Across South America, op. cit.*, p. 31.

124. Haring, *op. cit.*, p. 198.

125. Francisco Seeber, *Great Argentina, Comparative Studies between Argentina, Brazil, Chile, Peru, Uruguay, Bolivia, and Paraguay*, Buenos Aires, 1904, p. 216.

126. *Op. cit.*, p. 30, and following.

127. *Sociologia Argentina*, Madrid, 1913, p. 100

128. *Op. cit.*, p. 208.

129. *Op. cit.*, p. 190.

130. *Monroe Doctrine, op. cit.*, pp. 77–78.

131. Calderon, *Latin America, op. cit.*, p. 349.

132 *Ibid.*, p. 348.

133. Malagrida, *op. cit.*, p. 99.

134. *Op. cit.*, pp. 311–312. Seventy years ago similar opinions were published from the European standpoint by S. Dutot. Compare his *France et Brésil*, Paris, 1859, p. 211.

135. Calderon, *Latin America, op. cit.*, p. 344.

136. *Ibid.*, p. 340. Poincaré understands Calderon's programme to be transitional and minimum. "I believe that at heart M. Calderon regrets the excessive division of the States of South America. But the problem of unity, often brought to the fore in congresses and conferences, appears to him insoluble, and in default of this he would be content with intellectual alliances, with economic or fiscal unions, which would still permit the various republics to draw nearer to one another, to know one another better, and in time and on occasion to associate their defensive efforts." Preface to Calderon's *Latin America*, p. 13. It is true that Calderon's plan has a distinctly opportunistic character. Principally he is wavering between continentalism, Pan-latinism, and Hispano-Americanism.

137. *Latin America, op. cit.*, p. 392

138. *Ibid.*, pp. 398–399.

139. In the same manner Garcia Gadoy distinguishes between "Americanism" (continental) and "Nationalism" (peculiar of each republic).

140. Calderon, *Latin America, op. cit.*, p. 247.

141. Haring, *op. cit.*, p. 214.

142. *The Destiny of the Continent, op. cit.*, p. 284.

143. Padilla Castro, *op. cit.*, pp. 55–56, 123.

144. Recently in Portugal Francisco Ribeiro Salgado discusses the problem of a "Hispano-American bloc." *Op. cit.*, p. 48.

145. Raymond Leslie Buell, *The United States and Latin America.* A suggested programme. *Foreign Policy Association*, Vol. III, Special Supplement No. 4, p. 88.

146. *Ibid.* P. A. Martin means that there exists for Latin America "The dilemma of choosing between the League of Nations and the Monroe Doctrine." *Op. cit.*, p. 572.

147. Buell, *op. cit.*, p. 87. Several Latin-American writers are against participation in the League of Nations. Compare Carrion, *Los creadores de la Nueva América*, Madrid, 1928.

148. "While the United States did not become a member of the League of Nations, nineteen American States, including Canada, became members. Several Latin-American Republics have been members of the Council of the League. It is apparent that a special effort has been made on the part of the European Powers to bring about close political relations with the Latin-American States, and representative men of Latin America have been brought into more intimate contact with the leading figures of European diplomacy. Costa Rica has ceased to be a member of the League, and Brazil in 1926 gave preliminary notice of withdrawal. It is also true that several Latin-American States have not manifested deep interest in its proceedings, but the League of Nations is, and will remain, an important factor, which must have friendly but adequate recognition in considering our relations with our neighbours." Charles E. Hughes, *op. cit.*, p. 2.

149. Baltazar Brum's (Uruguay) plan of an American League finds new arguments through Briand's project. Nevertheless, it encounters sharp criticism in Moreno Quintana. *Politica Américana*, Buenos Aires, 1920.

150. Fraga, *op. cit.*, p. 433.

151. *Latin America, op. cit.*, p. 346.

152. Ugarte, *Le Prochain Congrés Pan-Américain*, La Revue, March 1, 1910.

153. Malagrida, *op. cit.*, p. 81.

154. Calderon, *La Creación, op. cit.*, p. 28.

155. L. Jiménez de Asua, *op. cit.*, p. 71.

156. Luis de Armiñan, *El Pan-américanismo*, Madrid, 1900, p. 15.

157. Ugarte, *La Patria Grande, op. cit.*, p. 32.

158. *Op. cit.*, p. 59.

159. *Archivo Historico Diplomatico Mexicano*, *op. cit.*, p. xxvii.

160. R. L. Lomba, Consul-General of Uruguay in France, was the initiator.

161. *Op. cit.*, pp. 8–9.

162. Compare *Revue de l'Amérique Latine*, Paris, May 1, 1930, p. 397.

163. Enrique Gay-Calbo, *La América indefensa*, Habana, 1925, pp. 95–100.

164. *Op. cit.*, pp. 116–117.

165. *Foreign Policy Association.* Sixth Pan-American Conference, New York, 1928, p. 80.

CHAPTER III

"Peligro Yanqui"

1. Viallate, *Economic Imperialism*, *op. cit.*, p. 32.
2. *Op. cit.*, pp. 102–103.
3. *Imperialism and World Politics*, New York, 1928, p. 470.
4. *Union Latino-Americana*, Paris, 1865.
5. *La Allianza fantastica: Yankees e Ingleses*, Santiago de Chile, 1866.
6. *Monroe Doctrine*, *op. cit.*, pp. 72–73.
7. *Le Pan-Américanisme et l'équilibre Américain*, Saint-Amand (Cher), 1897, pp. 5, 122.
8. *Ibid.*, pp. 175–176.
9. Enock, *op. cit.*, p. 491.
10. *La evolución*, *op. cit.*, pp. 127–128.
11. The emphasis of their own danger one can find by studying the German imperialism of the Kaiserreich. A typical example. In the year 1904 there appeared in English the well-known book *The Pan-Germanic Doctrine* (London and New York, Harpers, Inc.). The content of this book was annihilating to German policy. In the Harvard College Library one can find a copy inscribed as: gift to Hohenzollern Collection "in commemoration of the visit of his Royal Highness Prince Henry of Prussia—on behalf of his Majesty the German Emperor." There is also a certain flirtation on the part of the United States authors, who speak with preference of an "offensive of Yankee Imperialism," or "Dollar Diplomacy," and partly with pride, partly in expressed anti-capitalistic ways, study, describe, and investigate this apparition.

"The American raise the strongest claims against their fellow-citizens who are 'Imperialists.'" Harry T. Collings, *Die Kapitalexpansion der Vereinigten Staaten in Latin America*, Jena, 1927, p. 19

12. Benjamin H. Williams, *op. cit.*, p. 5.

13. *Problems of Expansion*, New York, 1900.
14. Haring, *op. cit.*, p. 80.
15. Jacques Anboyneau, *Le marché des capitaux en France de 1924 à 1926*, Paris, 1927, p. 169.
16. Moon, *op. cit.*, p. 471.
17. v. Schulze-Gaevernitz, *op. cit.*, p. 122.
18. Many investigators emphasized the peculiarity of the imperialism of the United States. Parker T. Moon characterizes it as "subtle." A modern French economist stresses that it "destroys the government of the small countries" (Jean Gachon, *La Pénétration des États-Unis dans l'Amérique Centrale.* Revue d'Économie politique, Paris, 1929, No. 4). On the other hand, Neering and Freeman do not recognize any difference between economic penetration and political intervention.
19. *Op. cit.*, Vol. I, p. 52.
20. *Wandlungen des Kapitalismus.* Verhandlungen des Vereins für Sozialpolitik in Zürich, 1928. München and Leipzig, 1929, p. 38.
21. Adolf Halfeld, *America und dcr Americanismus*, Jena, 1928, p. 50.
22. *Appendix to the Outlines, op cit.*, p. 4.
23. Halfeld, *op. cit.*, p. 54.
24. Charles E. Hughes recalls this point of view: "There seems to be a popular impression that bankers in our country make the loans. Of course, they merely place the loans. It is the people of the United States, from the Atlantic to the Pacific, who buy the foreign loans. . . . This sort of economic penetration may be regarded as the highest expression, from the material standpoint, of international confidence and good will." *Op. cit.*, pp. 57–58.
25. Compare Sven Helander, *Die Kapitalausfuhr Schwedens in "Die Anslandskredite," op. cit.*, p. 131.
26. *The Americans in Santo Domingo*, New York, 1928, pp. 166–176.
27. *Nuestros banqueiros en Bolivia.* Spanish translation, Madrid, p. 169.
28. Max Winkler, *op. cit.*, p. 43.
29. *Proceedings, op. cit.*, p. 168.
30. *Ibid.*, p. 173.
31. *La Concurrence Américaine, op. cit.*, pp. 85–86.
32. Coolidge, *op. cit.*, p. 146.
33. *Ibid.*, p. 303.
34. *La agonia Antillana, op. cit.*, p. 97.
35. *Across South America, op. cit.*, p. 32.
36. This moment of surprise is emphasized by H. H. Simmons, *The Myth of American Financial Imperialism*, New York, 1927. A following explanation of the origin of the "Peligro Yanqui" is quite naïve: "But the United States is known in Latin America chiefly by its movies, its jazz, and other aspects of its life which do not add to its prestige. Personal contacts are made chiefly by salesmen who

frequently leave a bad impression as to our education and ideas. Latin Americans resent the fact that apparently we are interested solely in commercial intercourse with them and not interested in cultural contacts as is the case with some of the most advanced European countries which send some of their finest scholars, publicists, and educators to lecture in the Latin-American countries." *Institute of International Education, Tenth Annual Report*, New York, October 1, 1929, p. 7.

37. Alemporte, *op. cit.*, p. 30. Compare also Kasdorf, *op. cit.*, p. 51.

38. Professor John H. Latané, in testifying before the House Committee on Foreign Affairs on January 12, 1927, said that the number of cases of intervention by the United States in the affairs of some other country probably runs up to a hundred. Particularly in the smaller countries of the Caribbean has the United States often intervened, controlling the affairs of the country by the force of American arms, sometimes continuing such control for a considerable number of years. Compare *Selected Articles on Intervention in Latin America*, compiled by Lamar T. Beman, The Handbook Series, Series II, Vol. V, p. v, New York, 1928.

39. Coolidge, *op. cit.*, p. 304.

40. Compare Georges Dovime, *Ne ratifions pas*, Paris, 1929, p. 100.

41. Compare G. G. Wilson, *The Monroe Doctrine after the War*, Boston, 1918.

42. "But with a sensitive people such as the Latin Americans, any assertion of authority or hegemony by the United States is immediately resented, and if exercised would be inimical to trade relations. The problem for the United States is not an easy one, involving as it does on the one hand the necessity for some moral intervention or mentorship, and on the other the desire for predominance in trade." Enock, *op. cit.*, p. 495.

43. *Op. cit.*, p. 11.

44. *Across South America*, *op. cit.*, p. 388.

45. *Report on Trade and Tariffs*, *op. cit.*, p. 22.

46. Warshaw, *The New Latin America*, New York, 1922, p. 163.

47. Introduction to Winkler, *op. cit.*

48. Calderon, *Latin America*, *op. cit.*, pp. 299–300

49. *Wilson Doctrine*, New York, 1914, p. 7.

50. *Report of the Sixth International Conference of American States*, held at Habana, Washington, 1928, p. 64.

51. Address by Secretary of State, Lansing, at the Second Pan-American Scientific Congress, 1915. *New Pan-Americanism*, *op. cit.*, Part II, p. 99.

52. Bingham, *Monroe Doctrine*, *op. cit.*, p. 106.

53. Buell, *op. cit.*, p. 85.

54. *La Patria Grande*, *op. cit.*, p 19.

55. Senator Henrik Shipstead, *Current History*, September 1927.

56. Bingham, *Monroe Doctrine*, *op. cit.*, p. 98.

CHAPTER IV

AN EXPERIMENT

1. José Ignacio Rodriguez, *Estudio historico sobre el origen, desenvolvimiento y manifestaciones prácticas de la idea de la anexión de la Isla de Cuba a los Estados Unidos de América*, Habana, 1900.
2. *Op. cit.*, p. 89.
3. Secretaria de Hacienda, Seccion Estadistica, *Importación en el ano 1928*, Habana, 1929.
4. Max Winkler, according to Cuban American Chamber of Commerce, estimates the United States' investments in Cuban Government Bonds to be $110,000,000, which seems to be incorrect, because the total national debt of Cuba (foreign and internal) has not reached the sum of $90,000,000 (*op. cit.*, p. 183). Jenks gives a much lower figure (*op. cit.*, p. 294)
5. Dr. Antonio L. Varvelde, *Produccion de Tobacco*, Habana, 1929, p. 10.
6. The English call the sugar trade "The lottery of the West Indies." "The price of sugar seems to be more mysterious and maliciously inconstant than cyclones, which run over our country, and which are far better known and investigated." José Manuel Cortina, *El Azúcar y la Nación Cubana*, Habana, 1926, p. 10.
7. "Cuba is progressing so rapidly that a guide-book which is not changed frequently will quickly become obsolete," says the author of the best guide to Cuba. (Terry's *Guide to Cuba*, Habana–London, 1929, p. v.) But the Cuban, generally speaking, is not aware of the great transformation of his country. The book of Ramiro Guerra, *Un cuarto de siglo de la evolución Cubana*, Habana, 1924, p. 14, gives an excellent picture of the economic development of Cuba in an interesting description combined with a thorough knowledge of facts. This is a work in the style of the famous investigation by Helferich into the prosperity of Germany. The reader interested in facts can find data in the above-mentioned book as well as in the work of Jenks.
8. Scott Nearing y José Freeman, *Dollar Diplomacy: A Study of Yankee Imperialism*. Spanish translation, Madrid, (?), p. 200.
9. *Ibid.*, p. 220.
10. Leland H. Jenks, *Nuestra Colonia de Cuba*. Spanish translation, Madrid, 1929.
11. *Ibid.*, pp. 291–297
12. *Ibid.*, p. 305.
13. *Ibid.*, p. 296.
14. *El latifundio en la economia Cubana*, Habana, 1929.
15. *Ibid.*, p. 14.
16. *Op. cit.*, p. 66.
17. *Azúcar y población en las Antillas*, Habana, 1927.

18. *Ibid.*, p. 10.

19. *Ibid.*, p. 19.

20. *Op. cit.*, p. 69.

21. In his last article in *Diario de la Marina*, January 2, 1930, the author is more realistic and outlines a plan of convention between Cuba and other sugar-producing lands.

22. *Funerales y responso*, La crisis politica, social y economica, Habana, 1926, p. 304.

23. *La Riqueza de Cuba*, Habana, 1927.

24. *Cuestiones economicas cubanas de actualidad*, Habana, 1927.

25. *La Agonia Antillana*, *op. cit.*

26. See also Ramiro Guerra: "Every cent that we save in the cost of production, at the expense of greater sacrifice and greater poverty of the working people of Cuba, is neutralized by one cent tariff increase in the United States." *Op. cit.*, p. 17.

27. "To live in the place where we work, or on our own farm—to earn little—but also to need little and produce all that we need . . . the type of life of small communities, of the self-sufficient, cannot be ours any more." Here Zamora continues with an annihilating criticism.

28. "Not only is our national capital insufficient, but it is also conservative and timid" (*op. cit.*, p. 23). The "dansa" showed that Cuban capital has already proved its enterprising attitude.

29. *La crisis del patriotismo.* Una teoria de las immigraciones, Habana, 1929.

30. *Op. cit.*, Introduction.

31. *Op. cit.*, p. 131.

32. *Camara de representantes. Discursos y trabajos del Dr. José A. Gonzalez Lanuza*, Habana, 1921, pp. 22, 800–801.

33. After finishing the writing of this, I had the opportunity of becoming acquainted with the dispassionate, practical work upon tariff union, rich in knowledge and obviously based on facts, which the Cuban Ambassador in Washington, Professor Orestes Ferrara, published in the first number of the new *Revista de la Habana* in 1930. It seems that this thought has already made some progress and been given serious consideration in Cuba.

34. Calderon, *Latin America*, *op. cit.*, p. 313.

35. *Op. cit.*, p. 210.

36. Jenks, *op. cit.*, p. 228.

37. Professor Jorge Roa considers Cuba as a neutralized island, and emphasizes that Cuban politics is always governed by laws of a higher order, namely, the laws dictated by the geographical situation of the island. *En el Surco de dos Razas*, Habana, 1924, p. 17.

38. Max Henriquez Urena, *The Yankees in Santo Domingo*, Madrid, 1929, pp. 8–9.

39. Jenks, *op. cit.*, p. 85.

40. Ramiro Guerra, *Un cuarto de siglo, op. cit.*, p. 99.

41. Dr. Antonio I. Varvelde, *Colonización e immigración en Cuba*, Academia de la Historia, Habana, 1923, p. 14.

42. Cortina, *op. cit.*, p. 8.

43. Terry, *op. cit.*, p. 35. And further, typically: "But the honest, thoughtful, grateful Cuban of the old regime, with a memory for past favours, says: 'The United States has been a godsend to Cuba, a generous fountain whence Cuba has drawn unthinkable benefits. What would have become of Cuba had the friendship of the United States been withheld?' "

44. *Op. cit.*, p. 42.

45. *Op. cit.*, p. 39.

46. Cortina, *op. cit.*, p. 18.

47. Jenks, *op. cit.*, p. 297.

48. *Op. cit.*, p. 68.

49. *Op. cit.*, p. 110.

50. *Ibid.*

51. *Op. cit.*, p. 110.

52. *Latin America, op. cit.*, p. 322.

53. *Op. cit.*, p. 318. One can find an analogous verdict in the anti-Yankee book by Guillermo Padilla-Castro (*op. cit.*, p. 51).

54. *La Revista de la Universidad*, Habana, January 1930, Vol. II, No. 2.

55. *La Solidaridad Latina en América*, Habana, 1897.

56. Only once in an advertisement of the Cuban Telefon Co. (subsidiary of the I.T.T.) could any indication be found of this importance of Cuba. The company has just announced new extensions to other countries of America and Europe, having completed the necessary plans to establish within a relatively short time telephonic communication between Buenos Aires and Montevideo, with extensions to Chile and Brazil, which permit communication with other countries of South America, Mexico, Cuba, and with the United States and Europe. "By its geographical position Cuba will be the key to transcontinental telephonic communication." According to Malagrida, the Antilles "should organize themselves into a single absolutely sovereign State. This State should become a link between Anglo-Latin America and Spanish America." *Op. cit.*, p. 474.

Besides, in the writings of Jorge Roa one can find the remark: "Geographically we are the centre of the continent" (*op. cit.*, p. 117); and "Cuba was and will be a laboratory of racial relations in America. There is ostensibly no other destiny for her."

57. *Latin America, op. cit.*, p. 321.

58. *Op. cit.*, p. 415.

59. *Op. cit.*, p. 20.

60. Some romanticists lend support to tariff-unionism. This is true of Emilio del Real y Tejera, author of the theory of the "natural market" (*La industria azucarera de Cuba*, Habana, 1928).

61. *El Centenario del Cadiz y la intimidad Ibéro-Américana*, Habana, 1913, p. 26.

62. *Ibid.*, p. 71.

63. *Ibid.*, p. 77.

64. *El Panamericanismo y el Panhispanismo*, Habana, 1916.

65. *Panhispanismo* (Prólogo de Rafael Altamira), Barcelona, 1926.

66. *Ibid.*, p. 120.

67. Compare with his latest publication, *El Panamericanismo y la opinion Europea*, Paris, 1930. Unconditionally accepting the Monroe Doctrine and official Pan-Americanism, he goes, however, too far, as does another Cuban writer, Jorge Roa, who completely justifies the Platt Amendment and the interventionist policy of the United States in Cuba (*En el surco*, *op. cit.*, p. 101).

68. Malagrida must admit that this idea is current only among a "select group" of intellectuals and politicians (*op. cit.*, pp. 475–476), who are, of course, of small importance.

69. *La Patria Grande*, *op. cit.*, p. 19.

70. Juan Leets, *United States and Latin America*. Dollar Diplomacy, New Orleans, 1912, p. 54. This publication is a personal accusation levelled against Secretary of State Philander C. Knox.

71. *Op. cit.*, p. xx.

72. *Op. cit.*, p. 7.

73. *Op. cit.*

74. *Op. cit.*, p. 17.

75. *Pan-Americanism and the International Policy of Argentina*, American Association for International Conciliation, New York, 1916.

76. "We shall welcome the aid of capital and the enterprising spirit of the United States, and I earnestly hope that the leading men of this country will pay more attention to the great possibilities open to American capital in every one of the South American countries." *The Pan-American Conferences and Their Significance*, Supplement to the Annales of American Academy of Political and Social Science, Philadelphia, 1906, p. 19.

77. "The Hispano- or Latin-Americanism can very well exist, not only in the display of fraternity among our republics having similar origin and language, but also on the ground of economic relations; its existence, however, must be in accord with Pan-Americanism and not opposed to Anglo-Americanism." *Historia de las doctrinas economicas in América y en especial en Chile*, Santiago de Chile, 1924, pp. 104–110.

78. *La lucha economica*. Estudio de economica social. Santiago de, Chile, 1909.

79. Enrique Gay Colbo, *La América indefensa*, Habana, 1925, p. 49.

80. *Mexico y la solidaridad américana*, Madrid, (?).

81. Introduction to Fernando Berenguer, *op. cit.*, p. 8.

82. *Op. cit.*, Vol. I, p. 54.

CHAPTER V

Future

(a) *Industrialization*

1. With regard to division into stages of evolution of economic development, Karl Bücher's scheme is being followed. The term "world economy" is being used in Bernhard Harms' sense

2. Bomfim, *op. cit.*, p. 125

3. John H. Latane, *The Diplomatic Relations*, *op. cit.*, p. 12. New historical investigations raise some doubts as to the exactness of this view. An investigation into the relations between Denmark and Iceland would present an interesting parallel to the colonial policy of Spain and Portugal.

4. Compare the following lines with Bingham: "Our own defects have been so repeatedly pointed out by foreigners, many of them with distressing unanimity, that we cannot afford to set ourselves up as judges of what South Americans should or should not do " *Across South America*, *op. cit.*, p. 387.

5. *Verhandlungen des Vereins für Sozialpolitik in Zürich*, 1928, München and Leipzig, 1929, p. 27.

6. v. Schulze Gaevernitz, *op. cit.*, p. 107

7. Compare Paul B. Souweine, *L'Argentine au seuil de l'Industrie*, Tournai-Paris, 1927, pp. 317–318; Alfred Funke, *Brasilien im 20 Jahrhundert*, Berlin, 1927, p. 415.

8. Letter of Thomas Jefferson to Benjamin Austin, from Monticello, January 9, 1816; quoted by Frederick List, *Outlines*, *op. cit.*, pp. 38–39.

9. *Ibid.*, p. 10.

10. *Ibid.*, p. 4. List's importance for America has unfortunately not been as yet sufficiently investigated. How clearly he foresaw the course of events may be judged from the following citation: "The whole American history of the next hundred years shall be contained in these three words, if you do not do what Jefferson said—place the manufacturer by the side of the farmer. This is the only means of preventing population and capital from withdrawing to the west. Ohio will soon be as populous as Pennsylvania, Indiana as Ohio, Illinois as Indiana; then they will pass over the Mississippi—next the Rocky Mountains—and at last turn their faces to China instead of England. Pennsylvania and all the eastern and middle States can increase in population, in arts and sciences, civilization and wealth, and the Union can grow powerful only by fostering the manufacturing interest. This, sir, I think the true *American political economy*." *Ibid.*, p. 24.

11. *Conflicto*, *op. cit.*, pp. 455–456.

12. *Ibid.*, p. 449.

13. *Estudios, op. cit.*, p. 334.

14. *Ibid.*, p. 95.

15. *Ibid.*, pp. 98–99. We can find in the works of Alberdi the first attempt ever made in the South American literature at an explanation of crises. His theory of crises is closely bound up with the credit theory. His economic views could be an interesting subject for investigation.

16. *Ibid.*, p. 391.

17. *Op. cit.*, p. 247.

18. *La Reconquista, op. cit.*, p. 102.

19. *Ibid.*, p. 104. The ideology of the agricultural state is poorly represented in the South American literature. The problem "Agricultural state *v.* Industrial state," which life is trying to solve, has not, strangely enough, come under discussion in South America. One can find in the writings of Francisco Seeber a peculiar mixture of industrialism and agricultural romanticism. J. H. Williams sees Argentina as an agrarian state: "In the period of our study Argentina was, and it still is, a purely agricultural and grazing country. It has no coal and iron in workable quantities. The development of manufactures on any considerable scale, aside from the elaboration of its food products, appears improbable. Argentine economic life seems destined for a long time to come to continue in the channel that it has pursued in the past, namely, an exchange of its agricultural and grazing products, either in the raw state or as elaborated food products, for the manufactured products of the outside world. The volume and the terms of this exchange will continue to be the index of its economic wealth and growth." *Argentine International Trade Under Inconvertible Paper Money, 1880–1900*, Cambridge, 1920, p. 178.

The Catholic Association for International Peace is against industrialization of South America. *Latin America and the United States*, Pamphlet No. 2, Washington, 1929, pp. 42–43.

20. One can hardly agree with Calderon, who sees in Porfizio Diaz of Mexico a leader comparable to "Bismarck in Germany and Witte in Russia."

21. Cooper, *op. cit.*, p. 255.

22. "Only the results of a complete industrial census can determine the development of manufacturing industries during the War. Undoubtedly many industries have increased. Whether the increase was beyond the normal tendency, and whether the stage of development reached will be maintained with the return of normal conditions, it is difficult to foretell. Undoubtedly the tendency, apparent before the War, of manufacturing to increase will continue in the future, in spite of the difficulties of obtaining capital, fuel, and iron. It is certain, however, that agricultural and animal products will be the dominating sources of economic wealth and the field for enterprise for many years to come." Smith, L. Brewster, and Collings, Harry T., *The Economic*

Position of Argentina During the War, Department of Commerce, Miscellaneous Series, No. 88, Washington, 1920, p. 71.

23. Paul B. Souweine, *op. cit.*, p. A (*avant propos*).

24. *Ibid.*, p. xxviii (Introduction).

25. *Ibid.*, p. B.

26. *Report of the Secretary of the Treasury to the President in the Second Pan-American Financial Conference at Washington, op. cit.*, pp. 75–78.

27. Cremer, M. A., *Selling in Brazil*, United States Department of Commerce, Bureau of Foreign and Domestic Commerce, 1925, pp. 2–3. The following characterization resembles the above described conditions in Argentina: "One of the characteristics of the people seems to be a desire to manufacture something. One will find doctors, lawyers, military men, and others who are ambitious to erect a plant for the manufacture of stockings, ties, or other commodities. Many of the immigrants from southern Europe who come to Brazil, probably with the idea of securing employment as agriculturists, drift into the cities to engage in various manufacturing activities on a small scale. There are throughout Brazil, therefore, thousands of persons operating small shops, making shoes, tanning leather, and working iron. In some sections of Rio de Janeiro, for example, one may pass through narrow streets, where each small building is crowded close to the next, and the sidewalks are so narrow that two persons cannot walk abreast, and find a shoe factory with probably twenty-five workmen, a cardboard box factory with six workmen, and another where probably eight men are making chairs and doors." *Machinery Markets of Brazil*, United States Department of Commerce, Bureau of Foreign and Domestic Commerce, Trade Information Bulletin, No. 383, 1926, p. 1.

28. M. J. A. Barboza-Carneiro, *Situation Économique et Financière du Brésil*, Memorandum presenté à la Conference Financière Internationale, Bruxelles, Septembre-Octobre, 1920, p. 36.

29. Dr. Walter Schuck, *Organisation und Betrieb des Brasilianischen, Importhandels*, Stuttgart, 1928, p. 27.

30. *Report on Trade and Tariffs in Brazil, Uruguay, Argentina, Chile, Bolivia, and Peru*, Washington, 1916.

31. Frank R. Rutter, *Tariff Systems of South American Countries*, Department of Commerce, Tariff Series, No. 34, p. 12.

32. *Ibid.*, p. 13.

33. Federal Trade Commission, *Report on Trade and Tariffs in Brazil, Uruguay, Argentina, Chile, Bolivia, Peru*, Washington, 1916, p. 26.

34. "The protectionist sentiment in Brazil is very strong. There is no political party or influential body of persons in the country which is opposed to protection. The rates of duty in the tariff are a wall intended to protect domestic industry. No statement is more misleading than the one frequently heard in the United States of America that the sole object of South American tariffs is to raise revenue.

In Brazil and elsewhere nascent industries are fostered and favoured, and duties are adjusted to suit the interest of him who wishes to make a venture into the field of national industry. The duties on pianos furnish a good example of the extent to which Brazilian legislators go in protecting industry. These duties are very high. They protect one piano factory at Curityba, the only piano factory in Brazil. This so-called factory is located in a building previously used for a dwelling, and at best it cannot build more than ten or twelve pianos at a time. There are other cases of this kind.

"It is difficult to make clear the exact nature of the ultra-protection of Brazil. It is one phase of that recognized practice of the Government helping the individual. Industries which hardly exist at all are protected by prohibitive duties. Sericulture is scarcely known in Brazil. Yet very high duties are levied on silk goods to protect a few mills that do not pretend to supply the domestic market. There are few sheep in Brazil. Yet high duties are maintained on woollen goods in order that a small domestic industry may continue to exist." Federal Trade Commission, *Report on Trade and Tariffs in Brazil, Uruguay, Argentina, Chile, Bolivia, and Peru*, *op. cit.*, p. 62.

35. *1928 Retrospecto Commercial do Jornal do Commercio, Rio de Janeiro*, 1929, p. 7. Compare also p. 65.

36. "The total capital invested in these plants is estimated at $3,899,000 American currency, and the annual production at about 5,800,000 pairs of shoes. A comparison with statistics of 1909 indicates that the number of factories and the number of employees has changed but little, although the capital has been doubled and the value of the output has increased 73 per cent. This result is due to the increased use of modern equipment and to the greater efficiency of the workmen." Arthur Redfield, *Brazil, A Study of Economic Conditions Since 1913*, Department of Commerce, Miscellaneous Series, No. 86, p. 64.

37.

PRODUCTION OF MATCHES IN BRAZIL

Year	Number of Factories	Boxes of Sixty Matches Produced (in Thousands)	Factories	Production
1911	30	524,988	100	100
1914	31	461,191	103	88
1917	25	497,759	83	95
1920	23	609,129	77	116
1923	23	792,250	77	151

1928 Retrospecto Commercial do Jornal do Commercio, Rio de Janeiro, 1929, p. 63. The Swedish trust could not monopolize this industry in Brazil as yet, despite the fact that some success has been achieved.

38. *Relatorio da Directoria do Centro Industrial de Fiacão e Tecelagem de Algodão*, Rio de Janeiro, 1929.

39. Compare Manuel Ugarte's *La Patria Grande*, *op. cit.*, p. 8.

40. *Op. cit.*, p. xix. On the other hand, as acute an observer as Enock thinks that "Mexico, Brazil, Peru. Argentina, Chile are names denoting an individuality and colourful character which the more prosaic and solid people of Anglo-America do not possess" (*op. cit.*, p. 10).

41. Bryce, *op. cit.*, p. 427.

42. Bryce, *op. cit.*, p. 426. An outstanding naturalist expresses unconsciously the same idea: he is attracted by the revival of old Germany or Europe of one hundred or more years ago. Guenther, *Das Antlitz Brasiliens*, Leipzig, 1927, p. 323.

43. Funke, *op. cit.*, p. 44.

44. Carlos O. Bunge, *Nuestra América*, Madrid, 1926, p. 180.

45. Fernando Ortiz, *op. cit.*, p. 40. Bryce is of a different opinion. "Argentina is the United States of the Southern Hemisphere" (*op. cit.*, p. 314). He does not, however, prove this contention. On the contrary, Bryce's further exposition first weakens and then contradicts this statement. He says: "Buenos Aires is something between Paris and New York. It has the business rush and luxury of the one, the gaiety and pleasure-loving aspect of the other" (p. 318). And after having compared Paris and the country with Europe, he states that here (in Argentina) "one feels much nearer to Europe than anywhere in South America" (p. 346).

46. *Op. cit.*, p. 27.

47. "Uruguay is in South America what Switzerland, Belgium, and Holland are in Europe." Reyes, *op. cit.*, p. 167.

48. Clark calls Lima "the Paris of the South" (*op. cit.*, p. 94). The comparison is exaggerated, though the European character of the city is rightly emphasized. But there seems to be no excuse for comparing Bolivia to "the Switzerland of South America" (p. 121).

49. Louis Gros, *L'Argentine pour tous*, Paris, (?).

50. Funke, *op. cit.*, p. 155.

51. Calderon exaggerates Brazil's achievements when he says that Brazil has "already attained independence through her national industry" (*La Creación de un Continente*, *op. cit.*, p. 192), although he correctly appraises the progress and possibilities of the country. On the other hand, Bryce, whose book on South America is thus far the greatest, and who is full of admiration for Brazil's natural beauty and riches, has underestimated the country's possibilities.

52. German Professor August Skalweit finds that the possibilities in South America are limited. His pamphlet is clearly influenced by the Argentine point of view and German interests. *Die Wirtschaftliche Emanzipation Süd Amerikas*, Jena, 1927 (Kieler Vorträge, No. 20).

53. Calderon, *Latin America*, *op. cit.*, p. 378.

54. Clark, *op. cit.*, p. 19.

55. *Republica Argentina*, Dirección General de Commercio e Industria, Buenos Aires, 1925, p. 11 (quoted from Souvaine, *op. cit* p. 5).

56. Arthur Redfield, *Brazil, A Study of Economic Conditions since 1913*, Department of Commerce, Miscellaneous Series, No. 86, Washington, 1920, p. 44.

57. *Ibid.*, p. 34.

58. Malagrida, *op. cit.*, p. 265.

59. Malagrida, *op. cit.*, p. 275.

60. *Latin America*, *op. cit.*, p. 378.

61. Entire South America, Argentina included, has no stock exchange of any importance. There is no large mortgage bank organization, except in Argentina, and, with the exception of the ABC States and Uruguay, there is no national organization of commercial credit in the remaining South American countries.

62. I refer to my investigation concerning Rio Grande do Sul in Brazil, which showed quite an unexpected degree of development of capital formation. See *Harvard Business Review*, January, 1931.

63. Ministerio de Relaciones Exteriores de Chile. *Los Capitales en Chile*, 1928, p. 6.

64. Compare Monterroyos, *op. cit.*

65. Achille Villate, *Economic Imperialism*, *op. cit.*, p. 60.

66. Calderon, *Latin America*, *op. cit.*, p. 75.

67. *La raza cósmica*, Paris, (?) p. 16.

68. *La creación*, *op. cit.*, pp. 59–60.

69. "To-day, like in the times gone by, it is not a question of whether one is born a German or a Roman, a Greek or a Latin; it is rather a question of education, of whether one is urbanized (Weltstadtler) or provincial." Spengler, *op. cit.*, Vol. I, p. 48.

70. Especially for Brazil, compare Cincinato Braga, *op. cit.*, p. 48

71. Helio Lobo, *A Democracia Uruguaya*, Rio de Janeiro, 1928, p. 45.

72. Indications in this direction are to be found in the writings of Francisco Ribeiro Salgado, *op. cit.*, p. 42. At the Pan-American Conference at Rio de Janeiro (1906) there was general agreement on "recommending the holding of an international American Coffee Congress at the city of São Paulo, Brazil. The Congress has not been held."

73. It is high time that a study concerning these attempts be undertaken. Indeed, mountains of material and statistical data in the various industries are waiting for the patient scholar.

74. *Op. cit.*, p. 73.

75. Frederick List has already defined with great precision the situation in 1827. "It is, however, not my intention to treat on European policy. I only went so far as to state generally the aim of Mr. Canning's policy, which is to counteract the continental powers of

Europe and to monopolize the South American market. In respect to this country Mr. Canning has not to fear a present manufacturing power but a rising one, which menaces the interest of the English manufacturing power in a threefold way: in the first place, in depriving the English manufactures of our interior market; secondly, in sharing with them the South American market; and thirdly, in increasing our internal and external shipping immensely, which is the basis of the future ascendancy of our naval power. There was no occasion, and there will perhaps not in the course of centuries reappear such an opportunity as the event of the emancipation of the South American people for raising the manufacturing power of the United States, in a few years wonderfully, and taking an equal standing in power and wealth with England by developing our internal and external shipping. Let only a few years pass and England will have taken exclusive ground in the south and will have raised her power and wealth by Mr. Canning's policy beyond all conception. There will then be no possibility for an American competition with England neither in industry nor in political power. In the relations, sir, between two rival nations, not to grow in strength and to become weak are synonyms." *Appendix to the Outlines, op. cit.*, pp. 5–6.

76. Calderon, *Latin America, op. cit.*, p. 382.

77. Alfons Goldsmidt, *Argentinien*, Berlin, 1929, p. 102.

78. J. H. Williams, *op. cit.*, p. 12.

79. *Ibid.*, p. 13.

80. Calderon says of Garcia Moreno of Ecuador: "His ideal was the monarchy of Philip II, the Jesuit Empire of Paraguay, the return of the Middle Ages, and a conventional peace." *Latin America, op. cit.*, p. 219.

81. Calderon, *Latin America, op. cit.*, p. 382.

82. Garcia Caminero, *op. cit.*, p. 66.

83. Compare the booklet *El Lazarillo* (1773)—a guide of the way from Buenos Aires to Lima.

84. Alberdi, *Estudios economicos, op. cit.*, p. 10.

85. "The sub-committee recognizes that the resources of Brazil are so large that properly to develop them not only can all the available domestic capital be used but also as much foreign capital as might be secured. At the present stage of development, it is our opinion that the best interests of the country require the use of as much domestic capital as possible in commercial and agricultural pursuits, and that railroad, public utility, and industrial development can best be financed by foreign capital." *Report of the Secretary of the Treasury to the President on the Second Pan-American Financial Conference at Washington, op. cit.*, p. 77.

86. B. H. Williams, *op. cit.*, p. 33.

87. Enrique Guy-Calbo, *La América indefensa*, Habana, 1925, p. 5.

88. *Op. cit.*, p. 375.

(*b*) *Politics*

1. Marriano A. Pelliza had already declared in the year 1885 that the plan of union in America which "was a Utopia in 1810," gained new assistance through the development of communication. "Now we have those things which we lacked in 1810 and 1825, namely the steamship, the telegraph, the railroad." *Federación social americana*, Buenos Aires, 1885, p. 8.

2.

EXPORTS FROM ARGENTINA

(*Values in U.S. Gold*)

To:

Year	Brazil	Uruguay	Paraguay	Bolivia
	$	$	$	$
1913	23,579,841	6,111,551	1,846,690	1,097,646
1925	32,252,259	5,453,033	5,953,642	1,130,525
1926	28,951,524	6,019,600	5,007,722	1,377,228
1927	36,392,096	5,655,634	5,432,220	1,631,693
1928	39,104,906	6,779,909	6,154,982	2,329,959

Source: *Pan-American Union*, letter of June 20, 1930.

3. Compare the attitude of the Argentine delegate, Honorio Pueyrredon, at the Havana Conference.

4. This comparison with Germany is, of course, not new. It was even drawn at the end of the nineteenth century in the vitriolic publication of Furey-Chatelain (*op. cit.*, p. 187). It was declared that one of the aims of the War was the economic liberation of the world from Germany's attempts at industrial and commercial hegemony. (Compare *L'Avenir de l'Expansion Économique de la France*, *op. cit.*) Compare the following lines: "Twenty years hence, and a syndicate of five or six big houses of Berlin will obtain the economic rule of the planet." (Henri Hauser, *op. cit.*, p. 9.) Replacing the word "German" by "United States" and "Berlin" by "New York," is that not a true statement when applied to the American danger? Careful reading of similar accusations confirms this analogy. The American policy of establishing "assembling plants" abroad is another example.

One Argentine writer declares: "Imperialism is actually a specific phenomenon of the German race, or virtually of the Teutons—the Germans, in reality, Anglo-Saxons and North Americans." J. Soraci, *Concepto del Panamericanismo*, Buenos Aires, 1917, p. 25.

5. An analogy is to be found in Napoleon's continental system at the beginning of the nineteenth century. Pentmann defines this policy as "a surrogate of a dictatorial customs union of the continental States

against England." *Die Zollunionsidee und ihre Wandlungen*, Jena, 1917, pp. 4–5.

6. Several other phenomena in the political life of Latin America resemble European conditions. Compare *supra*.

7. Did not the attitudes of several countries prior to the foundation of the German Empire or Italy appear insuperable? The misunderstanding between Chile and Peru is not so acute as between Bavaria and Prussia at that time. As an illustration of these half-forgotten contrasts, we can find in Thomas Mann's famous novel *Budenbrooks* a picture of the times when Munich was to the other Germany a foreign town with foreign language and customs. In South America, however, especially in Brazil, in spite of the great distances, lack of adequate communication, etc., "the difference between a Brazilian from Manãos and one from Santa Catharina is less than the difference between a Breton and a native of Marseilles; a German from Saxony differs more from one from Hamburg than a Venezuelan from an Argentine." Manoel Bomfim, *op. cit.*, p. 268.

8. *New Pan-Americanism*, Part III (World Peace Foundation), Boston, 1917, p. 153.

9. Malagrida, *op. cit.*, p. 432.

10. The Mexican, José S. Carranza, emphasized the importance of this fact. *Cuestiones Américanas*, Nuevos Capitulos, Liguge, 1912, p. 5.

11. "The single Republic of South America ceased to exist: The Brazilian Imperium," said Rojas Paul, the President of Venezuela.

12. Calderon, *Latin America, op. cit.*, p. 54.

13. *O Brasil actual*, Rio de Janeiro, 1929, p. 106.

14. Bryce, *op. cit.*, p. 419.

15. Clemenceau, *op. cit.*, p. 215.

16. Gunther, *op. cit.*, p. 334. This is one of the most intelligent books on Brazil.

17. Compare *Avenir de l'Expansion*, *op. cit.*, pp. 306–307.

18. Calderon exaggerates as usual in his statement that "between 1848 and 1862 the monarchy created the Brazilian nation." (*Latin America*, *op. cit.*, p. 190.) The nation is to-day still in the making.

19. "The conditions here noted may be thought to resemble those of the Southern States in the North American Union." Bryce, *op. cit.*, p. 414.

20. There was announced recently the publication of a history of many volumes on the Brazilian Literature, Arthur Motta, *Historia de Literatura Brasileira*.

21. *Op. cit.*, p. 267.

22. *Op. cit.*, p. 206.

23. Compare Helio Lobo, *Rio Branco e seu circulo de ouro* (in *Brasilianos y yanquis*).

24. It is sufficient to recall the rôle of Joaquim Nabuco.

25. For a statement of the attitude of Brazil towards the United

States prior the War, compare Bingham, *Across South America*, *op. cit.*, p. 14.

26. *1928 Retrospecto*, *op. cit.*, p. 36.

27. *Ibid.*, p. 36.

28. Amaro Cavalcanti, *Pan-American Questions*, Rio de Janeiro, 1913, pp. 41–42.

29. *Second Pan-American Financial Conference*, Washington, 1921, p. 53. (Address delivered by Dr. Carlos Cesar de Oliveira Sampaio, Chairman of the Brazilian Delegation.)

30. Elliott, *op. cit.*, p. 286.

31. Paul Adam, *Les visages du Brésil*, Paris, 1914, p. 239.

32. "From an economic as well as a political standpoint, therefore, the relation of the United States with Brazil must inevitably be closer than with a country like Argentina which exports chiefly beef and cereals, products we possess abundantly at home." Haring, *op. cit.*, p. 213. Compare Bingham, *Across South America*, *op. cit.*, p. 39; Harry T. Collings, *Die Kapitalexpansion der Ver. Staaten in Latin America*, Jena, 1927, p. 12 (Kieler Vorträge, No. 23).

33. "The social community that subsists among the nations of Spanish America does not extend either to Brazil or to the United States." This opinion of Moreno Quintana is traditional for Spanish South America (quoted by Haring, *op. cit.*, p. 112). For the Brazilian point of view, compare Baptista Pereira *Civilisacão contra Barbarie* and *O Brasil ea raça*, São Paulo, 1928.

34. This rôle of Brazil is not new, as Helio Lobo emphasizes in his numerous publications. Compare, for instance: *Brazilianos y Yanquis*, *op. cit.*, pp. 163–164, and *A passo de Gigante*, Rio de Janeiro, 1925, p. 51.

GEORGE ALLEN & UNWIN LTD
LONDON: 40 MUSEUM STREET, W.C.1
CAPE TOWN: 73 ST. GEORGE'S STREET
SYDNEY, N.S.W.: WYNYARD SQUARE
AUCKLAND, N.Z.: 41 ALBERT STREET
TORONTO: 77 WELLINGTON STREET, WEST

For Product Safety Concerns and Information please contact our EU representative GPSR@taylorandfrancis.com
Taylor & Francis Verlag GmbH, Kaufingerstraße 24, 80331 München, Germany

www.ingramcontent.com/pod-product-compliance
Ingram Content Group UK Ltd.
Pitfield, Milton Keynes, MK11 3LW, UK
UKHW022024061126
477531UK00002B/12
9781138551428